Yosemite Place Names

D0145178

YOSEMITE PLACE NAMES

The historic background of geographic names in
Yosemite National Park

Peter Browning

GREAT WEST BOOKS • LAFAYETTE, CALIFORNIA
1988

Copyright © 1988 by Peter Browning
All Rights Reserved

Cover design by Larry Van Dyke and Peter Browning
Front cover: Portion of the *Tuolumne Meadows* 15′ quadrangle
Back cover: Portion of Lt. McClure's *Map of the Yosemite National Park*, 1896

Printed in the United States of America

Great West Books
PO Box 1028
Lafayette, CA 94549

Library of Congress Cataloging-in-Publication Data

Browning, Peter, 1928–
    Yosemite place names : the historic background of geographic
    names in Yosemite National Park / Peter Browning.
        p.   cm.
    Bibliography: p.
    ISBN 0–944220–00–2 (pbk. : alk. paper) : $12.95
        1. Names, Geographical—California—Yosemite National Park–
    –Dictionaries.   2. Yosemite National Park (Calif.)—History, Local.
    I. Title.
    F868.Y6B83 1988   87–29793
    917.94′47′00321—dc 19   CIP

Contents

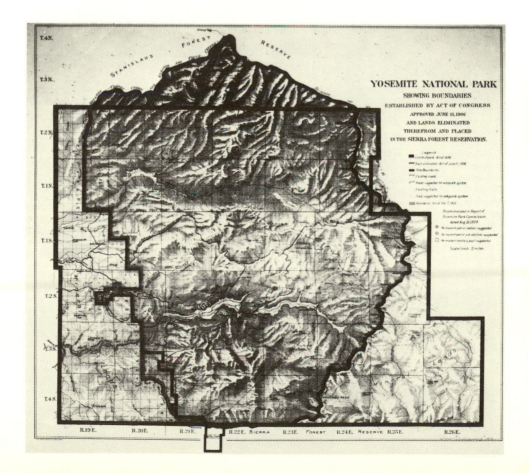

Illustrations

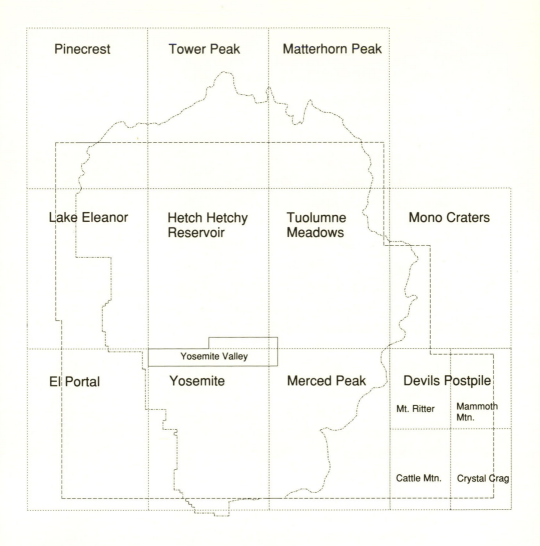

Pinecrest	Tower Peak	Matterhorn Peak
Lake Eleanor	Hetch Hetchy Reservoir	Tuolumne Meadows
El Portal	Yosemite	Merced Peak

Mono Craters

Yosemite Valley

Devils Postpile

Mt. Ritter Mammoth Mtn.

Cattle Mtn. Crystal Crag

Present boundary of Yosemite National Park ....

The park's boundary from 1890 to 1905 - - - - - - - - - - - - - - - -

Boundaries of topographic quadrangles ....

Boundary of Yosemite Valley 1:24,000 map _____

Preface

Some of the information in this volume is derived from my earlier book, *Place Names of the Sierra Nevada*, published in 1986 by Wilderness Press, Berkeley. Since then, additional research has revealed more information, which has enabled me to revise and enlarge some of the entries from that earlier book, and to add entries for names not previously covered.

Yosemite National Park has not always had its present boundaries. The original Yosemite Grant to the state of California, created in 1864, comprised Yosemite Valley and vicinity and the Mariposa Grove of Big Trees. In 1890 when the national park was created, the boundaries were drawn along township lines, without much regard to the topography or to land use and ownership. There was a great deal of resistance to the creation of a large park, especially by mining and timber interests. They used the same arguments that are still heard today when new parks are created or when wilderness areas are established: valuable resources are being 'locked up,' and a private preserve is being created for a group of selfish elitists.

In 1905, after fifteen years of political pressure and manipulation, the boundaries of the park were realigned. Some land on the west and southwest was taken from the park. It was not of park quality, and much of it was already in the hands of homesteaders and miners. The boundaries were expanded to the north, to encompass all the area up to the northern and northeastern ridges that constitute the headwaters of the Tuolumne River. (This region is on the *Matterhorn Peak*, *Tower Peak*, and *Pinecrest* quadrangles.) On the east and southeast the park lost a large area of spectacular wilderness that should have remained in the park. Included in this excision were Banner Peak, Mount Ritter, the Minarets, Devils Postpile (which became a national monument in 1911), and the headwaters of the North and Middle forks of the San Joaquin River. (These areas are on the *Devils Postpile* and *Merced Peak* quadrangles.) There are entries for all the names of places that were within the park from 1890 to 1905, excepting a few on the *Lake Eleanor* and *El Portal* quadrangles, west and southwest of the present park boundaries.

By its nature, research for a book of this sort is a solitary occupation. One reads dozens of books and periodicals, peruses obscure journals, and traces a multitude of faint clues through the musty archives in search of a few more items of obscure information. I also spent some hundreds of hours looking at nineteenth century newspapers on microfilm. Yet no matter how much one does alone, it isn't possible to do a thorough job without the help of many others. In particular I want to thank the staff of the Bancroft Library for being endlessly helpful and accommodating in fulfilling my endless requests for research materials. Those individuals to whom I am especially grateful for assistance and information are Mary Vocelka at the Yosemite Research Library; Barbara Lekisch, former librarian at the Sierra Club Library; N. King Huber at the US Geological Survey in Menlo Park; Shirley Sargent, the Yosemite author; and Jim Snyder, Yosemite National Park trail foreman and historian.

Francis P. Farquhar, in his 1926 *Place Names of the High Sierra*, was the pioneer in place-names research in the Sierra. The origin of many names in Yosemite would not be known had not Farquhar elicited the information from those who did the naming. Marjory Farquhar allowed me complete freedom to delve into the files that her husband had accumulated since publication of his 1926 book. Farquhar was intimately involved with the Sierra Nevada for sixty years as a climber, historian, and conservationist. By the time this book is published there will likely be a peak in Kings Canyon National Park named for Farquhar.

Introduction

On the evening of March 27, 1851, fifty-eight men of the Mariposa Battalion camped in Yosemite Valley near Bridalveil Fall. They were in pursuit of the Yosemite Indians, and were the first whites ever to have entered the valley.

Around their campfires that evening the surgeon of the detachment, Lafayette H. Bunnell, suggested that they ought to name the valley. After a period of "coarse jokes" and "ready repartee," Bunnell managed to engage the men in making a serious response. A variety of names was offered: canonical, scriptural, foreign, romantic. Bunnell didn't care for any of them. He presented a reasoned argument in favor of naming the valley "Yo-sem-i-ty," for the tribe that occupied it. This evoked an angry response from a man named Tunnehill, who cursed the Indians and suggested the name "Paradise Valley." Bunnell converted that remark into a joke at Tunnehill's expense, which drew a hearty laugh from the company. In that moment of relaxation another man suggested that a vote be taken. Bunnell explained why he thought the valley ought to be named Yo-sem-i-ty—and the vote adopting the name was nearly unanimous.

The Indians who inhabited Yosemite Valley had names for the major features and for the valley itself. Some of the names were descriptive, some were connected with legendary events, others referred to an area where a certain activity took place or a certain plant or tree grew. One thing they didn't do was to name features for Important People.

A few of these names have survived, often having been subjected to multiple interpretations and a variety of pronunciations. Some of them were placed on the wrong features due to the ignorance and arrogance of the first groups of white people in Yosemite.

The Indians' name for Yosemite Valley was *Ahwahnee*. *Pohono*, the name for Bridalveil Fall, now applies only to the Pohono Trail. *Ahwiyah*, the name for Mirror Lake, is found only on a rock spur below Half Dome. *Tenaya*, although the name of the Yosemite chief, was the name given to the lake by Lafayette Bunnell. Mono Pass was named not by the Mono Indians but by Lieutenant Tredwell Moore of the US Army. *Tioga* is an Indian name imported from New York and Pennsylvania. The *Tuolumne* name was given to the river by the Spanish in 1806 for a tribe of Indians that lived on the banks of the river in the Central Valley. Yosemite's other major river, the Merced, also was named by the Spanish in 1806. The several other features bearing the "Tuolumne" and "Merced" names were given those names by Americans many years later. The only other name the Spanish provided is *Mariposa*, which also originated in the Central Valley in 1806. *El Capitan* is Spanish, but the name was given by the Mariposa Battalion in 1851.

Many of the major features in and around Yosemite Valley were named by the Mariposa Battalion, in particular by Bunnell. The first tourist parties, in 1855 and 1856, bestowed a few names—such as Bridalveil Fall—but fortunately most of what they proposed did not survive. In 1863 the California Geological Survey (the Whitney Survey) named most of the prominent peaks in what would later become the national park. Some of their names were descriptive or evocative, such as Cathedral Peak, Unicorn Peak, and the Obelisk (now Mount Clark). Others were borrowed names, such as Tuolumne Meadows. Most of the peaks they named were for geologists and other scientists.

From the middle 1860s until about 1900 sheepmen and cattlemen named meadows and streams in their summer grazing territories. These were unofficial names, yet many have endured because they came to be in common use and thus were recorded by later generations of map-makers. The Wheeler Survey was in Yosemite Valley and the northern part of the park-to-be in 1878 and 1879. They provided a smattering of names, but more importantly they placed on their maps some of the names then being used by the sheepmen.

The US Army administered Yosemite National Park from its beginning in 1890 until the National Park Service was created in 1916. In the middle 1890s Lieutenants McClure and Benson explored, blazed trails, learned more names from sheepmen, and did some naming of their own. Joseph N. LeConte's map of 1893 and McClure's map of 1896 were the first comprehensive maps of the entire park as it existed at that time. McClure's and Benson's efforts marked the beginning of almost two decades of features being named by and for army personnel. Foremost among these namers was Colonel William W. Forsyth, acting superintendent of the park from 1909 to 1912, who named a number of peaks and other features—mainly in the northern part of the park—for army officers and, often, their wives. Robert B. Marshall of the US Geological Survey also was lavish with names. His inclination was to honor relatives and friends, and their wives and daughters. He had a penchant for naming lakes for women. Joseph N. LeConte created several maps between 1893 and 1904, and is responsible for a number of names. Other Sierra Club members provided a considerable number of names, especially after 1901 when the club began its annual outings.

Between 1891 and 1911 the Geological Survey published a series of standard 30-minute topographic maps on a scale of 1:125,000. Many names appeared for the first time, some of them given by the geographers and cartographers who created the maps. The first USGS map of Yosemite Valley and vicinity on a scale of 1:24,000 came out in 1907. This basic map is still in use today, and is now in its tenth edition.

Park Service rangers did most of the naming during the 1920s and 1930s—names that usually first appeared on the 15-minute series of quadrangles, which were published in the 1950s. There was a good deal of derivative naming done on that new series of maps: lakes, creeks, and meadows often being named because of their proximity to a peak or other major feature that had been named long before.

There are many names in Yosemite National Park whose precise origins are unknown—and will likely remain unknown. They were created informally many years ago by people who kept no written records. Often enough the reason for a descriptive name is easy to deduce, but neither the date of naming nor the namer is known.

In a number of instances where a feature is named for a homesteader or other owner of the land, I have given the location of the land in terms of section, township, and range. These references are abbreviated thus: sec. 24, T. 1 S., R. 19 E. Each section is one square mile. There are thirty-six sections in a township, which is a square—six sections on a side. Thus, Township 1 South, Range 19 East is easily found on the *Lake Eleanor* quadrangle. The range and township numbers are on the map borders in red, and every section is numbered. The homestead and patent records referred to are preserved on microfilm in the "control document index" files of the General Land Office at the Bureau of Land Management on Cottage Way in Sacramento.

James T. Gardiner (Gardner) of the Whitney Survey spelled his last name both ways at different times in his life. I have used the spelling "Gardiner" throughout, except when it appears as "Gardner" in quoted matter.

For some peaks and lakes, two elevations are given. All of these are on the *Devils Postpile* 15-minute quadrangle, and on the four 7.5-minute quadrangles that are replacing it. The first figure is in feet, from the 15-minute quadrangle; the second is in meters, from the 7.5-minute quadrangle. To convert meters to feet, multiply by 3.2808. To convert feet to meters, multiply by 0.3048. The topographic maps of the 7.5-minute series, on a scale of 1:24,000, that will cover all of Yosemite National Park, are presently scheduled to be published by the end of 1989.

Names are in boldface type, and the name or names of the topographic maps the features are on are in italic type. These quadrangle map names can be located on the reference map on page viii. In those instances where one basic name applies to several features, the names will appear thus: **Ackerson: Meadow, Creek, Mountain**, meaning that there is an **Ackerson Meadow**, an **Ackerson Creek**, and an **Ackerson Mountain**.

For the sake of economy of space I have frequently used abbreviations, which may be found in the following list. The list is repeated on page 231. Those that are references are also in the Bibliography.

BGN	The United States Board on Geographic Names
BL	The Bancroft Library, Berkeley
CHSQ	*California Historical Society Quarterly*
DAB	*Dictionary of American Biography*
DFG	California Department of Fish and Game
EB	*Encyclopedia Britannica*
GLO	The General Land Office
INF	Inyo National Forest
quad	A topographic quadrangle map
SC	The Sierra Club
SCB	*Sierra Club Bulletin*
StNF	Stanislaus National Forest
USFS	United States Forest Service
USGS	United States Geological Survey
YNN	*Yosemite Nature Notes*
YNP	Yosemite National Park
YRL	Yosemite Research Library

Yosemite Place Names

Acker Peak (11,015)   *Tower Peak*

William Bertrand Acker was in charge of national park affairs in the Department of the Interior before the National Park Service was created in 1916. (Farquhar: R. B. Marshall.) The name was given by the US Geological Survey, and first appeared on the *Dardanelles* 30' map, 1912.

Ackerson: Meadow, Creek, Mountain (5,249)   *Lake Eleanor*

Named for James F. Ackerson, a '49er. (Paden, 207.) The meadow was called "Wade's or Big Meadows" on Hoffmann and Gardiner's map, 1863–67. (On that same map, "Wade's Ranch" was midway between the present "Ackerson Meadow" and "Sawmill Mtn," and the present "Bald Mtn" was called "Wade's Mt.") At one time Hoffmann referred to the meadow as "Reservoir Meadows." (*Proceedings* 3, Oct. 21, 1867: 370.) The creek was called "Big Meadow Creek" on the 1880 GLO plat. Ackerson homesteaded 160 acres in sec. 24, T. 1 S., R. 19 E. in 1882. He patented another 180 acres in secs. 24 and 25 in 1884. The creek rises in the park. The other features were in the park from 1890 to 1905, and are now in Stanislaus National Forest.

Adair Lake   *Merced Peak*

Charles F. Adair (1874–1936), a park ranger from 1914 to 1935. He introduced golden trout into this lake, which gave him the right to name it after himself. (Bingaman, *Guardians*, 91.) The lake was once called "Obelisk Lake" because of its proximity to Mount Clark, which initially was called "The Obelisk" by the Whitney Survey. At one time the lake was known informally as "Cirque Lake."

Agnew Meadows   *Devils Postpile, Mammoth Mtn.*
Agnew Pass   *Devils Postpile, Mt. Ritter*
Agnew Lake (8,508)   *Mono Craters*

Theodore C. Agnew, a miner, settled in the meadow in 1877. "... South of this mineral belt [the North Fork District] in a low land, separated from the San Joaquin by a ridge, is quite a body of valley land, moist and rank with luxurious pasture plants, and known as Agnew's meadows. On the northeast edge of this well-fenced pasture, a site has been selected for the future town of this district, to be known as Highland City." (*San Francisco Mining and Scientific Press*, Aug. 23, 1879: 121.)

The town never came into being. "Agnew's House" is marked on the 1885 GLO plat. He tried several times to patent the land, but was refused because there was no accepted survey of that township. The survey that ostensibly was made in 1885 was declared fraudulent by the Department of the Interior in 1899. It was one of many so-called 'barroom surveys.' The surveyor sat in the tranquillity of a tavern, safe from the elements and hard work, and composed fictional field notes. Agnew performed valuable service by guiding army troops who were patrolling the park. (Farquhar.)

Lt. McClure's 1895 map simply had the word "Agnews" where the meadow is, and also named the pass. His 1896 map and Benson's 1896 map showed all three features. The meadow is in Inyo National Forest, but was within the park from 1890 to 1905. The pass and the lake are in the national forest.

Ahwahnee   *Yosemite Valley, Yosemite*

"A-wa'-ni, a large village standing directly at the foot of Yosemite Fall. This was the ruling town, the metropolis of this little mountain democracy, and the giver of its name, and it is said to have been the residence of the celebrated chief Ten-ai'-ya." (Powers, 365.)

"Ten-ie-ya . . . responded rather loftily: 'I am the descendant of an Ah-wah-ne-chee chief. His people lived in the mountains and valley where my people have lived. The valley was then called Ah-wah-nee. Ah-wah-ne-chee signifies the dwellers in Ahwahnee.'" (Bunnell, *Discovery*, 1911: 72.) "When these facts were communicated to Captain Boling, and Ah-wah-ne was ascertained to be the *classical* name, the captain said that name was all right enough for history or poetry, but that we could not now change the name Yosemite, nor was it desirable to do so." (Ibid., 73.)

Galen Clark said the name meant "deep grassy valley." Although it may have been the Indians' name for Yosemite Valley, it now applies only to the Ahwahnee Hotel and a bridge on a park road. Construction of the hotel began in the spring of 1926; it was opened on July 14, 1927. (Sargent, *Innkeepers*, 89–93.)

Ahwiyah Point   *Yosemite Valley, Hetch Hetchy Reservoir*

"Ahwiyah" was the Indian name for Mirror Lake (various spellings were used by early writers). It is now applied to a spur on the south wall of Tenaya Canyon below Half Dome, overlooking Mirror Lake. Galen

Clark said the name meant "quiet water." Although this is an old name, it did not appear on the *Yosemite Valley* map until the edition of 1938. The name "Old Man of the Mountains" was in use in 1875. (*Mariposa Gazette*, June 12, 1875.) Some earlier names that fortunately did not survive are "Acorn Peak" and "The Old Piute."

Alder Creek *Yosemite*

A tributary of the South Fork of the Merced River; crossed by the Wawona Road five miles north of Wawona. "Undoubtedly named for a native species of alder, *Alnus rhombifolia*." (YRL files.) A common name, in early use. (*Overland Monthly* 4 [Second Series], no. 22, Oct. 1884: 366; *Mariposa Gazette*, Sept. 2, 1857.) The name was on the 1863–67 Hoffmann and Gardiner map.

Alger: Lakes, Creek *Mono Craters*

R. B. Marshall of the USGS named the one lake (two lakes narrowly joined) in 1909 for John Alger, a packer for the Geological Survey. The creek name derives from the lakes. It was called "Little Rush Creek" in the 1880s. (*Homer Mining Index*, Aug. 23, 1884.) On the 1914 *Mt. Lyell* 30' map it was called "North Fork" (of Rush Creek). The lakes and the creek are in Inyo National Forest, but were in the park from 1890 to 1905.

Alkali Creek *Tuolumne Meadows*

A tributary of Conness Creek, north of the Tuolumne River. The origin of the name is not known. On the Wheeler Survey atlas sheet 56D, 1878–79, it was called "Middle Fork." Lt. McClure used the present name in 1894 (*SCB* 1, no. 5, Jan. 1895: 169), and had it on his maps of 1895 and 1896.

Alpine Lake *Merced Peak*

Named by Ansel F. Hall and Al Solinski on an exploring expedition, September 8–20, 1922. "300 feet higher than Iceberg Lake lies one of about the same proportions, which we called ALPINE LAKE. It is exceedingly impressive in its bleakly majestic setting. . . ." (YRL files.) The name first appeared on the *Merced Peak* quad, 1953. The lake is in Sierra National Forest, but was in the park from 1890 to 1905.

Alpine Lake *Tuolumne Meadows*

Named in 1932 by Al Gardisky "because of its elevation." (Spuller.) Although in Inyo National Forest, the lake was in the park from 1890 to 1905.

Alstot Lake   *Devils Postpile, Cattle Mtn.*

Origin unknown. The name appeared on the *Cattle Mtn.* quad, 1983. To find it on the *Devils Postpile* quad: it is a small lake next to the trail a mile southwest of Iron Mountain. It's in Sierra National Forest, but was in the park from 1890 to 1905.

Altha Lake (2,959 m.)   *Devils Postpile, Mt. Ritter*

Origin unknown. The name appeared on the *Devils Postpile* quad, 1953. The lake is 0.3 mile east of Garnet Lake. It is in Inyo National Forest, but was in the park from 1890 to 1905.

Amelia Earhart Peak (11,982)   *Tuolumne Meadows*

The name was proposed by the Rocketdyne Mountaineering Club for Amelia Earhart Putnam, who disappeared over the Pacific on an around-the-world flight in 1937. Approved by the BGN in 1967. The name is not on early editions of the *Tuolumne Meadows* quad; it first appeared on the 1968 edition. The peak is about 0.7 mile east by south from Ireland Lake.

Andrews: Peak (8,570), **Lake**   *Tower Peak*

The origin of the name is not known, but it may have been named for an army officer during the superintendency of Col. W. W. Forsyth. As a possibility, I suggest Lincoln Clarke Andrews, a cavalry officer and West Point classmate of Lt. Smedberg for whom Smedberg Lake was named. Andrews was promoted to captain in the 15th Cavalry on the same day in 1901 that Smedberg was promoted to captain of the 14th Cavalry. (Heitman, 166.) The peak was first named on the third edition of the *Dardanelles* 30' map, 1912. The lake's name appeared on the *Tower Peak* quad, 1956.

Anne Lake   *Merced Peak*

Origin unknown. A small lake, just north of Rutherford Lake and about 0.7 mile east of the park's eastern boundary. The name appeared on the *Merced Peak* quad, 1953. The lake was within the park from 1890 to 1905.

Anona Lake (2,773 m.)   *Devils Postpile, Cattle Mtn.*

Origin unknown. A small lake in Inyo National Forest about 0.5 mile east of Iron Mountain. It was first named on the *Devils Postpile* quad, 1953. It was within the park from 1890 to 1905.

Ansel Adams, Mount (over 11,760)   *Merced Peak*

Ansel Adams (1902–1984) is the preeminent American landscape photographer of the twentieth century. His wilderness portraits of Yosemite, the Sierra Nevada, Big Sur, and the Southwest awakened three generations to the unparalleled beauty of the American West. Adams had his greatest influence as a conservationist, using his photographs to demonstrate the need to preserve the remaining wild areas in the West. He was a director of the Sierra Club for thirty-seven years, and was the author of seven portfolios of original prints and more than thirty books. In his book *These We Inherit*, Adams wrote: "Our time is short, and the future terrifyingly long . . . . With reverence for life, and with restraint enough to leave some things as they are, we can continue approaching, and perhaps can attain, a new society at last—one which is proportionate to nature."

Adams first saw and photographed this peak in September 1921, when he described it as "undoubtedly inaccessible." On a Sierra Club outing in 1934, the peak was climbed for the first time by three men, who unofficially named it for Adams. Two days later, July 13, 1934, dedication ceremonies were conducted on the summit by a party of fifteen, including Ansel Adams and his wife, Virginia. (*SCB* 11, no. 3, 1922: 315–16, photo opp. 258; and *SCB* 20, no. 1, Feb. 1935: 104–5, photo plate VI.)

The name remained unofficial, since BGN regulations do not permit naming a geographic feature for a living person. It was approved by the BGN in December 1984. The name does not appear on present USGS maps, but will be on the *Mt. Lyell* 7.5′ map when it is published. The peak is at the headwaters of the Lyell Fork of the Merced River, 0.75 mile northeast of Foerster Peak.

Arch Rock   *Yosemite*

A natural tunnel on State Route 140 just north of the park entrance station. Referred to in early accounts as "Tunnel Rock" and "Arched Rocks." (*YNN* 34, no. 1, Jan. 1955: 2.) The most remarkable of all the "earthquake boulders" that have fallen from the walls of Yosemite Valley and the Merced River gorge. (Matthes, *Paper 160*, 108.)

Ardeth Lake   *Tower Peak*

Otto M. Brown, a YNP ranger from 1927 to 1946, named the lake for his wife. (Bingaman, *Guardians*, 103–4.)

Arndt Lake   *Tower Peak*

Named by Lt. H. C. Benson in 1896 for First Sergeant Alvin Arndt, Troop I, Fourth Cavalry, US Army. (Farquhar: Benson.) In September 1893 Arndt led a detachment of troops from Slide Canyon to Tiltill Valley, and learned from sheepmen of a route from Matterhorn Canyon to Hetch Hetchy Valley. (*SCB* 1, no. 5, Jan. 1895: 168.)

Arrowhead Spire   *Yosemite Valley*

Probably named in the late 1930s by Sierra Club climbers, who at that time called it simply "Arrowhead." (*SCB* 25, no. 1, Feb. 1940: 55.)

Artist: Point, Creek   *Yosemite Valley, Yosemite*

From Artist Point, on June 20, 1855, the artist Thomas Ayres drew the first picture of Yosemite Valley. Ayres, born in New Jersey, came to California in 1849, and accompanied James M. Hutchings on the first tourist trip to Yosemite Valley. (*San Francisco Daily California Chronicle*, August 18, 1855.) This point "on account of its impressive comprehensiveness, and near proximity to Yo Semite, has been selected, by all the leading artists, as the best general view. This should receive the name of 'Artist Point' . . . ." (Hutchings, *Tourist's Guide for 1877*: 85.) Ayres was lost at sea en route from San Pedro to San Francisco in April 1858.

Artist Point was mislocated on *Yosemite Valley* maps from 1907 through the edition of 1947; it was moved west one-fourth mile on the edition of 1958. The creek was first named on the fourth edition of the *Yosemite Valley* map, 1927.

Courtesy Yosemite Research Library, NPS

The first picture made in Yosemite Valley, by the artist Thomas Ayres on June 20, 1855.

Ashley Lake (2,909 m.) *Devils Postpile, Cattle Mtn.*

Origin unknown. A small lake in Inyo National Forest 0.6 mile north-east of Iron Mountain. The name appeared on the *Devils Postpile* quad, 1953. The lake was in the park from 1890 to 1905.

Aspen Valley *Lake Eleanor*

Named for an abundance of quaking aspen. The namer is not known, but the name has been in use since at least the time of the construction of the Tioga Road. (*Mammoth City Times*, Nov. 8, 1879.) In that same year Jeremiah Hodgdon built a two-story log cabin at the southeast end of the meadow. (Robert F. Uhte, "Yosemite's Pioneer Cabins," *SCB* 36, no. 5, May 1951: 51.) In 1881 Hodgdon patented 160 acres in sec. 28, T. 1 S., R. 20 E. See also **Hodgdon Ranch**.

Avalanche Creek *Yosemite*

The namer is not known, but may have been one of the members of the Whitney Survey who were in this vicinity in August and September of 1864. The name appears on the Wheeler Survey atlas sheet 56D, 1878–79, and the GLO plat of 1884.

Avonelle Lake *Tower Peak*

Otto M. Brown, a YNP ranger from 1927 to 1946, named the lake for his daughter. (Bingaman, YRL files.)

Babcock Lake (8,983) *Tuolumne Meadows*

Named by Lt. McClure in 1895 for John P. Babcock, chief deputy, California State Board of Fish Commissioners. (Farquhar: McClure.)

Badger Pass *Yosemite*

The namer is not known; the name first appears on the *Yosemite* quad, 1956. The pass is a high point on the old Glacier Point Road, half a mile east of the Badger Pass Ski Area.

Bailey Ridge *Tower Peak*

The origin of the name is unknown, but possibly it was named for an army officer by Col. Forsyth about 1910. George Frederick Bailey, who came up through the ranks, was commissioned as second lieutenant in the cavalry in 1901. (Heitman, 181.) The name appeared on the third *Dardanelles* 30' map, 1912.

Bald Mountain (7,261)   *Lake Eleanor*

The name was submitted to the BGN by the USGS in 1896. An earlier name was "Wade's Mountain," which is how it appeared on the Hoffmann-Gardiner map of 1863–67 and on the Wheeler Survey atlas sheet 56D, 1878–79. Both names are on Lt. McClure's 1896 map. Only the present name is on LeConte's 1900 map and all subsequent maps.

Banner Peak (12,945–3,943 m.)   *Devils Postpile, Mt. Ritter*

The peak was given the early name of "Mammoth Mountain" by the Whitney Survey, but that name didn't get on any maps. (Journal of James T. Gardiner, July 12, 1866; copy in Farquhar Papers, BL.) The present name was given in 1883 by Willard D. Johnson and John Miller of the USGS when they made the first ascent, for a magnificent cloud-banner streaming from the summit. (J. N. LeConte, *SCB* 11, no. 3, 1922: 248.) The peak is on the boundary between Inyo and Sierra national forests, but was within the park from 1890 to 1905.

Bartlett: Peak, Creek   *Pinecrest*

The origin of the name is not certainly known, but I think it quite likely that the peak was named for George True Bartlett by Col. W. W. Forsyth, acting superintendent of the park from 1909 to 1912. Bartlett was an artillery officer, and a classmate of Forsyth at West Point. Although in different branches of the army they had parallel careers, being promoted to higher ranks at the same time. (Heitman, 196.) The peak was named on the third *Dardanelles* 30' map, 1912. The creek was first named on the *Pinecrest* quad, 1956.

Basket Dome (7,612)   *Yosemite Valley, Hetch Hetchy Reservoir*

Galen Clark recited the legend of Tis-sa'-ack, who entered Yosemite Valley with her husband, carrying a great conical burden-basket. They hurried to the valley for water to slake their thirst. The woman was ahead, and when she reached Lake Ah-wei'-yah (Mirror Lake) she drank all the water before he arrived. He was angry, and beat her. She reviled him and threw her basket at him. And as they faced each other "they were turned into stone for their wickedness, and there they still remain. The upturned basket lies beside the husband where the woman threw it, and the woman's face is tear-stained with long dark lines trailing down. Half-Dome is the woman Tis-sa'-ack and North Dome is her husband, while beside the latter is a smaller dome which is still called Basket Dome to this day." (Clark, 87–90.)

Bath Mountain (10,558)   *Matterhorn Peak*
Origin unknown. The name appeared on the first *Bridgeport* 30' map, 1911.

Battalion Pass   *Yosemite*
The name was suggested by Chester Versteeg in 1953 for a pass on the Chowchilla Mountain Road, about three miles southwest of Wawona, believed to be on the route taken by Major James Savage and the Mariposa Battalion in 1851. (YRL files.) The pass is in Sierra National Forest, about two miles outside the park boundary.

Bear Lake   *Tower Peak*
While making a field survey, park rangers Gallison and Wallis saw a large bear at the lake. Because it was so "undomesticated"—unlike those of Yosemite Valley—they were favorably impressed, and named the lake in its honor. (YNP field survey, 1952.)

Bear Valley   *Tower Peak*
The namer is unknown. The name appeared on the third *Dardanelles* 30' map, 1912.

Bear Wallow Spur   *El Portal, Yosemite*
Origin unknown. The name first appeared on the *El Portal* quad, 1947. The feature is in Sierra National Forest, but was in the park from 1890 to 1905.

Bearup Lake   *Tower Peak*
"Named by Lieutenant N. F. McClure for a soldier in his detachment, 1894. Pronounced 'Beer-up.'" (Farquhar: McClure.) It is possible the name may be on the wrong lake. McClure's 1896 map shows it as being approximately where present-day Otter Lake is.

Beatitude, Mount   *Yosemite Valley, Yosemite*
Not on the maps. The point marked "Old Inspiration Point" was originally known as "Mount Beatitude." (See **Inspiration Point** and **Old Inspiration Point**.) "There is a truism that 'Some things can be done as well as others.' In our opinion a full description is not one of them. A passage in the good book says, 'Eye hath not seen, neither hath ear heard, neither hath it entered into the heart of man to conceive what there is laid up in heaven for those who love and serve God.' Now . . . we simply wish to apply the language to those who have the good fortune to see Yo Semite

from this stand-point." (Hutchings, *Scenes*, 1871: 144–45.) This is the point from which a contingent of the Mariposa Battalion had their first view of Yosemite Valley in 1851. (Bunnell, *Discovery*, 1911: 63.)

Beck Lakes (2,998 m. and 2,988 m.)   *Devils Postpile, Mt. Ritter*
John Beck named the lakes for himself about 1882. He was one of the owners of the Minaret Mines, located on the south slope of Iron Mountain. (Farquhar: Versteeg.) Beck apparently went to the area about 1873, and was convinced he had found one of the world's great iron deposits, ". . . an immense mountain of magnetic iron. . . . This is the richest iron ore in the world. The vein is 300 feet wide and 100 feet high. It is two miles long . . . ." (*Fresno Weekly Expositor*, Jan. 22, 1880.)

Beck had a prospecting hole at the outlet of the lower Beck Lake sometime during the 1890s. (USGS, letter from Arch Mahan of Red's Meadow, Oct. 7, 1953.) The lakes are in Inyo National Forest, but were within the park from 1890 to 1905.

Bench Canyon   *Merced Peak, Devils Postpile, Mt. Ritter*
Origin unknown. The creek in Bench Canyon is a tributary of the North Fork of the San Joaquin. The canyon has several benches—broad and nearly level—separated by steeper stretches. The name probably was given by the USGS during the 1898–99 survey for the *Mt. Lyell* 30' map; it is on the first edition, 1901, and is also on LeConte's map of 1900. The canyon is in Sierra National Forest, but was within the park from 1890 to 1905.

Bennettville (site)   *Tuolumne Meadows*
Named for Thomas Bennett, Jr., president of the Great Sierra Consolidated Silver Mining Company. It was expected that the budding town would grow into a fine metropolis; it was originally called "Bennett City." (*Homer Mining Index*, Feb. 18, 1882.) More than $350,000 was spent in building the town and developing the Great Sierra Mine, but not a penny's worth of gold, silver, or any other metal was taken out. Bennettville (also known as "Tioga") had a post office from March 1882 to November 1884. (*Post Offices*, 19.)

Benson Lake   *Tower Peak*
Benson Pass (over 10,080)   *Matterhorn Peak*
Harry Coupland Benson (1857–1924), army officer; stationed in Sequoia National Park, 1891–92; acting superintendent of Yosemite National Park, 1905–8; in Yellowstone National Park, 1909–10. (Heitman,

212.) He was noted for his fanatical devotion to duty, and thus acquired the nickname "Batty" Benson. (Paden, 232.)

Benson developed many trails in Yosemite. The old "Hs" on trees throughout the park north of the Tuolumne River were cut by Benson's troops. (Bingaman, *Pathways*, 36.) The names were given in 1895. (Farquhar: Benson.) A brief biography and portrait of Benson are in *SCB* 12, no. 2, 1925: 175–79.)

Bernice Lake (10,217)   *Tuolumne Meadows*

Bernice Carle Lewis, wife of Washington B. Lewis, the first civilian superintendent of Yosemite National Park, 1916–28. (Farquhar files.)

Big Creek   *Yosemite*

An early name, origin unknown, but in use since at least 1860. (Hutchings, *Illustrated* 4, no. 11, May 1860: 482.)

Big Horn Lake   *Tuolumne Meadows*

"Because Mrs. Spuller discovered the core of a set of Sierra Bighorn sheep at Finger Lake." (Spuller.) The lake is just outside the present park boundary, but was in the park from 1890 to 1905.

Big Meadow   *Yosemite Valley, Yosemite, El Portal*

Probably named by the Whitney Survey; it is on the Hoffmann and Gardiner map of 1863–67 as "Big Meadows."

"As the name implies, these are extensive grassy flats that afford excellent pasturage for stock, and where much of the grain-hay used in Yo Semite is produced." (Hutchings, *In the Heart*, 290–91.)

Big Meadow Creek   *Matterhorn Peak*

Origin unknown. A tributary of Piute Creek, north of Tuolumne Meadows. The name appeared on the first *Bridgeport* 30' map, 1911.

Big Oak Flat Road   *Lake Eleanor, El Portal, Yosemite*

The road reached the floor of Yosemite Valley on July 17, 1874, exactly one month after the Coulterville Road to the valley was opened. The name derives from the town of Big Oak Flat—which earlier was known as "Savage's Diggings," for Major Savage, commander of the Mariposa Battalion. (Paden, 124.)

"The oak from which Oak Flat takes its name was foully murdered. . . . When water was brought into Oak Flat, strange Gorillas, miners I should say, rushed in. . . . Encountering its widely spreading roots they cut them off piece by piece. . . . It withered and died, the limbs were cut for firewood. Then some one in a drunken frolic peeled from the trunk the bark, a foot in thickness. It was not enough to murder, but desecration must follow. So now, there only stands the immense bare, dead trunk, as you enter the town, elevated on a mound left by the washing away of the surrounding soil, a silent monument of shame. . . ." (*Sonora Union Democrat*, June 12, 1869.)

"Big Oak Flat is a little mining village, on a little flat. The 'big oak' which gave name to the place has been undermined and killed. . . . It was nearly ten feet in diameter, and in the days of its glory must have been a grand tree." (Brewer, *Up and Down*, 401.)

The Old Big Oak Flat Road between Crane Flat and Yosemite Valley was replaced by a modern road in 1940. The old road was used for downhill traffic only until October 1942, when the "zigzags" were destroyed by rockslides. (Paden, 299.)

The road was called the "Chinese and Yosemite Road" on the 1880 GLO plat, and "Groveland to Yosemite Road" on a 1906 GLO survey of the Yosemite National Park boundaries.

Bigelow: Peak (10,539), **Lake**   *Tower Peak*

Major John Bigelow, Jr., Ninth Cavalry, US Army, acting superintendent of Yosemite National Park in 1904. (Heitman, 217.) The peak was named first; the name appeared on the third edition of the *Dardanelles* 30' map, 1912. The lake was not named until the 1956 *Tower Peak* quad.

Biledo Meadow   *Yosemite*

There are two cabins at Biledo Meadow. The one made of round timbers was built by Thomas Biledo in 1890. (The name was correctly spelled Biledeaux, according to a YNP ranger who knew him.) Biledo was a French-Canadian who came to the region in the 1880s, and was employed by the Mount Raymond Mining Company. (Robert F. Uhte, "Yosemite's Pioneer Cabins," *SCB* 36, no. 5, May 1951: 51.)

Billy Lake   *Mono Craters*

Origin unknown. A tiny lake just west of Gem Lake. It is in Inyo National Forest, but was in the park from 1890 to 1905.

Bingaman Lake   *Mono Craters*

John W. Bingaman was a YNP ranger from 1921 to 1956. "In 1930 I was a Patrol Ranger in Tuolumne Meadows. I decided to plant an unnamed lake in my district. I took two pack mules loaded with 6,000 rainbow-fry, making a successful plant. By doing so I established the right to call the lake Bingaman." (Bingaman's handwritten statement in YRL files.)

Birch Lake *Lake Eleanor*
Origin unknown. The name first appeared on the present map.

Bishop Creek *Yosemite*
Samuel Addison Bishop (1825–1893), first sergeant in the Mariposa Battalion. The creek is named on the Hoffmann and Gardiner map, 1863–67; on the Wheeler Survey atlas sheet 56D, 1878–79, it appears as "Bishop's Creek."

Bishop came to California from Virginia in 1849. He later went to Owens Valley and settled on the creek that now bears his name, about three miles southwest of the later town of Bishop. He left the area in 1864, in 1866 became one of the first supervisors of Kern County, and in 1868 built the first San Jose streetcar line. (Farquhar; Gudde, *Place Names*, 30; *Historic Spots*, 117.)

Black Mountain *Matterhorn Peak*
Origin unknown. The name was on the first *Bridgeport* 30' map, 1911. The peak is in Toiyabe National Forest, but was within the park from 1890 to 1905.

Black Spring *Yosemite Valley, Yosemite*
"These take their name from the color of the rich alluvial through which the delightfully refreshing waters of two full-flowing cold springs hurry down a deep-cut gully. . . . This, in appearance, is only one spring, while in reality it is formed of two, that boil out from beneath a large flat rock about a hundred yards distant, on sides opposite to each other." (Hutchings, *In the Heart*, 400.) The name was on the first *Yosemite Valley* map, 1907.

Blackie Lake *Merced Peak*
The DFG surveyors of this lake in 1946 reported that warden Herb Black said the lake was sometimes called "Blackie Lake," after himself. (DFG survey.) The lake is in Sierra National Forest about half a mile outside the park, but was in the park from 1890 to 1905.

Blacktop Peak (12,710) *Mono Craters*
The origin is unknown, but it is obviously descriptive. The name

appeared on the first *Mt. Lyell* 30′ map, 1901. The peak is just outside the park boundary, but it was in the park from 1890 to 1905.

Bloody Canyon   *Mono Craters*
The canyon is on the route of an historic Indian trail across the Sierra, a route that was readily adopted by the first white explorers and travelers. (See **Mono Pass**, etc.)

"After crossing the pass [Mono Pass], the way leads down Bloody Canyon—a terrible trail. You would all pronounce it utterly inaccessible to horses, yet pack trains come down, but the bones of several horses or mules and the stench of another told that all had not passed safely . . . . It was a bold man who first took a horse up there. The horses were so cut by sharp rocks that they named it 'Bloody Canyon,' and it has held the name—and it is appropriate—part of the way the rocks in the trail are literally sprinkled with blood from the animals." (Brewer, *Up and Down*, 415–16.) The canyon is east of the park boundary in Inyo National Forest, but it was within the park from 1890 to 1905.

Blue Lake   *Matterhorn Peak*
One of the Virginia Lakes; origin of the name unknown. It appeared on the first *Bridgeport* 30′ map, 1911. The lake was bisected by the park boundary of 1890 to 1905, but it is now entirely in Toiyabe National Forest.

Blue Lake   *Merced Peak*
The namer is unknown; the lake is as blue as blue can be. It is at the headwaters of Bench Canyon, about 0.7 mile southeast of Foerster Peak on the park's southeast boundary. The name first appeared on the *Merced Peak* quad, 1953. The lake is in Sierra National Forest, but was within the park from 1890 to 1905.

Bluejay Creek   *Yosemite Valley, Hetch Hetchy Reservoir*
The name appeared on the first *Yosemite Valley* map, 1907; the namer is unknown. The creek is a tributary of Yosemite Creek.

Bohler Canyon   *Mono Craters*
Joseph Bohler homesteaded 160 acres in sec. 33, T. 1 N., R. 26 E. in 1872, and an additional 160 acres in secs. 27 and 34 in 1876. The headwaters of the creek in this canyon were in the park from 1890 to 1905.

Bond Pass (over 9,680)   *Tower Peak*
Named for Frank Bond of the General Land Office; a member of the

Yosemite National Park Boundary Commission in 1904; later, chairman of the US Board on Geographic Names. (Farquhar: R. B. Marshall.) The pass is on the northern boundary of the park.

Boothe Lake   *Tuolumne Meadows*
    Named for Clyde Boothe, a YNP ranger from 1915 to 1927. (Bingaman, *Guardians*, 93–94.) The lake was once the site of the Boothe Lake High Sierra Camp—which was later moved half a mile and renamed "Vogelsang."

Boundary Creek   *Devils Postpile, Crystal Crag*
    The namer is unknown, but the creek's name apparently derives from the fact that it begins near the boundary between Madera and Mono counties. The name was on the first *Mt. Lyell* 30' map, 1901.

Boundary Hill (over 8,480)   *Yosemite Valley, Hetch Hetchy Reservoir*
    A point on the boundary of the original Yosemite Grant. By the act of June 30, 1864, the federal government granted to the state of California as a state park the "'Cleft' or 'Gorge' known as the Yo-Semite Valley, and . . . the 'Mariposa Big Trees Grove.'" The grant was made "upon the express condition that the premises shall be held for public use, resort, and recreation." The name "Boundary Hill" was given by Lt. Macomb of the Wheeler Survey, and first appears on the survey's map of Yosemite Valley, 1883.

Boundary Lake   *Pinecrest*
    The namer of the lake is unknown; it is just inside the northwest boundary of the park. The name appeared on the *Pinecrest* quad, 1956.

Branigan Lake; Upper and **Middle Branigan Lake**   *Tower Peak*
    Branigan Lake was named in 1894 by Lt. N. F. McClure for a soldier of his detachment. Branigan was later killed in the Philippines. (Farquhar: McClure. See also *SCB* 1, no. 5, Jan. 1895: 183.) The names of the upper and middle lakes were added to the *Tower Peak* quad, 1956.

Breeze Creek   *Hetch Hetchy Reservoir, Tower Peak*
Breeze Lake   *Merced Peak*
    Both these features were named in 1896 for William F. Breeze of San Francisco, who assisted his brother-in-law, Lt. H. C. Benson, in compiling Benson's map of Yosemite National Park. (Farquhar: Benson.) At the time, Breeze worked as a draftsman for the San Francisco and San Joaquin Valley Railroad. (*San Francisco Directory*, 1896.)

Bridalveil: Fall, Creek   *Yosemite Valley, Yosemite*
Bridalveil: Meadow, Moraine   *Yosemite Valley*

Hutchings claimed that he suggested the name on his first visit to Yosemite, in 1855. "'Is it not as graceful, and as beautiful, as the veil of a bride?' to which Mr. Ayres rejoined, 'That is suggestive of a very pretty and most apposite name. I propose that we now baptize it, and call it, 'The Bridal Veil Fall,' as one that is both characteristic and euphonious.'" (Hutchings, *In the Heart*, 89.) Another who claimed the honor of naming the fall wrote: "We make bold to call it the Bridal Veil; and those who may have the felicity to witness the stream floating in the embrace of the morning breeze, will acknowledge the resemblance, and perhaps pardon the liberty we have taken in attempting to apply so poetical a name to this Queen of the Valley." (Warren Baer, editor, *Mariposa Democrat*, Aug. 5, 1856.)

There were some who didn't like the name at all. ". . . in 1856 it was christened 'Falls of Louise' by some explorers in honor of 'the first lady of our party that entered the valley.' Thank Heaven, the cataract wouldn't stand this nonsense; and it seemed to me to be pleading with us to have the 'Bridal Veil' folly thrown aside, that it might be known forever by its Indian baptism, 'Pohono.'" (Starr King, 47–48.) Another early name was "Cascade of the Rainbow." (Hutchings *Illustrated* 1, no. 1, July 1856: 3.)

The Indians did indeed call the fall "Pohono;" the name was still in use in 1863 when the Whitney Survey was there. (Brewer, *Up and Down*, 404.) See **Pohono Trail** for the differing explanations of the word's meaning.

The fall and the creek were named on King and Gardiner's map of 1865. The meadow was named on the first *Yosemite Valley* map, 1907; the moraine was named beginning with the eighth edition, 1958. "Bridalveil Moraine" might well be incorrectly located. It is near El Capitan Meadow, while the moraine near Bridalveil Meadow is unnamed. There are also six other moraines between the two meadows. (Information from N. King Huber, USGS; see Matthes, *Paper 160*, 56–57.)

Broderick, Mount (6,706)   *Yosemite Valley, Yosemite*

David Colbreth Broderick (1820–1859), US Senator from California, 1857–59. He was killed in a duel with David S. Terry, chief justice of the California Supreme Court, as the result of political differences. (*Historic Spots*, 412.)

The name was originally applied to what is now called "Liberty Cap," which was given that name in 1865. The King and Gardiner map of 1865 calls it "Cap of Liberty or Mt. Broderick."

Bruce, Mount (9,728)   *Merced Peak*

Albert O. Bruce patented 160 acres in sec. 35, T. 4 S., R. 21 E. in 1889, and another 160 acres in sec. 35 in 1892, giving him the north half of the section—covering all of what is now North Wawona. The name "Mount Bruce" was proposed by the Park Service in 1976 to commemorate the Bruce family, who pioneered in the Wawona area in the 1850s. (BGN, 1976.) The peak is on Buena Vista Crest, six miles southwest of Merced Peak. It is not named on early editions of the *Merced Peak* 15' quad.

Buck: Creek, Camp   *Merced Peak*

Buck Camp is said to have got its name because buck privates were sent there for duty—apparently an undesirable post. Both names were on the first *Mt. Lyell* 30' map, 1901. The former camp was located where Buck Creek crosses the trail; it is now the site of a summer ranger station.

Buckeye Pass (over 9,600)   *Matterhorn Peak*

The pass, on the northeast boundary of the park, gets its name from the Buckeye Mill Company, owned and operated by E. Roberts during the 1860s. (Maule.) The buckeye tree is not native to this area. One might speculate that the name was given for or by a native of Ohio. The name appeared on the first *Bridgeport* 30' map, 1911.

Buckhorn Meadow   *Devils Postpile, Cattle Mtn.*

Origin unknown; the name appeared on the *Cattle Mtn.* quad, 1983. To locate it on the *Devils Postpile* quad: it is in the lower left quadrant of the map, on a trail, half a mile southwest of the letter 'I' in the word "NA-TIONAL." It's in Sierra National Forest, but was in the park from 1890 to 1905.

Budd: Lake, Creek   *Tuolumne Meadows*

James H. Budd, governor of California, 1895–99. The creek was named first; the name appears on the first edition of the *Mt. Lyell* 30' map, 1901. The lake's name was ratified by a BGN decision in 1932. The creek was called "Cathedral Creek" in 1883, undoubtedly because it rose just east of Cathedral Peak. (*Homer Mining Index*, July 28, 1883.)

Buena Vista: Peak (9,709), **Creek, Lake, Trail**   *Yosemite*
Buena Vista Crest   *Merced Peak*

A common name; Spanish for "beautiful view." The peak's name is an early one: it appears on the Hoffmann and Gardiner map, 1863–67. The creek is named on the first *Yosemite* 30' map, 1897, and the other features are first named on the present maps. The name "Buena Vista Pass" has also been approved by the BGN, but is not on the *Yosemite* quad—no doubt due to lack of space. The pass is crossed by a trail just east of Buena Vista Lake, in sec. 12, T. 4 S., R. 22 E.

Bunnell: Cascade, Point (8,193)   *Merced Peak*

Lafayette Houghton Bunnell (1824–1903) proposed the name of Yosemite Valley and also named many other features in and near the valley. Bunnell was born in Rochester, NY, served in the Mexican War, and came to California in 1849. As a member of the Mariposa Battalion, he was one of the first white men to enter Yosemite Valley, on March 27, 1851. Bunnell's book, *Discovery of the Yosemite, and the Indian War of 1851, which led to that event*, went through four editions between 1880 and 1911.

Bunnell Point was formerly called "Sugarbowl Dome;" it was renamed shortly before 1920. (Hall, 82. The unnamed dome 0.7 mile west, on the other side of the Merced River, has also been known as "Sugarbowl Dome.") The BGN approved the names "Bunnell Point" and "Bunnell Cliff" in 1912. The latter name has not been used on maps. Bunnell Cascade (mistakenly spelled with one 'l' on the *Merced Peak* quad), on the Merced River at the head of Lost Valley, also had earlier names: "Washburn Cascade," "Diamond Shower Fall," and "Little Grizzly Falls." The present name was approved by a BGN decision in 1932.

Burro Pass (over 10,640)   *Matterhorn Peak*

The origin of the name is unknown. The pass was crossed by Lt. McClure in August 1894. It was not named then, nor did he name it. (*SCB* 1, no. 5, Jan. 1895: 175.) The name appeared on the Mono National Forest map in 1928.

Buttresses, The   *Devils Postpile, Crystal Crag*

The namer is unknown. The feature is a long north-south cliff in Devils Postpile National Monument. It was first named on the *Devils Postpile* quad, 1953. The area was within the park from 1890 to 1905, and was then in the national forest for six years until creation of the national monument in 1911.

Cabin Lake   *Devils Postpile, Mt. Ritter*

The site of a cabin built by David Nidever in the early 1900s. (INF archives. See **Nydiver Lakes**.) The lake is in Inyo National Forest, but was within the park from 1890 to 1905.

Courtesy Yosemite Research Library, NPS

Lafayette Houghton Bunnell, surgeon with the Mariposa Battalion,
the man who named Yosemite Valley.

California Falls   *Tuolumne Meadows*

Named in July 1892. ". . . then follow the river closely to the head of a
cascade of unrivaled beauty and grandeur. We named it the California
Cascade." (R. M. Price, "Through the Tuolumne Cañon," *SCB* 1, no. 6,
May 1895: 203.) Through confusion between Price and those who put his
names on their maps, what he named "California Cascade" is the present
Le Conte Falls. California Falls was called "Stella Falls" on LeConte's 1900
map. It was unnamed on the first two editions of the *Mt. Lyell* 30' map,
1901 and 1905, and had its present name beginning with the edition of
1910.

Camiaca Peak (11,739)   *Matterhorn Peak*

In the Yosemite Research Library files there is a copy of a handwritten note from Doug Hubbard about an Indian who gave him a piece of root to chew; it tasted like ginseng. The Indian said that when he was young he gathered large quantities of the root and took them to the Sioux country to trade for buffalo robes. "He told me his name was Cloudy Camiaca. . . . Later, when mapping a part of Yosemite National Park I applied it to rather a fine peak there. I thought I was playing quite a joke on Californians and at the same time giving Camiaca a final trip."

Unfortunately this information is not correct. When this part of the park's rearranged boundary was surveyed by A. F. Dunnington in 1906, the peak was already named. (Survey notes, YRL.) Hubbard was the park naturalist some fifty years later. The peak's name appeared on the first *Bridgeport* 30' map, 1911.

Camp Creek *Matterhorn Peak*

Origin unknown. The name appeared on the first *Bridgeport* 30' map, 1911.

Cargyle: Meadow, Creek *Devils Postpile, Cattle Mtn.*

Origin unknown. Both names were on the first *Mt. Lyell* 30' map, 1901. The features are now in Sierra National Forest, but they were within the park from 1890 to 1905.

Carlon Guard Station *Lake Eleanor*

Dan and Donna Carlon built the Carl Inn in 1916. It burned in 1920, was rebuilt, and burned again. The Park Service took over the land in 1932. (Paden, 213.)

Cascade Cliffs *Yosemite Valley*

"A huge massive granite formation on the south side of Little Yosemite Valley, about two miles east of Nevada Fall. Water cascades down these cliffs throughout much of the year." (*YNN* 34, no. 1, Jan. 1955: 4.) The name was on the first *Yosemite Valley* map, 1907. It is not on early editions of the *Merced Peak* quad, but appears on the 1972 edition. The cliffs are just south of the word "Valley" in the name Little Yosemite Valley.

"In few other places in the Yosemite region is the granite more continuously massive than in the Cascade Cliffs. Only one horizontal master joint divides the rock . . . . The dark streaks indicate the paths followed by the ribbon cascades . . . from which the cliffs take their name." (Matthes, *Paper 160*, caption, plate 45; also see p. 99.)

Cascade Lake   *Tuolumne Meadows*

Named by Everett Spuller in 1932 "because of the cascade coming down from the glacierette from North Peak." (Spuller.) The lake is just outside the northeast park boundary in Inyo National Forest, but was within the park from 1890 to 1905.

The Cascades   *Yosemite Valley, Yosemite*
Cascade Creek   *Hetch Hetchy Reservoir, Yosemite, Yosemite Valley*

"Nearly three miles below the valley, in the cañon, are two beautiful cascade falls of over seven hundred feet each. I named these falls the Cascades on a first exploration [in 1851], the name being suggested by their formation and twin-like appearance." (Bunnell, *Report*, 12–13.)

John Muir crossed Cascade Creek in 1869. "Never was a stream more fittingly named, for so far as I have traced it above and below our camp it is one continuous bouncing, dancing, white bloom of cascades." (Muir, *First Summer*, 140.)

The Cascades were called "Cascade Falls" on the first three editions of the *Yosemite Valley* map, 1907–22.

Castle Cliffs   *Yosemite Valley, Hetch Hetchy Reservoir*

The name is obvious, the origin unknown. The name is on the first *Yosemite Valley* map, 1907.

Castle Lake   *Devils Postpile, Mammoth Mtn.*

Origin unknown. A small lake about two miles south-southeast of Shadow Lake. The name appeared on the *Devils Postpile* quad, 1953. It is in Inyo National Forest, but was in the park from 1890 to 1905.

Cathedral: Peak (10,940), **Lakes, Pass, Fork** (of Echo Creek)
                                                  Tuolumne Meadows
Cathedral Range   *Tuolumne Meadows, Merced Peak*
Cathedral Creek   *Tuolumne Meadows, Hetch Hetchy Reservoir*

The peak was named by the California Geological Survey in 1863. "From a high ridge, crossed just before reaching this lake [Tenaya], we had a fine view of a very prominent exceedingly grand landmark through all the region, and to which the name of Cathedral Peak has been given. . . . The majesty of its form and its dimensions are such, that any work of human hands would sink into insignificance if placed beside it." (Whitney, *Geology*, 425.)

First ascent by John Muir, September 7, 1869. "This I may say is the first time I have been at church in California, led at here at last, every door graciously opened for the poor lonely worshiper." (Muir, *First Summer*, 336.)

The names of the other Cathedral features derive from the peak. The pass and one lake—the larger one—had been named by the time of the first *Mt. Lyell* 30′ map, 1901.

Cathedral Creek was called "Rocky Canyon Creek" in the early 1880s. (*Homer Mining Index*, July 22, 1882 and July 28, 1883.)

Courtesy The Bancroft Library
Cathedral Peak and upper Cathedral Lake. Photograph by Joseph N. LeConte.

Cathedral: Spires, Rocks   *Yosemite Valley, Yosemite*

James M. Hutchings named Cathedral Spires in September 1862. The California Geological Survey named "Cathedral Rock" in 1863. (Whitney, *Geology*, 410.) Both names are on King and Gardiner's 1865 map of Yosemite Valley.

"From one point, these spires appear symmetrical, of equal height, squarely cut, and rising above the edge of the cliff behind exactly like two towers of a Gothic cathedral." (Whitney, *The Yosemite Book*, 58.)

"The Cathedral Rocks and Spires, known as Poo-see-na-chuc-ka, meaning 'Mouse-proof Rocks,' from a fancied resemblance in shape to their acorn magazines or *caches*." (Bunnell, *Discovery*, 1911: 217.)

An earlier name for the rocks was "The Three Graces." (Hutchings, *In the Heart*, 400.)

Cecile Lake (3,121 m.) *Devils Postpile, Mt. Ritter*

Origin unknown; the highest large lake east of the Minarets. The name appeared on the *Devils Postpile* quad, 1953. The lake is in Inyo National Forest, but was within the park from 1890 to 1905.

Center Mountain (11,273) *Matterhorn Peak*

Probably named by the USGS during the 1905–9 survey for the *Bridgeport* 30' map; it is on the first edition, 1911.

Chain Lakes *Merced Peak*

A chain of three lakes in a row at the headwaters of the South Fork of the Merced River, just west of Gale Peak. The namer is unknown. The name appeared on the fifth *Yosemite* 30' map, 1911.

Cherry: Lake, Creek *Lake Eleanor, Pinecrest, Cherry Lake North*
Cherry Ridge *Pinecrest, Cherry Lake North*

The origin of the name is not known, but it is an old one: "Cherry Valley" is on the Wheeler Survey atlas sheet 56D, 1878–79. "Probably named for bitter cherry (*Prunus emarginata*) growing in the vicinity." (Hartesveldt, YRL files.) The lake is artificial; it was formed by damming Cherry Creek.

Chetwood Creek *Merced Peak, Devils Postpile, Cattle Mtn.*
Chetwood Cabin *Merced Peak*

Chetwood was an early cattleman. Although the Chetwood names do not appear on the *Mt. Lyell* 30' maps, François Matthes stopped at "Chetwood Cattle Camp" in July 1921. (Matthes, v. 25, July 24, 1921.)

Chilnualna: Creek, Fall, Lakes *Yosemite*

A name of uncertain meaning and unknown origin. Said to mean "leaping water." (YRL files.) The creek was named first; it was spelled "Chilnoialny" on the Hoffmann and Gardiner map, 1863–67, "Chilnoalna" by a GLO surveyor in 1883, and "Chilnooilny" by R. M. Price in 1892. (*SCB* 1, no. 1, Jan. 1893: 9.) The creek and the fall—with the present spelling—were on the first *Yosemite* 30' map, 1897. The name for the lakes was approved by the BGN in 1932.

Chinquapin *Yosemite*
Chinquapin Falls *El Portal*

For the bush chinquapin, *Castanopsis sempervirens*. Called "Chinquapin Flat" by Hutchings. (*In the Heart*, 474.) The name is on Lt. McClure's maps of 1895 and 1896 and on the first *Yosemite* 30' map, 1897. On the 1884 GLO plat it is called "Glacier Point Station." There is no longer a ranger station at the road junction, as shown on early editions of the *Yosemite* quad.

Chiquito: Creek, Lake, Pass (over 8,000)   *Merced Peak*

Chiquito is a Spanish diminutive. The creek was originally called "Chiquito Joaquin," meaning the "Little Joaquin"—a branch of the San Joaquin River. The name appears on Hoffmann and Gardiner's map of 1863–67. Gardiner referred to "Chiquita Joaquin." (Journal of James T. Gardiner, July 26, 1866; copy in Farquhar papers, BL.) All the present "Chiquito" names are on the *Mt. Lyell* 30' map, 1901. The pass is on the park's southern boundary. The lake and the creek are in Sierra National Forest, but the lake was bisected by the park's 1890–1905 boundary.

Chittenden Lake   *Merced Peak*

William A. Dill and Scott M. Soule of the DFG reported in 1946 that this lake is named after a Fresno family. A galvanized iron sign on a tree near the outlet read: "Chittenden Lake. Doris & Ruby. Mary & Ken. Corynne & Bob. July 5, 1930. El. 9,800."

The lake was named in the 1920s by Billy Brown, a packer. Corynne and Bob are the Chittendens; Mary and Ken are the Stanifords. (See **Stanford Lakes**.) Mr. Chittenden was a sheriff of Fresno County. (Letter from Barton A. Brown, M.D., Jan. 20, 1987.) The lake is in Sierra National Forest, but was in the park from 1890 to 1905.

Chittenden Peak (9,685)   *Tower Peak*

Hiram Martin Chittenden (1858–1917); military engineer and historian; graduated from West Point in 1884. He worked on road construction in Yellowstone National Park, 1891–93. In 1904–5 he was a member of the boundary commission for Yosemite National Park. He is best known for his definitive work, *The American Fur Trade of the Far West* (1902).

The peak probably was named by R. B. Marshall of the USGS, a friend of Chittenden's. On his maps of 1895 and 1896, Lt. McClure called the peak "Jack Main Mt.," a name derived from Jack Main Canyon, immediately to the west.

Church Tower   *Yosemite Valley, Yosemite*

According to the USGS the name originates with the Sierra Club; it was in use at the time of the first ascent, in 1935. (*SCB* 21, no. 1, Feb. 1936: 98.) It appeared on the maps in the 1950s.

Clarice Lake   *Devils Postpile, Mt. Ritter*

Origin unknown. It's a small lake just off the John Muir Trail southeast of Garnet Lake. The name appeared on the *Devils Postpile* quad, 1953. The lake is in Inyo National Forest, but was within the park from 1890 to 1905.

Clark, Mount (11,522)
Clark: Range, Canyon, Fork (of Illilouette Creek)   *Merced Peak*

Galen Clark (1814–1910), the first guardian of Yosemite State Park (1864), and discoverer of the Mariposa Grove. When he was in his forties he feared that he was going to die of a lung ailment. He went to the mountains for the sake of his health, built a cabin in the spring of 1857 at what became "Clark's Station" (now Wawona), and lived another 53 years.

The mountain was once called "Gothic Peak," and later, the "Obelisk," a name given by the Whitney Survey. The name "Mt Clark" is on the Hoffmann and Gardiner map, 1863–67.

"Mr. King, who, with Mr. Gardner, made the ascent of the peak says that its summit is so slender, that when on top of it they seemed to be suspended in air." (Whitney, *The Yosemite Guide-Book*, 1870: 109.) "We reached the summit and found it one block of granite with a flat top about four feet square, just big enough to set up my transit." (Journal of James T. Gardiner, July 12, 1866; copy in Farquhar Papers, BL.)

Clark Point   *Yosemite Valley*

On the south side of Merced Canyon, near Vernal Fall. The Yosemite Valley commissioners named the point in 1891 for Galen Clark. (*YNN* 34, no. 1, Jan. 1955: 4.) The name did not appear on the map until the ninth edition, 1970.

Clarks Valley   *El Portal*

Fred N. Clark patented 160 acres in secs. 28 and 33, T. 4 S., R. 19 E. in 1885. Although now well outside the park boundaries, the valley was in the park from 1890 to 1905.

Clouds Rest (9,926)   *Yosemite Valley, Tuolumne Meadows*

"Cloud's Rest . . . was so named by a squad from C Company, who had passed up the middle Branch [the Merced River], and were turned back by seeing the clouds gather on that peak for a snowstorm that followed that night, the second of our first entrance into the valley." (Bunnell, *Report*, 11; see also Bunnell, *Discovery*, 1880: 11.) That makes the date of naming March 28, 1851. Clouds Rest was mistakenly called "Tanaya Peak" on a GLO 1885 plat, surveyed in 1883.

"The undulating surface of the wall below Clouds Rest is an outstanding example of sheeting [exfoliation] that parallels the topographic surface; the sheets are concave in the bowl-shaped basins high on the cliff face and convex on the intervening spurs." (Huber, 34.)

Cockscomb (over 11,040)   *Tuolumne Meadows*
François E. Matthes, USGS, named this peak in 1919. "The writer does not claim to be a connoisseur in poultry; nevertheless, he believes that the likeness to a lobate cockscomb is fairly close." (*SCB* 11, no. 1, Jan. 1920: 26.) Called "Cockscomb Crest" and "Cockscomb Peak" before being given the present name.

Matthes was anticipated by an earlier writer who described it as an "immense mountain, whose shape reminds me of a gigantic fine-toothed comb, with most of the teeth broken, and the rest filled in with dirt." (*Mariposa Free Press*, Oct. 28, 1870.)

Colby Mountain (9,631)   *Hetch Hetchy Reservoir*
William Edward Colby (1875–1964), a member of the Board of Directors of the Sierra Club for forty-nine years, forty-seven of them as secretary and two as president. One of the most influential conservationists of the first half of the twentieth century; instrumental in enlarging Sequoia and creating Kings Canyon and Olympic national parks; first chairman of the California State Park Commission, 1927–36. (See "Remembering Will Colby" in *SCB* 50, no. 10, Dec. 1965: 69–78.)

The mountain was named by R. B. Marshall, USGS. (Farquhar: Marshall.) The name appeared on the fifth edition of the *Yosemite* 30' map, 1911.

Cold: Canyon, Mountain (10,301)   *Tuolumne Meadows*
Origin unknown. Both names were on the first *Mt. Lyell* 30' map, 1901.

Cold Creek   *Devils Postpile, Crystal Crag*
The namer is unknown; the creek is crossed by the trail about four miles south of Devils Postpile. It was first named on the *Devils Postpile* quad, 1953. Although in Inyo National Forest, the creek was within the park from 1890 to 1905.

Columbia Finger (over 10,320)   *Tuolumne Meadows*
"Columbia" has been used since the founding of the country as a poetic and patriotic name for the United States of America—derived from Christopher Columbus. (For perhaps the earliest known use of the name,

see George R. Stewart, *Names on the Land*, first Sentry edition, p. 171.) The peak was named "Columbia's Finger" on Lt. McClure's maps of 1895 and 1896.

Columbia Rock (5,031)   *Yosemite Valley, Yosemite*
". . . Columbia Rock, a bold bluff of the solid wall, affording a splendid near view of the bed of the Valley and the southern wall." (Article by John Conway, *Mariposa Gazette*, April 27, 1878.) Conway built the trail to the top of Yosemite Falls in 1873; the feature probably was named then.

Conness, Mount (12,590); **Conness: Creek, Lakes, Glacier**
Tuolumne Meadows
John Conness (1821–1909), a native of Ireland, came to the US in 1836; member of the California legislature, 1853–54, 1860–61; US senator, 1863–69; lived in Massachusetts from 1869 until his death.
The peak was named in 1863 by the Whitney Survey—for good reason. "Mount Conness bears the name of a distinguished citizen of California, now a United States Senator, who deserves, more than any other person, the credit of carrying the bill organizing the Geological Survey of California, through the Legislature." (Whitney, *The Yosemite Guide-Book*, 1870: footnote p. 100.) Conness also introduced the bill in the Senate that granted Yosemite Valley and the Mariposa Grove to the state.
The mountain is named on Hoffmann and Gardiner's map of 1863–67. The creek is named on the Wheeler Survey atlas sheet 56D, 1878–79. The lakes and the glacier are in Inyo National Forest, but were in the park from 1890 to 1905. They were first named on the *Tuolumne Meadows* quad, 1956.

Cony Crags (10,867 and 10,539)   *Merced Peak*
Named for the abundant "conies" (*Ochotona princeps muiri*), sometimes called "pikas" or "rock-rabbits," living in talus around the crags. (BGN, 1963.)

Cooney Lake   *Matterhorn Peak*
One of the Virginia Lakes; the origin of the name is unknown. It is in Toiyabe National Forest, but was within the park from 1890 to 1905.

Cora Lakes   *Merced Peak*
Cora Creek   *Merced Peak, Devils Postpile, Cattle Mtn.*
R. B. Marshall of the USGS named the lakes for Mrs. Cora Cressey Crow. (Farquhar: Marshall.) Just as a guess, Mrs. Crow may have been

Marshall's mother-in-law. See **Elizabeth Lake** for another appearance of the name "Crow." The name appeared on the third edition of the *Mt. Lyell* 30' map, 1910. The creek was first named on the *Devils Postpile* map, 1953. These features were within the park from 1890 to 1905.

Corral Meadow (77 Corral)   *Devils Postpile, Cattle Mtn.*
    In the 1870s a stock trail was built from Soldier Meadow directly across the canyon of the North Fork of the San Joaquin River to a corral in this meadow—constructed in 1877. At the time of the Mammoth mining boom Corral Meadow had the name of "Enslin's Sheep Camp." (*San Francisco Mining amd Scientific Press*, Aug. 16, 1879: 98.)
    The name "77 Corral" was on the *Mt. Lyell* 30' maps, was omitted from the *Devils Postpile* map, and has been restored on the *Cattle Mtn.* map. The area is in Sierra National Forest, but was within the park from 1890 to 1905.

Cottonwood Creek   *Hetch Hetchy Reservoir*
    This name is on the Hoffmann and Gardiner map, 1863–67, and therefore the creek may have been named by the California Geological Survey. It was used by Hoffmann in a letter to Whitney, Sept. 10, 1873. (Hoffmann correspondence, BL.)

Coulterville Road   *El Portal, Yosemite, Yosemite Valley*
    George W. Coulter opened a store in 1850 in the place that would later bear his name. He was one of the first commissioners appointed to manage the Yosemite Park grant, 1864. The Coulterville Road and the Big Oak Flat Road were in competition to reach Yosemite Valley; the former won out, reaching the valley floor on June 17, 1874, one month before the competitor. Thus the first wheeled vehicles entered Yosemite Valley over this road, although the Big Oak Flat Road eventually got the lion's share of the traffic. The best account of the building of the two roads is in Paden and Schlichtmann.

Coyote Rocks   *Hetch Hetchy Reservoir*
    Just north of the Tioga Road. Origin of the name is unknown.

Crane Flat; North Crane Creek   *Lake Eleanor*
Crane Creek   *El Portal*
    "This name [for the flat] was suggested by the shrill and startling cry of some sand-hill cranes we surprised as they were resting on this

elevated table." (Bunnell, *Discovery*, 1880: 316.) "It is often visited by blue cranes to rest and feed on their long journeys." (Muir, *First Summer*, 122.)

Bunnell's explanation probably is the correct one, but a differing opinion says that Crane Flat was named after a man named Crean. (Baron de Hubner, *A Ramble Around the World*, 1875: 177.)

Crane Flat and Crane Creek were named on the Hoffmann and Gardiner map, 1863–67; on that map North Crane Creek was called "Big tree Cr."—obviously because it flowed through the Tuolumne Grove of Big Trees.

Crater Creek *Devils Postpile, Crystal Crag*
Crater Meadow; Upper Crater Meadow *Crystal Crag*
The namer is unknown. The creek was named on the first *Mt. Lyell* 30' map, 1901. All the features are in Inyo National Forest, but were within the park from 1890 to 1905.

Crazy Mule Gulch *Matterhorn Peak*
The origin of the name is unknown; it was on the first *Bridgeport* 30' map, 1911. Lt. McClure's 1895 map shows two canyons in this area, which he called "Twin Canyons." His 1896 map omitted that name. See **Twin Cañons** in the Old Names list.

Crescent: Lake, Creek *Yosemite*
The lake name is an old one; it appears on the Hoffmann and Gardiner map, 1863–67. McClure's 1895 map shows it as "Duncan Crescent Lake," referring to a noted bear hunter. His 1896 map calls it "Crescent Meadow."

"Duncan is quite a hunter, and has killed some seventy grizzlies." (Tileston letter, June 22, 1871.) ". . . Duncan was rough in his ways, wanted to have his own way, and was generally hard to manage. I got along with him without a quarrel, though, which was doing well." (Tileston letter, Sept. 8, 1871.)

"The lake is in the exact form of a crescent, with both horns pointing westward. . . . On its border is a log cabin inhabited in summer by a mighty nimrod, Jim Duncan, who has killed forty or fifty bears within the past six years." (George B. Bayley, "Eleven Days in the High Sierra," *The Argonaut* 3, no. 24, Dec. 21, 1878.)

"A mile brought us to Crescent Lake . . . still partly covered with melting ice. At the northern end of the lake we came upon a forlorn little cabin, half-buried in a snow-drift. . . . Bones of deer and of other game were littered about the room, one end of which was cumbered with the wreck of a huge chimney of rock. . . . It was once the summer home of Jim

Duncan, a man whose fame as a hunter still lingers in the memory of old Sierra back-woodsmen." (Chase, 160.)

Crest Creek   *Mono Craters*
Origin unknown. The creek flows southeast from below Koip Crest to Gem Lake. It is in Inyo National Forest, but was within the park from 1890 to 1905.

Crocker Point (7,090)   *Yosemite Valley, Yosemite*
Named for Charles Crocker (1822–1888), one of the "Big Four" who financed and built the Central Pacific Railroad. (*YNN* 34, no. 1, Jan. 1955: 5.) The name appeared on the first *Yosemite Valley* map, 1907.

Crocker Ridge   *Lake Eleanor*
Henry Robinson Crocker (1827–1904), the proprietor of "Crocker's Station," later called "Crocker's Sierra Resort," fifteen buildings constructed between 1880 and 1887 on the Big Oak Flat Road. The resort lasted until about 1920. (Farquhar; also Paden, 207–12.) Crocker homesteaded 160 acres in sec. 33, T. 1 S., R. 19 E. in 1883. The area containing the ridge and Crocker's Station was within the park from 1890 to 1905, but is now in Stanislaus National Forest.

Crown Point (11,346)   *Matterhorn Peak*
A high point and USGS triangulation station on the northeast boundary of the park. It was named on August 30, 1905 by J. P. Walker who was surveying the relocated park boundary. (Field notes, YRL.) The name appeared on the first *Bridgeport* 30′ map, 1911.

Curry Village   *Yosemite Valley, Yosemite*
Formerly called "Camp Curry." David A. Curry (1860–1917) and Jennie Foster Curry (1861–1948) set up seven tents in Yosemite Valley in 1899, the beginning of Camp Curry and the present Yosemite Park and Curry Company. (Farquhar; *YNN* 34, no.1, Jan. 1955: 4.)

Dana, Mount (13,053); **Dana: Plateau, Lake**   *Mono Craters*
Dana: Meadows, Fork (of the Tuolumne River)
                                       Tuolumne Meadows, Mono Craters
Mount Dana was named in 1863 by the Whitney Survey for James Dwight Dana (1813–1895), professor of natural history and geology at Yale, 1849–90. Dana is considered the foremost geologist of his time; he provided the first comprehensive summary of North American geology.

In 1889, J. N. LeConte copied from a record he found on the summit: "State Geological Survey, June 28, 1863. J. D. Whitney, W. H. Brewer, Charles F. Hoffmann, ascended this mountain June 28th and again the 29th. We give the name of Mount Dana to it in honor of J. D. Dana, the most eminent American geologist. Approximate height 13,126 feet." (*SCB* 11, no. 3, 1922: 247.) Only Brewer and Hoffmann climbed the mountain on the 28th; Whitney was not feeling well. He and Brewer went up on the 29th. (Brewer, *Up and Down*, 408–9.) The ascent on the 28th was the first recorded one. "Up very early, and with Hoffmann started for Mt. Dana. Icy, over rocks and snow, and made the summit in 4 hours. So up by 10 A.M. and staid nearly 4 hours." (Brewer's diary, June 28, 1863, in BL.)

The peak appeared as "Dana Mt." on the first four editions of the *Mt. Lyell* 30' map; changed to "Mt. Dana" in 1922. Dana Fork was called "Dana Creek" on the Wheeler Survey atlas sheet 56D, 1878–79. The plateau was named on the first *Mt. Lyell* map, 1901. The name of Dana Meadows appeared on the third edition, 1910. Much earlier it was known as "Tioga Meadows." (*Homer Mining Index*, Oct. 1, 1881.)

Dark Hole   *Hetch Hetchy Reservoir*

The origin of the name is unknown. It was said to have been a stage station on the old Tioga Road. (Chase, 13.) This was a forest-ringed meadow, and was a favorite collecting area for early botanists. (YRL files.) On Lt. McClure's 1896 map it has the designation "D. H. Corrals." The present name is on the first *Yosemite* 30' map, 1897.

Davis, Mount (12,311–3,750 m.); **Davis Lakes**   *Devils Postpile, Mt. Ritter*

Lieutenant Milton Fennimore Davis (1864–1938), with the first troops assigned to guard the newly created Yosemite National Park, in 1891, at which time he made the first ascent of the mountain. (Heitman, 359.) The peak was named by Lt. McClure in 1894.

"I ascended the peak on Aug. 31, 1891. I took two days for the trip. Slept out without blankets at timber-line, making a fire of the last tree. I was accompanied most of the way by a Methodist preacher, Dr. E. W. Beers, of Anamosa, Iowa. The trip nearly killed him." (Letter, Davis to Versteeg, in Farquhar files.) "Beers gave out and did not cross the last gorge and make the last 2,000 feet." (*SCB* 12, no. 3, 1926: 305.)

Although McClure's 1896 map had the name as "Mt. Davis," it was "Davis Mt." on the *Mt. Lyell* 30' maps until the fifth edition, 1922. The lakes were not named until the *Devils Postpile* quad, 1953. The peak and lakes are in Inyo National Forest, but were in the park from 1890 to 1905.

Deadhorse Lake *Devils Postpile, Mt. Ritter*

A nice graphic name for an attractive alpine lake east of the Ritter Range and south of Minaret Lake. The namer is unknown; the name appeared on the *Devils Postpile* quad, 1953. The lake is in Inyo National Forest, but was within the park from 1890 to 1905.

Deadman: Pass, Creek *Devils Postpile, Mammoth Mtn.*

In about 1868 the headless body of a man was found near the creek. It was presumed to be Robert Hume, a miner from Carson City, who had been killed by his partner. The beginnings of this tale are in the story of the "Lost Cement Mines" in Mark Twain's *Roughing It*. The fullest details are in W. A. Chalfant's *Gold, Guns & Ghost Towns*. The name has been extended to "Deadman Summit" on US 395.

The creek and the pass were named on Lt. McClure's 1896 map, and were in the park from 1890 to 1905.

Deep Canyon *Hetch Hetchy Reservoir*

An old name, origin unknown. It was on Lt. McClure's maps of 1895 and 1896.

Deer Camp *Yosemite*

Origin unknown. The name first appeared on the *Yosemite* quad, 1956.

Delaney Creek *Tuolumne Meadows*

John Muir made his first sortie into the Sierra Nevada, from the foothills to Tuolumne Meadows, as a shepherd in the employ of Pat Delaney, in 1869. "Mr. Delaney has hardly had time to ask me how I enjoyed my trip, though he has facilitated and encouraged my plans all summer, and declares I'll be famous some day, a kind guess that seems strange and incredible to a wandering wilderness-lover with never a thought or dream of fame while humbly trying to trace and learn and enjoy Nature's lessons." (Muir, *First Summer*, 342.)

The creek was first named on Lt. McClure's map of 1895.

Detachment Meadow *Merced Peak*

The exact origin is unknown, but it undoubtedly dates from when US Army patrols first came this way in the 1890s. The name appeared on Lt. McClure's map of 1896. The area is in Sierra National Forest, but was within the park from 1890 to 1905.

Devil Peak (6,989) *Yosemite*
Devil Gulch *El Portal*
The origin of the names is unknown. They were on the Hoffmann and Gardiner map of 1863–67 as "Devil's Mt" and "Devil's Gulch." The peak is just outside the park boundary, in Sierra National Forest. The gulch also is in the national forest, but was partly within the park from 1890 to 1905.

Devils Dance Floor (6,836) *Yosemite Valley*
The name was applied in the 1930s by men at the Cascade Creek Camp of the CCC. One Sunday, with nothing better to do, some of them carried a Model T Ford on poles to this flat-topped summit. Someone must have commented that it looked as if they were doing a strange dance of the devils. (Letter from Douglass Hubbard to Shirley Sargent, July 7, 1955.) The name was in use locally for many years, but at last became official and appeared on the *Yosemite Valley* map in 1970.

Devils Postpile *Devils Postpile, Mammoth Mtn., Crystal Crag*
"Some miles farther down the river, near the place of crossing of the Mammoth trail, there is a splendid specimen of columnar basalt, which was photographed many years ago by Mr. J. M. Hutchings while crossing the mountains. In every scenic freak the sheepherder recognizes the handiwork of his Satanic majesty. The formation is therefore known to local fame as the Devil's Woodpile." (Theodore S. Solomons in *SCB* 1, no. 3, Jan. 1894: 74.)
President Taft proclaimed the "Devil Postpile National Monument" on July 6, 1911. (*SCB* 8, no. 3, Jan. 1912: 170–73, 226–27.) The feature was identified as "Devil Postpile" on the *Mt. Lyell* 30' maps from 1901 through the edition of 1944; it was changed to "Devils Postpile National Monument" on the ninth edition, 1948.

Dewey Point (7,385) *Yosemite Valley, Yosemite*
Admiral George Dewey commanded the American fleet in the one-sided victory over the Spanish fleet in the Battle of Manila Bay, May 1, 1898. He was the great American hero of his time; many thought he ought to be president. In a public interview on April 4, 1900, he said he would be "only too willing to serve. . . . Since studying this subject I am convinced that the office of President is not such a very difficult one to fill." Neither party brought up his name at its convention. (*DAB.*) The name appeared on the first edition of the *Yosemite Valley* map, 1907.

Dike Creek   *Devils Postpile, Mt. Ritter*

The origin is unknown, but my guess is that it was named for a 'dike' of igneous rock intruded into a mass of older rock. The name probably was given by USGS surveyors during the 1898–99 survey for the *Mt. Lyell* 30' map; it is on the first edition, 1901, and on LeConte's map of 1900. Although in Sierra National Forest, the creek was within the park from 1890 to 1905.

Dingley Creek   *Tuolumne Meadows*

One source said that the creek was named by the Wheeler Survey in the 1870s, but for whom was not known. (Letter, Col. Benson to Versteeg, in Farquhar files.) There was an A. S. Dingley who was born in 1858 in Stanislaus County where Oakdale now is. From about 1874 to 1877 he was in the stock business, "making a specialty of sheep." (*Biographical*, 396.) Dingley may have been one of the sheepmen who took his flocks into the Sierra in the summer, and established his range on the creek that now bears his name. The name is not on atlas sheet 56D; it first appears on Lt. McClure's 1895 map.

Discovery View   *Yosemite Valley*

The view from the parking lot at the east end of the Wawona Tunnel. This new name appeared on on the tenth edition of the *Yosemite Valley* map, 1977. It is the contemporary version of the several viewpoints that have preceeded it—the place from which one gets that first stunning view of the valley when entering from the southwest. Its predecessors were "Mount Beatitude" and "Old Inspiration Point" on the early horse trail pioneered by the Mann brothers in 1855–56, and the place presently named "Inspiration Point" on the old Wawona Road.

Diving Board   *Yosemite Valley, Yosemite*

"Never have I seen such a frightful precipice in all my experience. The edge which my hands grasped was not more than a few inches thick, and below there was nothing, absolutely nothing, but air down for 3,500 feet. Even the upper part of the cliff could not be seen, for evidently the rock upon which we were lying overhung the abyss. . . . To anyone who wants the experience of looking over a first-class precipice, without being caged in by gas-pipe railings, I can recommend this place above all others." (J. N. LeConte in *SCB* 9, no. 3, Jan. 1914: 134.) LeConte and James S. Hutchinson made this first ascent on July 26, 1912.

Doe Lake *Matterhorn Peak*
Origin unknown. The name was on the first *Bridgeport* 30' map, 1911.

Dog Lake *Tuolumne Meadows*
In 1898 Robert B. Marshall of the USGS named this lake because he found an abandoned sheepdog with a litter of puppies here. (Farquhar: Marshall.) The lake was first named on LeConte's map of 1900.

Doghead Peak (11,102) *Matterhorn Peak*
A descriptive name; origin unknown. Quite possibly named by early sheepmen. The name appeared on the first *Bridgeport* 30' map, 1911. The first mention in print is by Harold C. Bradley in *SCB* 8, no. 2, June 1911: 136–37.

Donohue: Peak (12,023), **Pass** (11,056) *Mono Craters*
The peak and the pass were named in 1895 by Lt. McClure for Sergeant Donohue, Troop K, Fourth Cavalry, when Donohue made the first ascent of the peak. (Farquhar: McClure; also letter, Brig. Gen. M. F. Davis to Chester Versteeg, Farquhar files.)

Dore: Cliff, Pass *Tuolumne Meadows*
Paul Gustave Doré (1832–1883), a noted French artist and illustrator, who had great popular success for many years, especially in America and England. Named by Israel C. Russell, USGS, about 1882. ". . . a scarp of grander proportions than those below crosses the trough and forms a wall of rock more than a thousand feet high. This rocky wall, together with the cliffs forming the eastern side of the gorge as far as Lake Cañon, has been named, in honor of the great French artist, the Doré Cliffs." (Russell, *Quaternary*, 332–33.)
Both features are in Inyo National Forest. The cliff was bisected by the park's 1890 to 1905 boundary. The pass, on the old trail from Lundy to Bennettville, was just outside the boundary.

Dorothy Lake; Dorothy Lake Pass (over 9,520) *Tower Peak*
Robert B. Marshall of the USGS named the lake for Dorothy Forsyth, daughter of Major William W. Forsyth, acting superintendent of Yosemite National Park, 1909–12. (Farquhar: Marshall.) The lake was called "Jack Main's Lake" by Lt. N. F. McClure in 1894. (*SCB* 1, no. 5, Jan. 1895: 181.) The name "Dorothy Lake" first appeared on the third edition of the *Dardanelles* 30' map, 1912. "Dorothy Lake Pass" was added on the *Tower Peak* quad, 1956.

Double Rock (9,782) *Hetch Hetchy Reservoir*

Although this descriptive name did not appear on a map until 1956, it was used by François Matthes—who may have named it when he made the first ascent, in 1916. (Matthes, v. 20, Aug. 4, 1916.)

Eagle: Peak (7,779), **Creek** *Yosemite Valley, Yosemite*
Eagle: Peak, Creek, Meadows *Yosemite Valley, Hetch Hetchy Reservoir*
Eagle Tower *Yosemite Valley*

Eagle Peak is the highest of the Three Brothers. It was called "Eagle Point" by Joseph LeConte in 1870. (*Ramblings*, 70.) It also had that name on the Wheeler Survey atlas sheet 56D, 1878–79, but on the survey's map of Yosemite Valley, 1883, it had its present name.

One source states that Eagle Peak was named in 1870. ". . . the lady whom I married a year later [1871] was in that excursion to Eagle Peak. She was the first white woman ever there, and she suggested the name 'Eagle Peak' to Mr. Muir at the time, and he kept his promise to her that it should thereafter be so known. Before that it was simply the highest of the 'Three Brothers.'" (Letter, Nelson F. Evans, The Prudential Insurance Company of America, to Mrs. Helen Muir Funk, Dec. 28, 1914; a condolence letter, four days after Muir died.)

"This was so named from its being such a favorite resort of this famous bird of prey. . . . I once had the pleasure of conducting the Rev. J. P. Newman, D.D., and Rev. Sutherland, D.D. (each, then, of Washington D.C.), to its wondrous summit, when, after a long, and evidently constrained silence the former suddenly ejaculated, 'Glory! Hal-le-lu-jah— Glory! Hal-le-lu-jah!' (the doctor was a Methodist, you know) then turning around, the tears literally streaming down his cheeks, he thus expressed himself: 'Well, Mr. H., if I had crossed the continent of America on purpose to look upon *this one view*, I should have returned home, sir, perfectly satisfied.'" (Hutchings, *In the Heart*, 479.)

"Eagle Tower" appeared on the Wheeler Survey's map of Yosemite Valley, 1883, "Eagle Creek" on the *Yosemite Valley* map in 1927, "Eagle Peak Creek" and "Eagle Peak Meadows" on the *Yosemite* and *Hetch Hetchy Reservoir* quads in 1956.

Earthquake Meadow *Devils Postpile, Cattle Mtn.*

Origin unknown. The name first appeared on the *Cattle Mtn.* quad, 1983. To find it on the *Devils Postpile* quad: it is three miles southwest of Iron Mountain at a trail junction just above the letter 'T' in the word "NATIONAL." It is in Sierra National Forest, but was in the park from 1890 to 1905.

Courtesy The Bancroft Library

Hetch Hetchy Valley, Tueeulala Falls, Wapama Falls,
from Surprise Point, by Joseph N. LeConte, 1894.

Echo: Peaks (over 11,040), **Lake**   *Tuolumne Meadows*
Echo Creek   *Tuolumne Meadows, Merced Peak*
Echo Valley   *Merced Peak*

Echo Peak and Echo Creek probably were named by the Wheeler Survey; both names are on atlas sheet 56D, 1878–79. The peak remained singular until the fifth edition of the *Mt. Lyell* 30′ map, 1922. The lake name first appeared on the *Tuolumne Meadows* quad, 1956, and the valley name on the *Merced Peak* quad, 1953.

Ediza Lake (2,824 m.)   *Devils Postpile, Mt. Ritter*

The origin of the name is unknown. Although it was not named on the early maps, it was once referred to as "Little Shadow Lake"—obviously because it was a couple of miles up Shadow Creek from Shadow Lake. (*Eleventh Report*, 223.)

Edna Lake   *Merced Peak*

Named by R. B. Marshall, USGS, for Edna Bowman, later Mrs. Charles J. Kuhn. (Farquhar: Marshall.)

Edson Lake   *Yosemite*

The name was proposed by Yosemite National Park rangers Bingaman and Ernst, possibly for another ranger; they spelled it "Edison." (YRL files.)

Edyth Lake   *Pinecrest, Tower Peak*

Major William W. Forsyth named the lake in 1910 for Edyth Nance, daughter of Colonel John T. Nance. (Farquhar; see **Nance Peak**.) The name was on the *Dardanelles* 30' maps as "Edith Lake" from 1912 through 1947, although the spelling was officially changed to "Edyth" by a BGN decision in 1932. However, in a letter to the National Park Service in 1979 the woman in question spelled her name with an 'i.' (YRL files.)

But it is "Edyth" on the maps.

Ehrnback Peak (11,240)   *Tower Peak*

Lt. Arthur R. Ehrnbeck, US Army, made a report in 1909 on a comprehensive road and trail project for Yosemite National Park. (Farquhar; see Appendix A, *Report of the Acting Superintendent of Yosemite National Park,* 1909.)

El Capitan (7,569); **El Capitan: Gully, Meadow**   *Yosemite Valley, Yosemite*

The name was given by the Mariposa Battalion in 1851. "The native Indian name . . . is *To-tó-kon oo-lah*, the Sandhill Crane, a chief of the First People. (C. Hart Merriam in *SCB* 10, no. 2, Jan. 1917: 206.)

"The famous cliff, El Capitan, is a Spanish interpretation of the Indian name To-tock-ah-noo-lah, meaning the 'Rock Chief.'" (Bunnell, *Report,* 1889–90: 9.) "Upon one occasion I asked [Tenaya], 'Why do you call the cliff Tote-ack-ah-noo-la?' The Indian's reply was, 'Because he looks like one. . . . Come with me and see.'. . . As the Indian reached a point a little above and some distance out from the cliff, he triumphantly pointed to the perfect image of a man's head and face, with side whiskers, and with an expression of the sturdy English type, and asked, 'Does he not look like Tote-ack-ah-noo-la?' The 'Rock Chief,' or 'Captain,' was again Sandino's [the interpreter's] interpretation of the word while viewing the likeness." (Bunnell, *Discovery,* 1911: 214–15.)

There is also a legendary explanation that is repeated throughout Yosemite literature. Galen Clark said that Tul-tok-a-nú-la is from the measuring worm (tul-tok'-a-na) which crawled up the face of the rock to rescue two small boys who were beyond being saved by any other creatures of the valley. (Clark, 92–95.)

According to one source, the original English name was "Crane Mountain," not for the reason given above but for the sandhill cranes that entered the valley by flying over the top of El Capitan. (*YNN* 34, no. 1, Jan. 1955: 6.) And finally, Hutchings' *Illustrated* 1, no. 1, July 1856: 3, called it "Giant's Tower."

El Portal   *El Portal*

Spanish for "The Gateway." It was named in 1907 by officials of the Yosemite Valley Railroad. The railroad company had hoped to build the line into the valley itself, but could not get the right-of-way from the federal government. It settled for building a wagon road from El Portal to the valley. (Johnston, *Railroads*, 15.) The GLO plat of 1884 shows "Wharton's Ranch" where El Portal now is. (Leonidas G. Wharton homesteaded 160 acres in secs. 16 and 17, T. 3 S., R. 20 E. in 1884.) Although the community is about a mile west of the present park boundary, it was within the park from 1890 to 1905.

Elbow Hill (over 9,200)   *Tuolumne Meadows*

A descriptive name, probably applied by the Wheeler Survey. It is in the sketchbook of J. Calvert Spiller, topographical assistant with Lt. Macomb, and is on atlas sheet 56D, 1878–79.

Eleanor, Lake (Reservoir)   *Lake Eleanor*
Eleanor Creek   *Pinecrest, Lake Eleanor*

The lake was named in the 1860s by the Whitney Survey for Eleanor Goddard Whitney (1856–1882), daughter of Josiah Dwight Whitney, state geologist and director of the first California Geological Survey. The name is on the Hoffmann and Gardiner map, 1863–67. The name of the creek first appears on the Wheeler Survey atlas sheet 56D, 1878–79.

The small natural lake occupied the center part of sec. 35 and a small part at the upper left of sec. 36, T. 2N., R. 19 E. The dam that converted it into a reservoir for San Francisco was built in 1917–18; it raised the lake level thirty-five feet.

Electra Peak (12,442)   *Merced Peak*

Probably named by the USGS (but for whom or what is unknown) in 1898–99 during the survey for the *Mt. Lyell* 30' map, published in 1901. The USGS determined the altitude by triangulation, as reported by J. N. LeConte, "Elevations."

Elephant Rock   *Yosemite Valley, Yosemite*
Origin unknown. The point juts out from the cliffs on the south side of the Merced River below Turtleback Dome. The name first appeared on the fourth edition of the *Yosemite Valley* map, 1927, but was already in use as early as 1920. (Hall, 14.)

Elevenmile Creek   *Yosemite*
Named for a stage station on the old Wawona Road, eleven miles from Wawona. It was shown as "Eleven Mile Sta." on the Wheeler Survey atlas sheet 56D, 1878–79, a designation it had on McClure's 1896 map; on his 1895 map it was "11-Mile House." On the first six editions of the *Yosemite* 30' map, 1897–1929, it was simply called "Eleven Mile." On the next edition, 1938, that name was dropped and "Elevenmile Creek" appeared. On McClure's 1896 map the creek was called "North F.B.C."—meaning the North Fork of Bishop Creek.

Elizabeth Lake (9,508)   *Tuolumne Meadows*
R. B. Marshall of the USGS named the lake in 1909 for Elizabeth Crow Simmons, a niece. (Farquhar: Marshall.) The name appeared on the third edition of the *Mt. Lyell* 30' map, 1910. (See **Cora: Lakes, Creek**.)

Ellery Lake (9,489)   *Mono Craters*
For Nathaniel Ellery, the State Engineer in charge of constructing the road from Mono Lake to Tioga Pass in 1909. (Farquhar; see also *SCB 7*, no. 3, Jan. 1910: 195–96.) The original name was "Rinedollar Lake," for a man of that name who had a mine nearby. (USGS.) The present name appeared on the third edition of the *Mt. Lyell* 30' map, 1910.

Emerald Lake   *Devils Postpile, Mt. Ritter*
Origin unknown. A small lake next to the John Muir Trail just southeast of Thousand Island Lake. The name first appeared on the *Devils Postpile* quad, 1953. The lake is in Inyo National Forest, but was in the park from 1890 to 1905.

Emerald Pool   *Yosemite Valley, Yosemite*
Named in 1856. "The descent between the Nevada and the Vernal Falls is about three hundred feet, and in its rapid flow into the 'Emerald Pool' it is broken into countless liquid diamonds." (Bunnell, *Report*, 1889–90: 12.)
That same summer one of the early tourist parties attempted to apply a more prosaic name to the pool. "This lake has been called 'Frances,' in honor of Mrs. Jane Frances Neal—she being the first lady who had visited

this lake, and who speaks of the landscape as having fully repaid her for all the fatigue she endured in ascending to the plateau. Let no one attempt to change the name, but rather add some other record of her courage and her love of the beautiful and grand." (*Mariposa Democrat*, August 5, 1856.)

". . . the smallest of all the glacial lakes in the Yosemite Region . . . unfilled and in precisely the same condition as at the end of the glacial epoch. The explanation is found in the very smallness of the basin, in the smoothness of its sides and bottom . . . and in the great momentum with which the water of the Merced River rushes into the pool as a result of its descent in the Silver Apron. (Matthes, *Paper 160*, 104.) Although it is an early name, "Emerald Pool" did not appear on a map until the first *Yosemite Valley* sheet, 1907.

Emeric: Lake, Creek   *Tuolumne Meadows*

These two features were named in 1896 by Lt. N. F. McClure for Henry F. Emeric, president of the California Board of Fish Commissioners. (Farquhar.)

At one time François Matthes used the name "Emeric Crest" to refer to—I assume—the gap northwest of Emeric Lake on the way to Echo Creek. (Matthes, v. 23, July 31, 1919.)

Emily Lake   *Devils Postpile, Mammoth Mtn.*

Origin unknown. A small lake 1.5 miles south-southeast of Shadow Lake. It was first named on the *Devils Postpile* quad, 1953. The lake is in Inyo National Forest, but was within the park from 1890 to 1905.

Empire Meadow   *Yosemite*

The origin is unknown, but it is an old name. It's on Alder Creek, about four miles upstream from the Wawona Road. It appears on the Hoffmann and Gardiner map of 1863–67 as "Empire Camp." Whitney's *The Yosemite Guide-Book*, 1874, p. 83, cites Empire Camp, "not now inhabited."

McClure's maps of 1895 and 1896 have the name, but then it drops from view until the eighth edition of the *Yosemite* 30′ map, 1951, where it appears as a plural: "Empire Meadows."

Evelyn Lake (10,328)   *Tuolumne Meadows*

Named for a daughter of Major William W. Forsyth, acting superintendent of Yosemite National Park, 1909–12. (Farquhar: R. B. Marshall.) The name first appeared on the third edition of the *Mt. Lyell* 30′ map, 1910.

Excelsior Mountain (12,446)   *Matterhorn Peak*

Probably named by the USGS during the survey for the *Bridgeport* 30'
map, in 1905. It is on the first edition of the map, 1911, but is not in
LeConte's "Elevations." The name already existed at the time of the YNP
boundary survey in 1906. (YRL files.)

Fairview Dome (9,731)   *Tuolumne Meadows*

Possibly named by the Wheeler Survey; the name is on atlas sheet 56D,
1878–79. McClure's map of 1895 calls it "Soda Springs Buttes," but notes
that it is also called "Fairview Dome." John Muir wrote, ". . . a majestic
dome which long ago I named the *Glacier Monument.*" (Muir, *Parks*, 87.) In
another book Muir said he named it "Tuolumne Glacier Monument."
(Muir, *The Yosemite*, 178.) In 1905 the present name was in use, but it was
sometimes called "Tuolumne Monument." (*SCB* 5, no. 3, Jan. 1905: 219.)

"The summit is burnished and scored . . . the scratches and striae in-
dicating that the mighty Tuolumne Glacier swept over it as if it were only
a mere boulder in the bottom of its channel." (Muir, *The Yosemite*, 179.)

Falls Creek   *Tower Peak, Lake Eleanor, Hetch Hetchy Reservoir*

Lt. McClure used the name in 1894, calling it "Falls River." (*SCB* 1,
no. 5, Jan. 1895: 181.) He had it on his maps of 1895 and 1896 as "Fall
River." The origin of the name is obvious: it's the stream that becomes
Wapama Falls. The USGS submitted the name to the BGN in 1896; it was
approved that same year, and had its present form on the first *Dardanelles*
30' map, 1898.

Falls Ridge   *Tuolumne Meadows*

The namer is not known, but the reason for the name is plain. The
ridge is south of the Tuolumne River, overlooking California, Le Conte,
and Waterwheel falls.

Fantail Lake   *Tuolumne Meadows*

Named by Everett Spuller, in 1932, because of its shape. (Spuller.) The
lake is in Inyo National Forest, at the headwaters of Mine Creek,
northwest of the site of Bennettville. It was within the park from 1890 to
1905.

Fawn Lake   *Tower Peak*

Origin unknown. The name was ratified by the BGN in 1932, and appeared on the final edition of the *Dardanelles* 30' map, 1947. Prior to 1932
the local usage was "Spotted Fawn Lake."

Fern Lake (2,675 m.)   *Devils Postpile, Cattle Mtn.*

No doubt named because there are ferns there, but the namer is unknown. The lake was first named on the *Devils Postpile* quad, 1953. It is in Inyo National Forest, but was in the park from 1890 to 1905.

Fern Spring   *Yosemite Valley, Yosemite*

The namer is unknown. "At the foot of the mountain [entering the valley via the Mariposa Trail] you arrive at 'Fern Spring.' The cooling, bower-like shade of the trees and shrubs, and the clear and sparkling brightness of the water, bubbling up among rocks and green-matted foliage, may . . . tempt an indulgence in too hearty a draught. This, however, should be studiously resisted . . . as persons unaccustomed to the pure cold water of Yo-Semite are in danger of being uncomfortably troubled with diarrhoea." (Hutchings, *Scenes*, 1871: 86–87.) The name is on the 1883 Wheeler Survey map of the valley.

Fernandez: Pass (10,175), **Creek, Lakes**   *Merced Peak*

First Sergeant Joseph Fernandez, Troop K, Fourth Cavalry, US Army, was with Lt. Harry C. Benson in the exploration of the headwaters of the Merced River, 1895–97. He was also in the park later, when Benson was the acting superintendent. Benson named the pass. (Farquhar: Benson.) The creek and the lakes were first named on the *Merced Peak* quad, 1953. Fernandez Pass is on the southeast boundary of the park. The other features are in Sierra National Forest, but were in the park from 1890 to 1905.

Finger Lake   *Tuolumne Meadows*

Everett Spuller named it in 1932 for its shape. (Spuller.) The lake is in Inyo National Forest about half a mile from the park boundary, but it was in the park from 1890 to 1905.

Finger Peaks (highest is over 11,440)   *Matterhorn Peak*

A descriptive name for three fingers of rock sticking straight up. Probably named by the USGS during the 1905–9 survey for the *Bridgeport* 30' map. The name appears on the first edition, 1911.

Fireplace: Bluffs, Creek   *Yosemite Valley, Yosemite*

Fireplace Bluffs is a descriptive name, but you have to be in the right place to appreciate it. From Inspiration Point on the Pohono Trail, look across the canyon of the Merced—and the reason for the name is obvious. The namer of the bluffs is unknown. The name appeared on the first edition of the *Yosemite Valley* map, 1907; the first use I have found in print was in 1893. (*SCB* 1, no. 4, May 1894: 134.) The creek was first named on the fourth edition of the *Yosemite Valley* map, 1927.

Fisher Lakes   *Tower Peak*

The name was approved by a BGN decision in 1965, but the decision didn't say for what or whom the name was given. It probably is for Charles K. Fisher, who surveyed the lakes for the DFG in 1952. (DFG survey.) Not named on early editions of the *Tower Peak* quad. It is a group of five small lakes just north of Lertora Lake—near the left-center edge of the map.

Fissures, The   *Yosemite Valley, Yosemite*

An old descriptive name for a feature on the Pohono Trail, just east of Taft Point. "A cleft or split in the rock . . . one thousand feet deep, five feet wide at the top and front, and grows gradually narrower as it extends downward and backward into the mountain." (*Bancroft's Tourist Guide*, 1871: 31.) J. M. Hutchings credited the photographer Eadweard J. Muybridge with discovering the fissures in 1867. (Hutchings, *Scenes*, 1871: 143.) The name was confirmed by the BGN in 1932, but it did not appear on any map until the *Yosemite* 15-minute quad, 1956.

These unusual gashes in the cliff's edge probably are due to rock that was "peculiarly susceptible to weathering, having been minutely sheared and slivered by faulting movements that took place under great pressure shortly after the granite had solidified." (Matthes, *Paper 160*, 110.)

Flat Lake   *Merced Peak*

Origin unknown. All lakes being flat, the name must be because the ground around the lake is flat. The name appeared on the *Merced Peak* quad, 1953. The lake is in Sierra National Forest, 1.2 miles east of the park's southeast boundary. It was in the park from 1890 to 1905.

Fletcher Creek   *Tuolumne Meadows, Merced Peak*
Upper Fletcher Lake; Fletcher Peak (11,408)   *Tuolumne Meadows*

The creek and the lake were named in 1895 by Lt. McClure for Arthur G. Fletcher, of the State Board of Fish Commissioners, who was instrumental in stocking the streams and lakes in the park. (Farquhar: McClure.) The creek and "Fletcher Lake" were named on the first edition of the *Mt. Lyell* 30' map, 1901. The peak was first named on the ninth edition, 1948. It had formerly been called "Baker Peak," after a cook at the Boothe Lake High Sierra Camp. (BGN, 1932.) However, it may have been

François Matthes who named it long before that. ". . . what I call Fletcher Mtn." (Matthes, v. 18, August 25, 1914.)

There is no reason to have an "Upper" lake unless there is a "Lower" one; there is not one on contemporary maps, nor has such a name been on older maps. The present "Townsley Lake" (which see) was once called "Upper Fletcher Lake." It was called "Fletcher Lake" on LeConte's 1900 map. The BGN decision of 1932 gave the name "Fletcher Lake" to the lake in sec. 34, T. 1 S., R. 24 E.—but that one is "Townsley Lake" on the map. The present "Upper Fletcher Lake" is in sec. 33.

If you don't have that straight in your head, you aren't allowed to go there.

Flora Lake   *Pinecrest*

Named about 1910 for Miss Flora Coleman of Mannsboro, Virginia, a cousin of R. B. Marshall of the USGS. (Farquhar files.) The name did not appear on a map until publication of the *Pinecrest* quad, 1956.

Florence, Mount (12,561)   *Merced Peak*
Florence: Creek, Lake   *Tuolumne Meadows, Merced Peak*

The peak was named for Florence Hutchings, daughter of James Mason Hutchings. "Florence Hutchings, and her brother, whose short legs were projected to larboard and starboard from the saddle . . . led off the cavalcade. Let us give the girl, for her own and her father's sake, some graceful mountain height, and let it be called Mt. Florence." (Taylor, 237–38.) Florence was the first white child born in Yosemite Valley, August 23, 1864, and she died there on September 26, 1881. (See Sargent, *Pioneers*, 34–37.)

The peak was named on Lt. McClure's maps of 1895 and 1896. The creek was named on the first *Mt. Lyell* 30' map, 1901, and the lake's name appeared on the 15-minute quads in the 1950s.

Foerster: Peak (12,432), **Creek**   *Merced Peak*

Lewis Foerster (1868–1936), a corporal in Troop K, Fourth Cavalry, on duty in the park in 1895 under the command of Lt. McClure. "In the policing of these wonderful recreation grounds, his service was outstanding, and it was in recognition of his achievements and because of his close association with the particular region, that I gave his name to a prominent peak on the park boundary and placed it on the map that I was then preparing." (McClure, in a memorial to Foerster, in *SCB* 22, no. 1, Feb. 1937: 102–3.)

Foresta *El Portal, Yosemite*

Foresta Falls *El Portal*

In 1913 A. B. Davis bought 200 acres, called himself the Foresta Land Company, and built a summer resort. The place was designed to appeal to people of culture, and seemed to promise "seminar discussions under the peacefully thought-provoking surroundings of Yosemite National Park." It was a sort of summer Chatauqua, known as the "Foresta Summer Assembly." But it didn't pay off. Davis abandoned it in 1915 and returned to his home in New York. Three years later the main hotel building burned under mysterious circumstances. Foresta is now a subdivision—an inholding within the national park—with a scattering of summer homes and cottages. (*YNN* 34, no. 3, March 1955: 43–45.)

Courtesy Yosemite Research Library, NPS

Major William Woods Forsyth and family at the Wawona Tunnel Tree, 1911.

Forsyth Peak (11,180)   *Tower Peak*

William Woods Forsyth (1856–1933), US Army, acting superintendent of the park, 1909–12. Robert B. Marshall, topographer on the *Mt. Lyell* 30' map, was a close friend of Forsyth. He named this peak and a "Forsyth Pass" on the Forsyth Trail between Clouds Rest and Tenaya Lake, and also named individual features for each of Forsyth's four daughters and two sons-in-law. (Farquhar, *History*, 216.)

The so-called pass isn't that at all. It is where the trail goes over a ridge about half a mile west-southwest of the Sunrise Lakes. Matthes used the name in 1913 (Matthes, v. 17, August 9, 1913), and Ansel Hall had it in his guidebook in 1920. (Hall, 37, 65, 69.)

Four-Mile Trail   *Yosemite Valley*

In 1871 James McCauley (who about four years later built the "Mountain House" at Glacier Point) hired John Conway to build a trail from the valley to Glacier Point. Conway had superintended construction of the "Zigzag" on the Big Oak Flat Road. (Paden, 285.) "At the entrance of the trail we found a small toll-house, kept by a far-seeing Irishman, named Macaulay, who built the trail. It cost $3,000 and it took eleven months of steady, hard labor to build it." (Jackson, 127.) The toll was one dollar. Later, rebuilding of the trail lengthened it to about five miles. On the map it is labeled the "Glacier Pt-Fourmile Trail." The trail is shown, but not named, on the *Yosemite* 15-minute quad.

Fraser Lakes   *Tower Peak*

The name was approved by a BGN decision in 1965. The decision didn't state for whom the lakes were named, but probably for J. C. Fraser of the DFG. (DFG survey.) It is a group of four small lakes about 0.3 mile south of the center of Emigrant Lake. Not named on early editions of the *Tower Peak* quad.

Frog Creek   *Tower Peak, Pinecrest, Lake Eleanor*

The creek flows southwest from Otter Lake into Lake Eleanor. The namer is not known. The name first appeared on McClure's map of 1896 and on the first *Yosemite* 30' map, 1897. It was ratified by the BGN in 1932 as accepted local usage.

Frog Lakes   *Matterhorn Peak*

The origin of the name is unknown; it first appeared on the *Matterhorn Peak* quad, 1956. The lakes are in Inyo National Forest, but were within the park from 1890 to 1905.

Frying Pan Lake *Merced Peak*

Charles K. Fisher of the DFG reported in 1948 that the name was given in 1940 by John Handley, formerly of the DFG's Madera hatchery. (DFG survey.) No reason was given for the name, but it probably is for the lake's shape, which is almost perfectly round. The lake is in Sierra National Forest, but was within the park from 1890 to 1905.

Gale: Peak (10,693), **Lake** *Merced Peak*

Captain George Henry Goodwin Gale (1858–1920), Fourth Cavalry, US Army; acting superintendent of Yosemite National Park in 1894, and of Sequoia and General Grant national parks, 1896–97. (Heitman, 442.) The peak was named by Lt. McClure in 1894, and appeared on his map of 1896. (Farquhar: McClure.) The lake was named for the peak in 1946 by a DFG survey party under William A. Dill. (DFG survey.) The peak is on the southeast park boundary, and although the lake is in Sierra National Forest it was within the park from 1890 to 1905.

Gallison Lake (over 10,400) *Tuolumne Meadows*

Arthur L. Gallison, a YNP ranger from 1916 to 1953, planted fish in the lake in 1916. The name was proposed by rangers Bingaman and Eastman. (Bingaman, *Guardians*, 93.)

Garnet Lake (9,678–2,950 m.) *Devils Postpile, Mt. Ritter*

Origin unknown. On all maps of the 1890s it was called "Badger Lake," while the name "Garnet Lake" was applied to what is now Shadow Lake. The lake is in Inyo National Forest, but was in the park from 1890 to 1905.

Gaylor: Lakes, Peak (11,004) *Tuolumne Meadows*

Andrew J. Gaylor, born in Texas in 1856; a packer with the US Cavalry in his youth; Yosemite National Park ranger, 1907–21. He died of a heart attack at the Merced Lake ranger station while on patrol. (Bingaman, *Guardians*, 13, 85.) The name was initially given to the lakes. It was later extended to the peak, as suggested by David Brower, and verified by Walter A. Starr, Sr. as being in common use. (USGS.)

At the time of the Tioga mining boom the peak and the entire ridge north and south of it were known as "Tioga Hill." (*Homer Mining Index,* Oct. 1, 1881; Jan. 28, 1882.)

Gem Lake (9,052–2,761 m.)   *Mono Craters, Devils Postpile, Mt. Ritter*
Gem Pass (over 10,480)   *Mono Craters*

The lake was originally named "Gem-o'-the-Mountains" by Theodore C. Agnew, an early miner. (See **Agnew Meadow**, etc. Farquhar: N. F. McClure.) The USGS shortened the name, and also applied it to the pass, during the 1898–99 survey for the *Mt. Lyell* 30' map. The lake has been dammed, and is a reservoir for Southern California Edison. Both the lake and the pass are in Inyo National Forest. The park's eastern boundary from 1890 to 1905 went through the western edge of the lake and directly across the pass.

Gertrude Lake   *Devils Postpile, Cattle Mtn.*

Origin unknown. A very small lake three miles west of the Devils Postpile boundary. On the *Cattle Mtn.* quad you can see that it is shaped like a tuning fork; certainly more like that than like Gertrude. The name appeared on the *Devils Postpile* quad, 1953. The lake is in Inyo National Forest, but was within the park from 1890 to 1905.

Gibbs, Mount (12,764); **Gibbs: Canyon, Lake**   *Mono Craters*

Oliver Wolcott Gibbs (1822–1908), professor of science at Harvard, 1863–67, and a lifelong friend of J. D. Whitney.

"Started for the summit [of Mount Dana] but took the next peak s. of Mt. Dana, fearing O. [Frederick Law Olmstead] could not reach the other. This I managed to get his horse up, so that he rode to the top, where we lunched. He named the peak Mt. Gibbs." (Brewer diary, August 31, 1864, in BL.) Brewer and Olmstead made the first ascent. Olmstead was chairman of the first Board of Commissioners to manage the Yosemite Grant, 1864.

Gibbs Canyon was named by Israel C. Russell in the early 1880s. (Russell, *Quaternary*, 336.) Gibbs Lake was first named on the *Mono Craters* quad, 1953. Both the lake and the canyon are in Inyo National Forest.

Gibson, Mount (over 8,320)   *Hetch Hetchy Reservoir*

Origin unknown, but probably named by or for a sheepman. The name was given to Lt. McClure in 1894 as one that already existed. (*SCB* 1, no. 5, Jan. 1895: 182.) McClure put the name on his 1896 map, and it has been on maps ever since.

Gin Flat   *Lake Eleanor*

"As related to me by Mr. John B. Curtin, construction of the Big Oak Flat Road was primarily done by Chinese labor. Various camps along the route were supplied by Chinese merchants from Jamestown. Delivering one consignment . . . a barrel of Chinese gin . . . dropped and burst wide open. That locality is still known as *Gin Flat*." (Letter, J. H. Wegner to Douglass Hubbard, May 25, 1961, in YRL.) For a somewhat different version, see Paden, 229. The name first appeared on Lt. McClure's map of 1896.

These and similar stories constitute the traditional lore about the naming of Gin Flat. However, it seems that none of them is true—or that if the episode is correct then the circumstances and the date are wrong. The Old Big Oak Flat Road was built past Gin Flat to Yosemite Valley in 1874, yet the name "Gin Flat" was in use at least ten years earlier. ("A Month in the Sierras," *Sonora Union Democrat*, Oct. 1, 1864.)

Givens: Meadow, Creek, Lake   *Merced Peak*

E. T. and Bob Givens first went to what is now named Turner Meadow in 1856. They were the first stockmen to pasture their stock in any part of what later became Yosemite National Park. They ran cattle at first, and later had sheep. (Homer Robinson notebook, YRL.) "Givens lived on the Morgan Canyon Road, near Auberry Valley, and ran sheep on the meadow." (Letter from Versteeg, in Farquhar files.) The meadow and the creek—a tributary of the South Fork of the Merced—were named on Lt. McClure's 1896 map. Givens Lake was first named on the ninth edition of the *Mt. Lyell* 30' map, 1948.

Glacier Point (7,214)   *Yosemite Valley, Yosemite*

The precise origin of the name is unknown. Clarence King wrote, concerning his activities with the Whitney Survey in 1864, from atop Sentinel Dome: "A little way to the east, and about a thousand feet below the brink of the Glacier Point . . . ." (King, 151.) That doesn't say who named it or when, although King and Gardiner had it on their 1865 map of Yosemite Valley. One might note that it is a different *sort* of name than all the others in and around Yosemite Valley up to that time. It is scientific/geologic; all the others are romantic, quasi-Indian, fanciful, patriotic, or for a presumed Great Man. That sort of circumstantial evidence seems to point to someone on the Whitney Survey as the namer.

"The name of 'Glacier Point' is said to be Pa-til-le-ma, a translation of which I am unable to give." (Bunnell, *Discovery*, 1911: 217.) Gudde states that Glacier Point was named by the Mariposa Battalion in 1851 (Gudde, *Place Names*, 120), and cites Bunnell—but Bunnell made no such claim.

Glacier Point was indeed covered by a glacier during an earlier glaciation, but was above the ice during the most recent (Tioga) stage. It could have been named for features that were mistaken for evidence of recent glaciation. (Matthes, *Paper 160*, 63–64; Huber, *Bulletin 1595*, 52.)

Gladys Lake   *Devils Postpile, Mammoth Mtn.*

Origin unknown. A small lake on the John Muir Trail a mile southeast of Shadow Lake. The name appeared on the *Devils Postpile* quad, 1953. The lake is in Inyo National Forest, but was in the park from 1890 to 1905.

Courtesy Yosemite Research Library, NPS

Gabriel Sovulewski, foreman of the park's trail system for thirty years. See **Grace Meadow** and **Mildred Lake**.

Glen Aulin   *Tuolumne Meadows*

James McCormick, later the executive secretary of the US Board on Geographic Names, said that R. B. Marshall of the USGS asked him to suggest a name for a beautiful little valley. "I at once suggested Glen Aulin, 'beautiful valley or glen,' and wrote it for him in this way, that it might be correctly pronounced—the *'au'* as in *author*. The correct Gaelic (Irish) orthography is *Gleann Alainn.*" (Letter, McCormick to Farquhar, Feb. 11, 1926.) The name appeared on the fourth edition of the *Mt. Lyell* 30' map, 1914. Glen Aulin is the location of one of the High Sierra Camps, opened in 1924.

Grace Meadow   *Tower Peak*

Named for Grace Sovulewski, daughter of Gabriel Sovulewski who came to the park as quartermaster sergeant with the US Army. He returned as a civilian employee in 1906, and during the following thirty years was largely responsible for the development and maintenance of the park's trail system. Grace married Frank B. Ewing, a park ranger from 1916 to 1950. (Bingaman, *Pathways*, 44–45.) "Grace Meadow" appeared on the third edition of the *Dardanelles* 30' map, 1912.

Grand Canyon of the Tuolumne River   *Hetch Hetchy Reservoir*

The nine miles of the river from Muir Gorge to the Hetch Hetchy Reservoir. John Muir called it the "Great Tuolumne Canyon" in *Overland Monthly*, August 1873. It was called "The Grand Cañon of the Tuolumne" by R. M. Price when he and another man went down through it in July 1892. (*SCB* 1, no. 1, Jan. 1893: 9–16.) The name has been on the maps since the first *Yosemite* 30' sheet, 1897.

Grand Mountain (9,491)   *Hetch Hetchy Reservoir*

"Grand Mt. stands right at the mouth of the Cathedral Cañon (I mean the cañon omitted on the map) that is on the lower side of it. Grand Mt. certainly is a Grand Mt., bare granite nearly to the summit." (Letter, Charles F. Hoffmann to J. D. Whitney, Sept. 10, 1873, in BL.) In this letter Hoffmann said that Grand Mountain was named by John Muir. Apparently Muir did not convey this information to other people. The mountain was called "Tuolumne Castle" by R. M. Price in 1894 (*SCB* 1, no. 6, May 1895: 205) and by Theodore S. Solomons in 1896 (*Appalachia* 8, no. 2, 1896: 173).

Granite Creek: East Fork and **West Fork**   *Merced Peak*

Origin unknown; probably named by sheepmen, cattlemen, or miners. The name was in use at least as early as the Mammoth mining boom. (*Mammoth City Herald*, Sept. 24, 1879.) The name appears on McClure's and Solomons' maps of 1896. The creek, a tributary of the San Joaquin River, is outside the park, but its headwaters were within the park from 1890 to 1905.

The location of Granite Creek Campground probably is the place formerly called "Granite Meadows." (*Eleventh Report*, 219.)

Granite Lakes (about 10,400)   *Tuolumne Meadows*
Formerly part of the Gaylor Lakes. The present name was approved by the BGN in 1962 on the recommendation of the park naturalist and the Sierra Club. The northwest two lakes are the Granite Lakes—just west of the park boundary and the Great Sierra Mine.

Granite Stairway   *Devils Postpile, Cattle Mtn.*
An old name, apparently given by early travelers. ". . . the trail crosses one of the numerous grassy flats which abound through this part of the mountains, to wind around and over a rough, rocky ridge, known as the 'Granite Stairs.'" (*Eleventh Report*, 219.)

Grant Lakes   *Hetch Hetchy Reservoir*
Origin unknown, but a likely supposition is that they were named for General, and President, U. S. Grant. The name appeared on the map in Whitney's *Yosemite Guide-Book*, 1871.

Gravel Pit Lake   *Lake Eleanor*
One wonders how a romantic name such as this has found its way into a national park. Does it have a permit? From the way the lake appears on the topo map (treeless, reached by a road) undoubtedly the name commemorates a sinister event. Be thankful you know nothing more about it.

Gravelly Ford   *Merced Peak*
An old name, descriptive of the river bed where the Chiquito Pass Trail crosses the South Fork of the Merced River. It appears as early as Lt. McClure's map of 1896.

Gray: Peak (11,574), **Creek**   *Merced Peak*
The peak was named by the Whitney Survey for the color of its upper portion. (Whitney, *The Yosemite Book*, 97.) The name first appears on the Wheeler Survey's atlas sheet 56D, 1878–79. It was confirmed by a BGN decision in 1897. The creek was named from the peak; its name appears on the first edition of the *Mt. Lyell* 30' map, 1901.

In a peculiarity of naming, the streams that flow into the Merced River from Triple Divide Peak, Merced Peak, and Red Peak are named for their respective peaks: "Red Peak Fork," etc., but the stream from Gray Peak, which has been known for decades as "Gray Peak Fork," has no official name on contemporary maps. However, it did have that name on all editions of the *Mt. Lyell* 30′ map, from 1901 to 1948.

Grayling Lake   *Merced Peak*
Named when grayling were first planted in the lake, in 1930. (YRL.)

Great Sierra Mine   *Tuolumne Meadows*
One cabin and a couple of shafts are all that remain of the endeavors of the Great Sierra Consolidated Silver Company in the 1880s. (See **Bennett-ville**.) The old cabin, just west of the Sierra crest, can be reached by a moderate hike from Tioga Pass, and commands spectacular views.

Green Mountain (8,602)   *Devils Postpile, Merced Peak*
Origin unknown, but undoubtedly descriptive since it is forested. Matthes used the name in 1921 (Matthes, v. 25, July 24, 1921), but the name didn't appear on maps until publication of the 15-minute quads in 1953. Green Mountain is in Sierra National Forest, but was in the park from 1890 to 1905. There are eight other summits in California bearing the same name.

Green Treble Lake   *Tuolumne Meadows*
Apparently a misnomer. According to Everett L. Spuller, in 1932 he named the largest lake "Treble" because there were three lakes in the group. The one adjacent to that he called "Green Lake," after a forest ranger of that name who was at the Lee Vining ranger station for many years. But on the topo map the two names have inadvertently been made one. So if you think the name "Green Treble" doesn't make sense, you're right. The lakes are in Inyo National Forest, but were in the park from 1890 to 1905.

Greenstone Lake   *Tuolumne Meadows*
Named in 1932 for the green-colored rocks around it. (Spuller.) In Inyo National Forest, but in the park from 1890 to 1905.

Grey Butte (11,365)   *Matterhorn Peak*
Origin unknown. The name appeared on the first *Bridgeport* 30′ map, 1911. By a BGN decision of 1932 the spelling was changed to "Gray," evidently due to the objection of Farquhar to the original spelling. (BGN case brief, 1970.) But the spelling never was changed on any map, and a 1970 decision officially made it "Grey" again. Although the distinction seldom is made these days, in the recent past "grey" was considered to be

the British spelling and "gray" the American one. At one time François Matthes used the "Gray" spelling in his diary. (Matthes, v. 40, August 23, 1936.)

Grizzly Creek   *Merced Peak*
The creek, which heads in Grizzly Lake well south of the park boundary, flows into the park and joins the South Fork of the Merced River. It acquired its present name through a BGN decision in 1968. It had the name "Quartz Creek" as early as the first edition of the *Mt. Lyell* 30' map, 1901—a name that was ratified by the BGN in 1932 and that apparently derived from nearby Quartz Peak. But the 1968 name report stated that no one used the name "Quartz Creek," and recommended the change. The customers are always right.

Grizzly: Peak (over 10,320), **Meadow**   *Tower Peak*
Origin unknown. The peak was named on the first *Dardanelles* 30' map, 1898. The meadow's name first appeared on the *Tower Peak* quad, 1956, as did the name for Grizzly Lake, in Toiyabe National Forest a mile east by north from the peak.

Grizzly Peak (6,219)   *Yosemite Valley, Yosemite*
Origin unknown. It may have been because its shape looked like the hump of a grizzly, or because it was a "grizzly" (difficult) climb. (*YNN* 34, no. 1, Jan. 1955: 7.) Hutchings quotes a letter from Charles A. Bailey, who made the first ascent about 1885 and indicated that it was a "hard and perilous climb." They did things differently in those days, and Bailey went on to say: "The first ascent of Grizzly Peak accomplished, I left my card, and water bottle, as mementos of my visit." (Hutchings, *In the Heart*, 454–55.)
It was called "Grizzly Pt" on the Wheeler Survey map of 1883, and "Grizzly Point" on all the *Yosemite* 30' maps until 1951, but was already "Grizzly Peak" on the first *Yosemite Valley* map, 1907. Before the "Grizzly" name became the thing, it was once referred to as "Sentinel Rock." (*Mariposa Democrat*, August 5, 1856.)

Grouse Creek   *Yosemite*
"Grouse" is one of the more overused geographic names in the Sierra and in California. There are fifteen "Grouse Creeks" in the state, and a grand total of sixty places whose names begin with the word "Grouse." This one may have been named by the Whitney Survey; it is on the Hoffmann and Gardiner map, 1863–67. Later there was a Grouse Creek

Stage Station where the old Wawona Road crossed the creek. That name was still in use in the second decade of this century. (Matthes, v. 18, June 11, 1914.)

Grouse Lake   *Yosemite*

"One day, after a long tramp [in September 1857], I stopped to rest by the side of a small lake about eight miles from the present site of Wawona, and I then named it Grouse Lake on account of the great number of grouse found there." (Clark, 95.)

Clark related an Indian legend about the lake. A boy had been drowned there long ago, and the Indians did not dare to go in the lake for fear the boy would seize their legs and pull them down to share his fate. Clark said he was told that story only because he had heard a distinct wailing cry at night, and asked the Indians what it was.

Gunsight   *Yosemite Valley, Yosemite*

Named by park rangers. One looks up the lower Cathedral Rocks gully and sees the Leaning Tower centered in the sights. (*SCB* 25, no. 1, Feb. 1940: 118–19.)

Half Dome (8,842)   *Yosemite Valley, Yosemite*

"Spencer [Pvt. Champion H. Spencer, Company B, Mariposa Battalion] looked a good long while at that split mountain, and called it a 'half dome.' I concluded he might name it what he liked, if he would leave it and go to camp; for I was getting tired and hungry and said so." (Narrative of Third Sergeant Alexander M. Cameron, in Bunnell, *Discovery*, 1911: 161.) And there you have the romantic story of the naming of Half Dome. The date was March 27, 1851, the day the Mariposa Battalion entered— and 'discovered'—Yosemite Valley.

The valley and Half Dome had actually been seen two years earlier by a couple of bear hunters. ". . . while farther beyond a rounded mountain stood the valley side of which looked as though it had been sliced with a knife as one would slice a loaf of bread and which Reamer and I called the Rock of Ages." (Diary of William Penn Abrams, BL.)

"The names 'North Dome,' 'South Dome,' and 'Half Dome' were given by us during our long stay in the valley from their localities and peculiar configuration. Some changes have been made since they were adopted. The peak called by us the 'South Dome' has since been given the name of 'Sentinel Dome,' and the 'Half Dome,' Tis-sa-ack, represented as meaning the 'Cleft Rock,' is now called by many the 'South Dome.' The 'Half Dome' was figuratively spoken of as 'The Sentinel' by our Mission

Indians, because of its overlooking the valley." (Bunnell, *Discovery*, 1880: 212.) Although Half Dome briefly was called "South Dome" (because it was across from North Dome) the name "Half Dome" was soon firmly established; it was on the King and Gardiner map of 1865. There were, of course, the inevitable attempts at interpreting Indian names and legends.

"Tissaack, South Dome in Yosemite, is . . . the name of a woman who according to tradition was transformed into the mountain." (Kroeber, 62. See **Basket Dome**.)

"Tis-se-yak, South Dome. This is the name of a woman who figures in a legend. . . . The Indian woman cuts her hair straight across the forehead, and allows the sides to drop along her cheeks, presenting a square face, which the Indians account the acme of female beauty, and they think they discover this square face in the vast front of South Dome." (Powers, 364.)

"Until the fall of 1875 the storm-beaten summit of this magnificent landmark was a *terra incognita*, as it had never been trodden by human feet. . . . This honor was reserved for a brave young Scotchman, a native of Montrose, named George D. Anderson, who by dint of pluck, skill, unswerving perseverance, and personal daring, climbed to its summit, and was the first that ever successfully scaled it. This was accomplished at 3 o'clock P.M. of October 12, 1875." (Hutchings, *In the Heart*, 456–57.)

Some early suggested names (doubtless we would think any one of them appropriate had it always been there) were "Goddess of Liberty," "Mt. Abraham Lincoln," and "Spirit of the Valley."

Contrary to the evidence of one's eyes, there never was another half of Half Dome, nor has Half Dome ever been covered by a glacier. Its sheer front is due to exfoliation in a zone of nearly vertical joints, and its rounded back is the result of exfoliation continued for millions of years. In fact it seems probable that the front of Half Dome was formed mainly between glacial periods. During earlier stages of glaciation the ice reached to within 500 feet of the top, but during the later (Tioga) stage it didn't even reach the base of the cliff. (Matthes, *Paper 160*, 116.)

Half Moon Meadow   *Hetch Hetchy Reservoir*
The namer is unknown, but it obviously is named for its shape. The name first appeared on the 1929 YNP map; it was ratified by the BGN in 1932 because it was in common use.

Hanging Basket Lake   *Tuolumne Meadows*
A somewhat fanciful but nevertheless descriptive name that first appeared on the *Tuolumne Meadows* quad, 1956. It's a snow-melt lake without a permanent outlet, sitting in a cirque east of Fletcher Peak.

Happy Isles   *Yosemite Valley, Yosemite*
"There are three islets just above the bridge which have never been given a place in the Yosemite geography . . . and commemorative of the emotions which I enjoyed when exploring them, I have named them the *Happy Isles*, for no one can visit them without for the while forgetting the grinding strife of *his* world and being happy." (Letter, W. E. Dennison, Guardian of Yosemite Valley, Oct. 25, 1885, in YRL files.) Earlier called "Island Rapids" by James M. Hutchings. (*YNN* 34, no. 1, Jan. 1955: 8.)

Harden Lake   *Hetch Hetchy Reservoir*
Apparently named by the Whitney Survey for James ("Johnny") Hardin who had a ranch and sawmill, and later a small stopping place on the Big Oak Flat Road, at what is still named "Harden Flat," just off state route 120. (Paden, 202–4.) The names "Hardins Ranch" and "Hardins Lake" are on Hoffmann and Gardiner's map of 1863–67. The BGN ratified the name "Harden Lake" in 1897, designated it as "Helen Lake" in 1932, but reversed that decision in favor of "Harden Lake" once more, in 1937.

Harriet Lake   *Merced Peak*
Possibly named by R. B. Marshall, USGS. It appears on the maps at the same time as other lakes named by Marshall for women (Edna, Evelyn, Marie). It first appeared on the third edition of the *Mt. Lyell* 30' map, 1910. One might speculate that it was named for Harriet Monroe, a long-time Sierra Club member who was on a number of the club's outings, including the one to Yosemite National Park in 1909. (Memorial in *SCB* 22, no. 1, Feb. 1937: 101.)

Hart Lakes   *Yosemite*
Three small lakes at the headwaters of Buena Vista Creek, a mile east by south from Ostrander Lake. Origin unknown. The name first appeared on the *Yosemite* quad, 1956.

Haystack Peak (10,015)   *Tower Peak*
A descriptive name, probably given by the Wheeler Survey; it is on atlas sheet 56D, 1878–79. McClure's 1896 map has the name on what is now Chittenden Peak. LeConte's 1900 map has it correctly located.

Hazel Green: Creek, Ranch   *Lake Eleanor*
"The next camp named [after 'Deer Flat'] was 'Hazel Green,' from the number of hazel bushes growing near a beautiful little meadow." (Bunnell, *Discovery*, 1911: 321.) The naming was in 1856 when Bunnell,

George Coulter, and others were constructing a trail from Coulterville to Yosemite Valley. The creek is a tributary of North Crane Creek. The location of the ranch is just outside the park boundary, but it was within the park from 1890 to 1905.

Headquarters Meadow   *Devils Postpile, Cattle Mtn.*
Origin unknown, but it may have been from when the US Army was patrolling the park between 1891 and 1916. The name appeared on the *Cattle Mtn.* quad, 1983. To locate it on the *Devils Postpile* quad: it is on the trail one mile west of Corral Meadow. It's in Sierra National Forest, but was in the park from 1890 to 1905.

Helen, Lake   *Matterhorn Peak*
Named in 1932 by Al Gardisky for a "lady friend." (Spuller.) The lake is on Mill Creek a mile east of the park boundary; it was in the park from 1890 to 1905.

Helen, Lake   *Tower Peak*
The lake is in Toiyabe National Forest, but is included because it was named by R. B. Marshall in 1909 for Helen Keyes, daughter of Colonel Forsyth and wife of Lt. Edward A. Keyes. (Farquhar: Marshall. See **Forsyth Peak** and **Keyes Peak**.) The name appeared on the third edition of the *Dardanelles* 30' map, 1912.

Helen Lake   *Mono Craters*
R. B. Marshall of the USGS named the lake in 1909 for Helen Coburn Smith, daughter of George Otis Smith, director of the USGS, 1907–31. (Farquhar: Marshall.) The name appeared on the third edition of the *Mt. Lyell* 30' map, 1910.

Hemlock Crossing   *Devils Postpile, Mt. Ritter*
Origin unknown. This is the spot where a trail crosses the North Fork of the San Joaquin, and there had better be some hemlocks there. The name appeared on the *Devils Postpile* quad, 1953. The location is at the left center edge of that quad, in Sierra National Forest. It was in the park from 1890 to 1905.

Henness Branch   *El Portal*
Henness Ridge   *Yosemite*
James A. Hennessy, a native of Ireland; the name was misspelled "Henness" by the Wheeler Survey. Hennessy grew vegetables for early

Yosemite visitors at what is now El Portal. The GLO plat of 1884, secs. 17 and 18, T. 3 S., R. 20 E., shows "House, Barn, Hennessy's Ranch," about 0.5 mile east of what is named "Rancheria Flat" on present maps. The area was in the park from 1890 to 1905.

"Mr. Hennessy has under cultivation about nine acres, from which he produces the choicest fruits and vegetables. . . . Mr. Hennessy's place proper contains about fifteen acres, which was no doubt once an island of the river. . . ." (*Mariposa Gazette*, July 23, 1881.)

Hetch Hetchy Reservoir   *Lake Eleanor, Hetch Hetchy Reservoir*
Hetch Hetchy Dome (6,165)   *Lake Eleanor*

"Named from a Central Miwok word denoting a kind of grass or plant with edible seeds abounding in the valley." (Kroeber, 42.)

"Hetch Hetchy is the name of a species of grass that the Tuolumne Indians used for food, and which grows on the meadow at the lower end of the valley. The grain, when ripe, was gathered and beaten out and pounded into meal in mortars." (Sanchez, 230–31.)

"Hatchatchie Valley (erroneously spelled Hetch Hetchy)." (Powers, 357.)

". . . In the Indian language used by Tenaya, Hetchy means 'tree.' At the end of the valley where the trail from the ridge comes in . . . there are twin yellow pine trees, and the Indians, therefore, called the valley 'Hetchy Hetchy,' or 'The Valley of the Two Trees.'" (Versteeg from J. V. Wolff, supervisor of Stanislaus National Forest, 1920s, in Farquhar files.)

"The valley was first visited, in 1850, by Mr. Joseph Screech, a mountaineer of this region, who found it occupied by Indians." (Charles F. Hoffmann, "Notes on Hetch-Hetchy Valley," *Proceedings* 3, Oct. 21, 1867: 368–70. Hoffmann received this information in conversation with Screech.) "The Pah Utes still visit it every year for the purpose of getting the acorns, having driven out the western slope Indians, just as they did from the Yosemite." (Whitney, *The Yosemite Guide-Book*, 1870: 110.)

"Hetch Hetchy Valley" and "Hetch Hetchy Fall" are on Hoffmann and Gardiner's map of 1863–67. The valley was called "Hatch Hatche Meadows" on the 1880 GLO plat and in the surveyor's field notes. On July 5, 1883, Joseph Screech patented 160 acres—the SE quarter of sec. 9—in T. 1 N., R. 20 E. On the same day, Nate Screech patented 160 acres in sec. 10.

Hetch Hetchy Dome was not named on the maps until the eighth edition of the *Yosemite* 30' sheet, 1951. It had been described, but not named, many years earlier by John Muir. "Facing Kolana, on the opposite side of the valley, is a rock 1,800 feet high, which presents a sheer, precipitous front like El Capitan, of Yosemite. . . . " ("Hetch-Hetchy Valley," *Overland Monthly*, July 1873: 45–46.)

Whatever the name "Hetch Hetchy" means—grass, seeds, trees—it is no longer relevant; everything is covered by water. O'Shaughnessy Dam was built between 1919 and 1923, and was raised another eighty-five feet during the years 1935–38.

Hidden Lake   *Tuolumne Meadows*

A small lake south of Snow Flat that cannot be seen from the trail. (BGN, 1932.) The name appeared on the first *Mt. Lyell* 30' map, 1901.

Hite Cove   *El Portal*

John R. Hite, frontiersman, explorer, miner, and "squawman," discovered a rich mine at this location in 1861. (Chamberlain, 128–33.) The name is on the Hoffmann and Gardiner map, 1863–67, as "Hite's Cove."

Hodgdon Ranch   *Lake Eleanor*

On the Old Big Oak Flat Road less than a mile inside the park boundary. Jeremiah Hodgdon settled here in 1865. It served as the headquarters for his summer cattle camp. (Paden, 214–16.)

He also fed and housed travelers to Yosemite Valley, in a crude sort of way. "Three, four, five in a room; some on floors, without even a blanket. . . . Food? Yes. Junks of beef floating in bowls of fat, junks of ham ditto, beans ditto, potatoes as hard as bullets, corn-bread steaming with saleratus, doughnuts ditto, hot biscuits ditto; the whole set out in indescribable confusion and dirt, in a narrow, unventilated room, dimly lit by two reeking kerosene lamps. . . . Not in the wildest and most poverty-stricken little town in Italy could such discomfort be encountered." (Jackson, 95–96.)

Hoffmann, Mount (10,850); Hoffmann Creek   *Hetch Hetchy Reservoir*

"Climbed a peak over 10,000 feet high which we called Mt. Hoffmann, and had one of the sublimest views I have ever had of the Sierra." (Brewer diary, June 24, 1863, in BL.)

Charles Frederick Hoffmann (1838–1913), born in Germany, came to California in 1858. He was topographer and cartographer with the Whitney Survey throughout its entire existence, 1860–74. Hoffmann and James Gardiner produced the *Map of a portion of the Sierra Nevada adjacent to the Yosemite Valley*, 1863–1867. Hoffmann's other important maps, published by the Whitney Survey, were *Topographical Map of Central*

California together with a part of Nevada, 1873, and *Map of the Region adjacent to the Bay of San Francisco*, 1873.

There are portraits of Hoffmann in *SCB* 11, no. 4, 1923, plate CXI; and *SCB* 12, no. 2, 1925, plate XLIV.

Holcomb Lake (2,889 m.)   *Devils Postpile, Mt. Ritter*

Origin unknown. The lake is 0.5 mile south of the Beck Lakes, and was first named on the *Devils Postpile* quad, 1953. It is in Inyo National Forest, but was within the park from 1890 to 1905.

Hooper Peak (over 9,520)   *Tuolumne Meadows*

Origin uncertain, but possibly named for Major Burchell Hooper. (YRL.) It is not known whether Hooper was related to Major Forsyth or to some other army officer who might have named the peak. Hooper was in the US cavalry during the Civil War. (Heitman, 541.) The name appeared on the third *Mt. Lyell* 30' map, 1910.

Hoover: Lakes, Creek   *Merced Peak*

Three lakes north of Buena Vista Crest, and the creek flowing from them, were named for President Herbert C. Hoover by Forest S. Townsley, probably in the late 1920s. Townsley was at that time chief ranger of the park, and a friend and fishing companion of Hoover. See **Townsley Lake**.

Hoover Lakes   *Matterhorn Peak*

Theodore Jesse Hoover, a brother of former President Hoover, professor of mining and metallurgy at Stanford, 1919–41. In 1904–5 Hoover was the manager of the Standard Consolidated Mining Co. of Bodie. An engineer of the company named the lakes in 1905. (Farquhar: T. J. Hoover.)

The lakes are about a mile outside the park's northeast boundary, in the Hoover Wilderness of Toiyabe National Forest. From 1890 to 1905 they were mainly within the park, with the park's northern boundary cutting through the middle of the northernmost lake. The name "Hoover Lake," applying to the upper lake, was on the first *Bridgeport* 30' map, 1911.

Horizon Ridge (8,262)   *Yosemite*

Origin unknown, but no doubt because it's the ridge one sees on the horizon from—who knows where. The name appeared on the first *Yosemite* quad, 1956.

Horse Ridge   *Yosemite*

Origin unknown, but possibly a name given by cattlemen before

Yosemite National Park was created in 1890. The name was on Lt. McClure's maps of 1895 and 1896.

Hummingbird Lake   *Tuolumne Meadows*
Named in 1932 by Al Gardisky because at one time he saw many hummingbirds there. (Spuller.) The lake is in Inyo National Forest 0.5 mile north of Saddlebag Lake. It was within the park from 1890 to 1905.

Courtesy Yosemite Research Library, NPS
James Mason Hutchings, writer, publisher, foremost publicist of Yosemite's wonders, organizer of the first tourist trip to Yosemite Valley, in 1855.

Hutchings Creek   *Merced Peak*
On the first eight editions of the *Mt. Lyell* 30' map (1901–1944) this stream was called "North Fork of Lyell Fork" of the Merced River. On the

ninth edition, 1948, it was changed to "Hutching Creek," which is how it appears on most editions of the *Merced Peak* quad. It was considered to have been named for Florence Hutchings, daughter of James Mason Hutchings. The BGN in 1978 decided that the name should be "Hutchings," and that it is for James, not his daughter. See **Florence, Mount**, etc.

Iceberg Lake (9,773–2,979 m.)   *Devils Postpile, Mt. Ritter*
    The lake is fed by a small glacier and a permanent snowfield, and often has ice floating in it until late summer. It probably was named by Ansel F. Hall and Al Solinski during an exploring expedition, September 8–20, 1922. (YRL files.) The name was first used in print in 1924. (*SCB* 12, no. 1, 1924: 30.) It appeared on the *Devils Postpile* quad, 1953.

Illilouette: Fall, Creek, Ridge, Gorge   *Yosemite Valley, Yosemite*
    "*Tululowehäck*. The cañon of the South Fork of the Merced, called the Illilouette in the California Geological Report, that being the spelling given by Messrs. King and Gardner,—a good illustration of how difficult it is to catch the exact pronunciation of these names. Mr. Hutchings spells it Tooluluwack." (Whitney, *Yosemite Guide-Book*, 1870: 17.)
    "This cañon is called by Professor J. D. Whitney the 'Illilouette,' a supposed Indian name; but I have never questioned a single Indian that knew anything whatever of such a word; while every one, without exception, knows this cañon either by Too-lool-a-we-ack or Too-lool-we-ack; the meaning of which, as nearly as their ideas can be comprehended and interpreted, is the place beyond which was the great rendezvous of the Yo Semite Indians for hunting deer." (Hutchings, *In the Heart*, 440.)
    "I think it advisable to call this the Glacier Fall, and, therefore, give it that name. . . . The name of 'Illeuette' is not Indian, and is, therefore, meaningless and absurd." (Bunnell, *Discovery*, 1880: 203.)
    Everyone tripped over the name. On the 1884 GLO plat it is spelled "Illionette" and "Illioneth." The creek was still called "Tu-lu-la-wi-ak or South Cañon" as late as the Wheeler Survey map of the valley, 1883. Lt. McClure had it as "Illilouette River" on his 1896 map. The fall was called "Sth Fork Fall" on a map in the *Sacramento Daily Union*, Sept. 30, 1865.
    The name for Illilouette Ridge was recommended by E. M. Douglas, a geographer with the USGS, on March 1, 1907. (BGN.) The gorge was first named on the fourth edition of the USGS map of the valley, 1927.

Indian: Canyon, Canyon Creek   *Yosemite Valley, Hetch Hetchy Reservoir*
    "It was up this cañon that the Indian prisoners escaped in 1851 . . . from which circumstance originated the name; and it was down this that

the avenging Monos crept, when they substantially exterminated the Yo Semite tribe in 1853." (Hutchings, *In the Heart*, 375.)

"This ravine became known to us as 'Indian Cañon,' though called by the Indians 'Le-Hamite,' 'the arrow-wood.' It was also known to them by the name of 'Scho-tal-lo-wi,' meaning the way to *'Fall Creek.'*" (Bunnell, *Discovery*, 1880: 169.)

Powers said the Indians used a generic word for canyon—Ma'-ta—and held up both hands to indicate perpendicular walls. (Powers, 364.)

"Indian Cañon" is on King and Gardiner's map, 1865. The creek was at first called "Indian Creek;" the name was changed by a BGN decision in 1932 to avoid confusion with another Indian Creek, which flows into the Merced River near El Portal. James M. Hutchings built a horse trail up Indian Canyon in 1874, but it didn't last more than a couple of years.

Indian Cave   *Yosemite Valley, Yosemite*

Formed by huge boulders piled on top of each other; said to have been occupied by the Yosemite Indians as a winter shelter. Ansel Hall said the Indians named the cave "Hol'-low'," but sometimes called it "Lah-koo'-hah," which meant "Come out!" (Hall, 22.) The name has been on the valley map since the first edition, 1907. On the *Yosemite* 15-minute quad and the Wheeler Survey map of 1883 it is simply marked "Cave."

Indian Creek   *Yosemite, El Portal*

A common name but an old one. The creek crosses the Wawona Road near Chinquapin and joins the Merced River above El Portal. It was named by early travelers, the Mariposa Battalion, or the Whitney Survey. The name is on the Hoffmann and Gardiner map, 1863–67.

Indian Meadow   *Devils Postpile, Cattle Mtn.*

Origin unknown. About 1.8 miles south of Cattle Mountain. The name first appeared on the *Devils Postpile* quad, 1953. The place is in Sierra National Forest, but was in the park from 1890 to 1905.

Indian: Rock (8,522), **Ridge**   *Yosemite Valley, Hetch Hetchy Reservoir*

Both these names probably derived from nearby Indian Canyon. Indian Rock is one of the points on the boundary of the original grant of Yosemite Valley in 1864. Although it is shown on the 1865 and 1863–67 maps of the Whitney Survey, it is not named until the Wheeler Survey map of the valley, 1883. "Indian Ridge" is on the first *Yosemite* 30' map, 1897.

Inferno Lakes   *Pinecrest*

Origin unknown. The lakes are on the northeast boundary of the park, about nine miles north of Hetch Hetchy Reservoir. The name first appeared on the *Pinecrest* quad, 1956.

Inspiration Point   *Yosemite Valley, Yosemite*

A viewpoint on the old Wawona Road, less than a thousand feet above the east end of the Wawona Tunnel. It can be reached by trail from the parking area at the east end of the tunnel. The original Inspiration Point is no longer marked on the maps. What is called "Old Inspiration Point" was actually "Mount Beatitude." (See the entries for those two names.) It is somewhat depressing rather than inspiring to know that there are eighteen places in California named Inspiration Point.

Ireland: Lake (10,735), **Creek**   *Tuolumne Meadows*

Named by Lt. Benson for Dr. Merritte Weber Ireland of the US Army Medical Corps, who was on duty in the park in 1897. Later, Ireland was surgeon general of the army for thirteen years. (Farquhar: Benson.)

On Lt. McClure's 1896 map the creek was designated as "Mt. McClure Fork T.R."—which uses the long-standing misspelling of "Maclure" to name this fork of the Tuolumne River. Both the creek and the lake had their present names on the first *Mt. Lyell* 30' map, 1901.

Iron: Mountain (11,149–3,318.2 m.), **Creek, Lake**

Devils Postpile, Cattle Mtn.

The mountain probably was named by C. S. J. (John) Beck in the mid-1870s. (*Fresno Weekly Expositor*, Jan. 22, 1880. See **Beck Lakes**.) The name is on the Wheeler Survey atlas sheet 56D, 1878–79. Iron Creek is named on the first edition of the *Mt. Lyell* 30' map, 1901. Iron Lake is first named on the *Devils Postpile* quad, 1953.

Iron: Creek, Mountain   *Yosemite*

Origin unknown. Both names first appeared on the *Yosemite* quad, 1956. The features are outside the park, but were within the park from 1890 to 1905. (These should not be confused with the Iron Mountain and Iron Creek southeast of Wawona in Sierra National Forest.)

Iron Spring   *Yosemite Valley, Yosemite*

The red stains from this spring can be seen from Glacier Point. It was called "Chalybeate Spring" on the Wheeler Survey map, 1883. ("Chalybeate" means water impregnated with the salts of iron.)

"I once visited this spring in company with the eminent English chemist, Dr. F. R. Lees, of Leeds, and he pronounced it the finest and most valuable chalybeate spring he had ever seen." (Hutchings, *In the Heart*, 391.)

Called "Mineral Springs" on the first five editions of the *Yosemite Valley* map, 1907–29. The name has been deleted from the valley maps since the edition of 1958.

Irwin Bright Lake   *Hetch Hetchy Reservoir*

Robert Bright stated that this lake was named for his deceased son Irwin, who planted thirty-seven rainbow trout in the lake. (USGS.) A BGN decision in 1932 spelled the first name "Irving;" this was corrected to "Irwin" by a 1960 decision. The lake had formerly been known as "Lily Lake" and "Saddle Horse Lake."

The Bright family ran cattle in this area in the 1880s, before Yosemite National Park was created. Three other features in the vicinity have names given by the Bright family. (See **Pleasant Valley**, **Saddle Horse Lake**, and **Table Lake**. Information from Jim Snyder, Yosemite trail foreman and historian.)

Isberg: Pass, Peak (10,996), **Lakes**   *Merced Peak*

Lt. N. F. McClure named the pass in 1895 for the native Norwegian in his command who discovered it while they were exploring for a route from the Merced River to the Minarets region. The peak was named from the pass. The pass was named on McClure's 1896 map; the peak was named on the first *Mt. Lyell* 30' map, 1901; and the lakes were first named on the *Merced Peak* quad, 1953.

When the BGN ratified the names for the pass and the peak in 1932 they were erroneously spelled "Ishberg." This misspelling didn't get on maps until forty years later, when the 1972 edition of the *Merced Peak* quad had it for the peak and the lakes—but not the pass. King Huber of the USGS pointed out the error, and the correct spelling has been restored on subsequent editions.

The pass and the peak are on the park's southeast boundary, and although the lakes are in Sierra National Forest they were in the park from 1890 to 1905.

Island Pass (over 10,160)   *Devils Postpile, Mt. Ritter*

Probably named because it is crossed by the trail from Rush Creek to Thousand Island Lake. Most likely named by the USGS during the 1898–99 survey for the *Mt. Lyell* 30' map; it is on the first edition, 1901. The first use of the name in print is by J. N. LeConte in 1909. (*SCB* 7, no. 1, Jan. 1909: photo opp. 6.)

Jack Main Canyon   *Tower Peak*

"Some years ago I was discussing a trip I had made through Jack Main Canyon with Mr. C. H. Burt. . . . He told me that as a boy he had often herded sheep through Jack Main Canyon and volunteered the information that the canyon was named after an old sheep-herder who ranged sheep in that region whose name was Jack Means. Mr. Burt said that the name of the canyon as it appeared on the maps was incorrect; that all the early sheep and cattle men in that region called the canyon 'Jack Means Canyon,' and that the present name of the canyon was a corruption of that name." (Letter, W. H. Spaulding to Farquhar, in *SCB* 12, no. 2, 1925: 126.)

The name first appears on Lt. McClure's map of 1895. On that same map he had the name "Jack Main's Mt." on what is now Chittenden Peak. On his 1896 map McClure called that same mountain "Haystack Peak." The present Haystack Peak is several miles away.

Jawbone Creek   *Pinecrest, Cherry Lake North*

In the late 1860s a Frenchman named Jarbau had a cabin at the confluence of what are now named Jawbone and Skunk creeks. Oldtimers called the northerly creek "Jarbau Creek," a name that was transformed into "Jawbone." (StNF files.) Lt. McClure called it "Pile Creek" on his 1895 map, but had the present name on his 1896 map—the same year it was approved by the BGN. The creek is in Stanislaus National Forest, but passed through the northwest corner of the park's 1890 to 1905 boundary.

Joe Crane Lake   *Merced Peak*

I don't know who Joe Crane is, or was—perhaps a packer. The name first appeared on the *Merced Peak* quad, 1953. The lake is about a mile east-southeast of Post Peak. It is in Sierra National Forest, but was in the park from 1890 to 1905.

Johnson: Lake, Creek   *Yosemite*

Origin unknown, but probably named for an early sheepman or cattleman. The lake is named on Lt. McClure's map of 1896. The creek is first named on the *Yosemite* quad, 1956.

Johnson Peak (11,070)   *Tuolumne Meadows*

Named in the 1890s by R. B. Marshall, USGS, for a survey-party teamster who was useful as a guide because he had been with Professor Davidson's party at Mount Conness in 1890. (Farquhar: Marshall.)

Johnston: Lake, Meadow *Devils Postpile, Mammoth Mtn.*
In 1919, Taylor Johnston, with his father and brother, began mining in this area. They also built roads, and started a resort at Reds Meadow. Stephen T. Mather, the first director of the National Park Service, suggested that Minaret Lake and Minaret Meadow be renamed to honor the Johnston family for the work they had done. (BGN Case Brief, 1962.) The names did not appear on maps until the 1950s, and were initially misspelled "Johnson." The spellings were corrected beginning with the *Devils Postpile* quad, 1960. The features are in Inyo National Forest, but were within the park from 1890 to 1905.

Kendrick Peak (10,390) *Tower Peak*
Kendrick Creek *Tower Peak, Pinecrest*
Colonel Forsyth named the peak in 1912 for Henry Lane Kendrick (1811–1891) professor of chemistry at the US Military Academy from 1857 to 1880. (Farquhar: H. C. Benson; Heitman, 591.) The name appeared on the third edition of the *Dardanelles* 30′ map, 1912. The creek was called "East Fork Eleanor Creek" on the *Dardanelles* 30′ maps from 1898 through 1924; it was changed to its present name on the fifth edition, 1939.

Kerrick Canyon *Tower Peak*
Kerrick Meadow *Matterhorn Peak*
James D. Kerrick took sheep into the mountains about 1880. The canyon was named first, by the Wheeler Survey. (Letter, Col. Benson to Versteeg, in Farquhar files.) Versteeg said that John Lembert gave the name to Lt. McClure in 1894. (Farquhar files.) The name is on McClure's maps of 1895 and 1896. The meadow is named on the first *Bridgeport* 30′ map, 1911.

Keyes Peak (10,670) *Tower Peak*
Colonel Forsyth named the peak in 1912 for his son-in-law, Lt. Edward A. Keyes. (Farquhar: Benson; Heitman, 596. See the second **Helen, Lake.**)

Kibbie Lake *Pinecrest*
Kibbie Creek *Lake Eleanor, Pinecrest*
Kibbie Ridge *Lake Eleanor, Pinecrest, Cherry Lake North*
The name has always been misspelled on maps and in print. Horace G. *Kibbe* planted trout in Lake Eleanor and Lake Vernon in 1877, and lived at

Lake Eleanor for many years. (Versteeg, from Benson and McClure, in Farquhar files; also Bingaman, *Pathways*, 34.) The correct spelling of the name was known: R. B. Marshall used it in a letter to the acting Yosemite superintendent, Major John Bigelow, Sept. 6, 1904. (YRL files.)

Kibbe discovered Lake Eleanor and its valley in 1860, and said "there was no trace of civilized man ever having set foot in it." (*Tuolumne Independent* (Sonora), May 12, 1877.)

"Lake Eleanor was stocked in early days by a cattleman named Kibbie, who packed the fish from Cherry Creek to the lake, carrying them in coal-oil cans." (Walter A. Starr in *SCB* 20, no. 1, Feb. 1935: 58.) Kibbe homesteaded 175 acres in secs. 34 and 35, T. 2 N., R. 19 E. in 1883—land that is now under the waters of Lake Eleanor Reservoir.

LeConte's map of 1893 had "Kibbie" (a building) at Lake Eleanor. McClure's maps of 1895 and 1896 had that and the creek's name. The lake and the creek were named on the first *Dardanelles* 30' map, 1898. The ridge wasn't named until the 15-minute maps were published in 1956.

King Creek   *Devils Postpile, Mt. Ritter, Cattle Mtn., Crystal Crag*

An early name, origin unknown. The name already existed at the time of the Mammoth mining boom. (*San Francisco Mining and Scientific Press*, Aug. 16, 1879: 98.) One newspaper had it as "King's Creek," as though named for a person. (*Fresno Weekly Expositor*, June 9, 1880.)

The creek originates in the Beck Lakes and flows into the Middle Fork of the San Joaquin at the southwest corner of Devils Postpile National Monument. It was first named on LeConte's map of 1893. The creek is in Inyo National Forest, but was within the park from 1890 to 1905.

Knoblock Cabin   *Merced Peak*

Knoblock was a cattleman early in this century. François Matthes encountered him at the Chetwood Cattle Camp in 1921. "Talked with H. H. Knoblock and his wife. He tells me how to reach Detachment Meadow and the Soda Springs." (Matthes, v. 25, July 24, 1921.) The name first appeared on the *Merced Peak* quad, 1953. The area is in Sierra National Forest, but was in the park from 1890 to 1905.

Koip: Peak (12,979), **Crest**   *Mono Craters*

Named by Willard D. Johnson, USGS, about 1883. (Farquhar: J. N. LeConte.) "Koip Peak, between Mono and Tuolumne counties, is probably, like near-by Kuna Peak, named from a Mono Indian word. *Koipa* is 'mountain sheep' in the closely related Northern Paiute dialect." (Kroeber, 45.) The bighorn sheep that were native to this area died out several decades ago. Recently a number of sheep were reintroduced into the Lee Vining Creek area, and in July 1987 it was reported that five of the animals had moved south to former bighorn sheep range at Parker Creek and Parker Lake—a few miles northeast of Koip Peak.

The peak's name was spelled "Kó-it" on the map in the USGS *Eighth Annual Report*, 1886–87, (Part I, Plate XVII), but spelled "Koip" in the same report (p. 275, et seq). LeConte had both the peak and the crest as "Ko-ip" on his 1893 map. Lt. McClure had "Koip Pk." on his 1896 map. The correct spelling for both features was ratified by the BGN in 1901. The peak is in Inyo National Forest, but was in the park from 1890 to 1905.

Kolana Rock (over 5,760)   *Lake Eleanor*

"Standing boldly out into the valley, from the southern wall, is the rock *Ko-la-na* . . . forming the outermost of a group corresponding in every way with the Cathedral Rocks of Yosemite. On the authority of the State Geological Survey, it is 2,270 feet in height." (John Muir, "Hetch-Hetchy Valley," *Overland Monthly*, July 1873: 45.) The name appeared on the fifth edition of the *Yosemite* 30' map, 1911. An earlier name was "Sugar Loaf." (R. M. Price in *SCB* 1, no. 1, Jan. 1893: 15–16; and on LeConte's map of 1893.)

K P Pinnacle   *Yosemite Valley*

A Sierra Club name, probably derived from Henry Knoll and Jack Pionteki, who in 1941 made the first ascent. (USGS.) The name appeared on the eighth *Yosemite Valley* map, 1958.

Kuna Peak   *Mono Craters*
Kuna: Creek, Crest, Lake   *Mono Craters, Tuolumne Meadows*

Kuna Peak was named by Willard D. Johnson, USGS, in 1882 or 1883. (Farquhar: J. N. LeConte.) Johnson was the cartographer who worked with Israel C. Russell on his study of the Mono Basin. (Russell, *Quaternary*, 98, 131.)

"Kuna Peak . . . is probably named from the Shoshonean word *Kuna*, usually meaning 'fire' but appearing in the Mono dialect of the vicinity with the signification of 'fire-wood.'" (Kroeber, 45.)

In 1976 the US Forest Service maintained that the peak's name was not correctly located on maps, and proposed that it be moved about half a mile southeast. This was accepted by the BGN. Therefore, all maps before that time show the peak's name incorrectly placed. On the *Mono Craters* quad, it should now be on the park boundary south of the center of the glacier that is west of Koip Peak. For the sake of precision, the coordinates are: 37° 48' 43" N., 119° 12' 19" W. The latest edition of the *Mono Craters* quad (1978) has the name in its new location.

The peak and Kuna Crest were named on Johnson's map (Russell, *Quaternary*, following p. 272), as they were on LeConte's 1893 map. Only the peak was named on McClure's maps of 1895 and 1896. The peak and the creek were named on the first *Mt. Lyell* 30' map, 1901. The crest and the lake were first named on the 15-minute quads in the 1950s.

Lady Lake   *Merced Peak*
Origin unknown. The lake is 0.7 mile east-northeast of Madera Peak, and was first named on the *Merced Peak* quad, 1953. It is in Sierra National Forest, but was within the park from 1890 to 1905.

Laura Lake (2,928 m.)   *Devils Postpile, Mt. Ritter*
Origin unknown; between Garnet Lake and Shadow Lake, east of the John Muir Trail. It was first named on the *Devils Postpile* quad, 1953. The lake is in Inyo National Forest, but was in the park from 1890 to 1905.

Laurel Lake   *Lake Eleanor, Pinecrest*
The name is an obvious one, for the mountain laurel around the shore, but the namer is unknown. The lake is on Frog Creek east of Lake Eleanor, and was named on McClure's maps of 1895 and 1896.

Leaning Tower   *Yosemite Valley, Yosemite*
"A tower-shaped and leaning rock, about three thousand feet in height, standing at the southwest side of the [Bridalveil] fall, sometimes called the 'Leaning Tower,' nearly opposite 'Tu-tock-ah-nu-lah' [El Capitan], has on its top a number of projecting rocks that very much resemble cannon. . . . We once took the liberty of christening this 'Tu-tock-ah-nu-lah's Citadel.'" (Hutchings, *In the Heart*, 408.)

The tower was named on the Wheeler Survey map of the valley, 1883.

Le Conte Falls   *Tuolumne Meadows*
Joseph LeConte (1823–1901), professor of geology and natural history at the University of California at Berkeley, 1869–1901.

The falls was named in 1894. "Cross this ledge well to the right and gradually approach the river, which can be followed to the head of what is in many respects the most majestic cascade in the whole cañon, the Le Conte Cascade, so named by us in honor of our most esteemed Professor, Joseph Le Conte." (R. M. Price, "Through the Tuolumne Cañon," *SCB* 1, no. 6, May 1895: 204.)

Somehow, a confusion occurred among the namer of the falls and the map-makers who used his information. What Price named "Le Conte Cascade" is indeed the most majestic one in the canyon—but it's the one that is now named "Waterwheel Falls." The present Le Conte Falls is the one originally named "California Falls," which is the way it appeared on McClure's maps of 1895 and 1896 and on LeConte's map of 1900. It was unnamed on the first two editions of the *Mt. Lyell* 30' map, 1901 and 1905, and had its present name beginning with the edition of 1910.

Courtesy The Bancroft Library

The LeConte family on the Vernal Fall bridge. Joseph LeConte on horseback; Joseph N. LeConte and his wife Marion at the left.

Le Conte Point (6,410)   *Hetch Hetchy Reservoir*

Joseph Nisbet LeConte (1870–1950), a charter member of the Sierra Club, professor of engineering mechanics at the University of California at Berkeley, 1895–1937. The point was named by R. B. Marshall, USGS, in 1911. The name didn't appear on maps until publication of the *Hetch Hetchy Reservoir* quad, 1956.

John Muir described the point long before it had a name. "The upper end of the Yosemite Valley is closed by the great Half-Dome Rock. The upper end of Hetch-Hetchy is closed in the same way, by a rock differing from Half-Dome only in those features that are directly referable to peculiarities of physical structure. . . . In front of this head-rock, the

Tuolumne River forks, just as the Merced forks in front of Half-Dome."
("Hetch-Hetchy Valley," *Overland Monthly*, July 1873: 47–48.)

Joseph N. LeConte was one of the foremost explorers of the Sierra
Nevada. He hiked and climbed from 1889 to 1928, wrote extensively
about his travels, was an expert photographer, and compiled a number of
very important maps. (See the Bibliography. Memorials in *SCB* 35, no. 6,
June 1950: 1–8; and *American Alpine Journal* 7, no. 4, 1950: 484–86.)

Lee Vining Creek   *Tuolumne Meadows, Mono Craters*
Lee Vining Peak (11,691); **Lee Vining** (town)   *Mono Craters*

"Leroy Vining and a few chosen companions, with one of Moore's
scouts as guide, went over the Sierra to the place where the gold had
been found [in 1852], and established themselves on what has since been
known as Vining's Gulch or Creek." (Bunnell, *Discovery*, 1880: 278.) But
Vining returned to the Mariposa vicinity for a time; he was mining at
Washington Flat on the Merced River in 1856. (*Daily San Joaquin
Republican*, March 11, 1856.) In March of 1859 Vining wrote a latter to the
Mariposa Gazette, which was reprinted in the *San Francisco Daily Evening
Bulletin* of May 4. It closed: "You might do worse than come over here. If
you *do* come, bring grub, because you will want a *little* until you get
acclimated . . . . I am writing by fire light, and haven't had a drink since I
left Mariposa."

In the early 1860s Vining built a sawmill on the creek now named for
him, and sold lumber in Aurora, Nevada. During that same period,
Vining and others mined for gold along Bohler Creek and in Horse
Meadow. (*Homer Mining Index*, July 1, 1882.)

Vining came to a peculiar end. "At that time the crowd of miners and
gamblers used to congregate at the Exchange Saloon [in Aurora], where
frequent shooting-scrapes would occur. Whenever trouble started everyone would get out of the room. On one of these occasions a gun went off
in the crowd and Lee Vining went out the door . . . and started up the
street toward the Odd Fellows Hall. Shortly after someone found him
lying on the walk dead, and upon examination it was found that the pistol
had gone off in his pocket, shooting him in the groin, from which he had
bled to death." (Letter, C. F. Quimby to Maule, Sept. 1927, in *SCB* 13, no. 1,
Feb. 1928: 84.)

On the A. W. Von Schmidt plat of 1857, the lower part of Lee Vining
Creek, where it flows into Mono Lake, was called "Rescue Creek."
Hoffmann's map of 1873 shows "Vining's Cr." The Wheeler Survey atlas
sheet 56D, 1878–79, calls it "Vining Creek." All the editions of the *Mt. Lyell*
30' map, 1901 to 1948, show "Leevining Creek" and "Leevining Pk."

Spelling the name as two words was put into effect on the 15-minute maps, a decision ratified by the BGN in 1955.

The headwaters of the creek were within the park from 1890 to 1905, and although the rest of the creek as well as the peak and the town are in Inyo National Forest, they are included here because of their historical significance to the region.

Lehamite Creek   *Yosemite Valley, Hetch Hetchy Reservoir*
Lehamite Falls   *Yosemite Valley*

"The cliff along the east side of Indian Cañon was known as Le-hamite, and designated the place of the arrow wood, as we might say, the oaks." (Bunnell, *Report*, 1889–90: 11.) The word could have been confused with the name of one of the Indian villages, about 0.4 mile east of Indian Canyon, which was given as Le-sam'-ai-ti. (Powers, 365.)

On the Wheeler Survey map of 1883, the creek is named "Little Winkle Branch." Variations of that name were on LeConte's map of 1893 and on McClure's maps of 1895 and 1896. The first five editions of the *Yosemite Valley* map (1907–29) called it "East Fork of Indian Creek." It changed to its present name on the sixth edition, 1938, and "Lehamite Falls" was added.

Leidig Meadow   *Yosemite Valley, Yosemite*

Mr. and Mrs. George Leidig built a two-story hotel in the valley in 1869. Their son Charles was born the same year—the first white boy born in Yosemite Valley. (*YNN* 34, no. 1, Jan. 1955: 10.) Charles Leidig (1869–1956), appointed Special Forest Agent in 1898; guide and scout for the US troops in summer; one of the guides for President Theodore Roosevelt's party in May 1903. (Bingaman, *Guardians*, 87–88.)

Leidig's Hotel was torn down in 1888 by order of the Yosemite Valley Commissioners because it was "unsightly." (Sargent, *Innkeepers*, 14.) The name first appeared on the *Yosemite Valley* map in 1922.

Lembert Dome   *Tuolumne Meadows*

John Baptist Lembert settled in Tuolumne Meadows sometime before 1882; he was visited in that year by a member of the crew surveying the original Tioga Road. Lembert was living in an eight-by-ten-foot cabin built directly atop one of the soda springs; water bubbled up in the center of the cabin. ("Surveying the Tioga Road," *YNN* 27, no. 9, August 1948: 109–12.)

Lembert raised angora goats, until he lost them in a snowstorm in the winter of 1889–90. Thereafter he made his living by collecting butterflies

Courtesy Yosemite Research Library, NPS

John Baptist Lembert, in Yosemite Valley. Photograph by Fiske.

and botanical specimens, which he sold to museums. On June 28, 1895, he gained legal possession of the property when he homesteaded 160 acres: the southwest quarter of sec. 5, T. 1 S., R. 24 E. He was murdered in his cabin in the Merced Canyon, below Yosemite Valley, in the winter of 1896–97. The Soda springs property was sold to the McCauley brothers in 1898 by Lembert's brother. J. J. McCauley sold it to the Sierra Club in 1912, which in turn sold it to the National Park Service in 1973. (For a detailed history of Lembert and a description of the property, see *SCB* 9, no. 1, Jan. 1913: 36–39.)

The dome was called "Soda Spr. Dome" on the Wheeler Survey atlas sheet 56D, 1878–79, but all maps since that time have used Lembert's name or a variation of it. John Muir called it "Glacier Rock." (Muir, *Picturesque*, drawing on p. 18; in the reprint edition, *West of the Rocky*

Mountains, p. 22.) The name was spelled "Lambert" on many early maps and in references. It is spelled that way on the first five editions of the *Mt. Lyell* 30' map, 1901–22; corrected on the edition of 1927.

Lewis Creek   *Tuolumne Meadows, Merced Peak*

Washington Bartlett Lewis (1884–1930), first civilian superintendent of the park, 1916–28. It was under his administration that the major development of roads and trails, the construction of buildings for headquarters and personnel, and the installation of public-utility systems was accomplished—the foundation for, and often the actual structures and systems, that exist today. (Obituary in *SCB* 16, no. 1, 1931: 60–62.)

The creek was called "McClure Fork" (of the Merced river)—although it should have been spelled "Maclure"—on the *Mt. Lyell* 30' maps from 1901 to 1929; changed to the present name on the edition of 1944.

Lewis, Mount (12,296)   *Mono Craters*

Named in 1930 for Washington B. Lewis (see the previous entry) by Robert B. Marshall of the USGS. (See also **Johnson, Mount**.)

"I was so pleased to know that your plans for naming a mountain for Dusty had gone through. . . . Even Carle was thrilled to know that there was to be a mountain in Yosemite, named for his daddy." (Letter, Bernice Lewis to Marshall, Nov. 18, 1930. In Marshall Papers, BL, Part I, Box IV. See also **Bernice Lake**.) Ironically, Mount Lewis is in Inyo National Forest, just outside the park's eastern boundary, although it was within the park from 1890 to 1905.

Liberty Cap (7,076)   *Yosemite Valley, Yosemite*

"Owing to the exalted and striking individuality of this boldly singular mountain . . . it had many godfathers in early days; who christened it Mt. Frances, Gwin's Peak, Bellows' Butte, Mt. Broderick, and others; but, when Governor Stanford . . . was in front of it with his party in 1865, and inquired its name, the above list of appellations was enumerated, and the Governor invited to take his choice of candidates . . . he responded 'Mr. H., I cannot say that I like either of those names very much *for that magnificent mountain*; don't you think a more appropriate one could be given?' Producing an old-fashioned half-dollar with the ideal Cap of Liberty well defined upon it, the writer suggested the close resemblance in form of the mountain before us with the embossed cap on the coin; when the Governor exclaimed, 'Why! Mr. H., that would make a most excellent and appropriate name for that mountain. Let us so call it.' *Thereafter it was so called*; and as everyone preferentially respects this name, all others have been quietly renunciated." (Hutchings, *In the Heart*, 445. See also **Broderick, Mount**.)

Galen Clark gave the Indian name as Mah'-ta, said to mean "Martyr Mountain." (Clark, 108.)

"Hundreds or, for aught we could feel, thousands of feet below us thundered the river. On the far side of it rose up Mah-tah . . . two thousand feet above the fall we were climbing to reach. What patriot first called this peak 'Cap of Liberty' considerate history forgets." (Jackson, 119.)

It was called "Cap of Liberty or Mt. Broderick" on King and Gardiner's map of 1865, and "Cap of Liberty" on the Wheeler Survey's atlas sheet 56D, 1878–79 and map of the valley, 1883, on LeConte's map of 1893, and on Solomons' map of 1896. But Lt. McClure's map of 1896 had "Liberty Cap"—and it's been that way ever since.

Lillian Lake *Merced Peak*

Origin unknown. A large lake about 1.2 miles east-southeast of Gale Peak on the park's southeast boundary. The name appeared on the third edition of the *Mt. Lyell* 30' map, 1910, which makes one think that it may have been named by R. B. Marshall of the USGS, who had a penchant for naming lakes for women. The lake is in Sierra National Forest, but was in the park from 1890 to 1905.

Lily Lake *Devils Postpile, Cattle Mtn.*

Origin unknown. The name appeared on the tenth edition of the *Mt. Lyell* 30' map, 1950. This tiny lake is next to the trail up the North Fork of the San Joaquin. It's in Sierra National Forest, but was within the park from 1890 to 1905.

Lion Point (8,866–2,704 m.) *Devils Postpile, Crystal Crag*

May have been named by the USGS during the 1898–99 survey for the *Mt. Lyell* 30' map; the name is on the first edition, 1901. The summit is in Sierra National Forest, but was in the park from 1890 to 1905.

Little Bear Lake *Pinecrest*

Origin unknown. The name did not appear on USGS maps until publication of the *Pinecrest* quad, 1956.

Little Crane Creek *El Portal*

The creek rises about a mile south of Crane Flat and flows southeast to

Crane Creek. The namer is unknown; the name first appeared on Lt McClure's 1895 map.

Little Yosemite Valley *Yosemite Valley, Yosemite, Merced Peak*
Named on March 28, 1851 by a few men from Captain Dill's company of the Mariposa Battalion. (Bunnell, *Report*, 11.) "A small squad climbed above Vernal and Nevada Falls. . . . These men were the first discoverers of Little Yosemite Valley. . . . Their names have now passed from my memory." (Bunnell, *Discovery*, 1880: 85.) The name is on King and Gardiner's map of 1865, and on Hoffmann and Gardiner's map of 1863–67 but with just the words "Little Yosemite."

The name is appropriate, both as to the valley's appearance and the way in which it was formed, and in the fact that it was once occupied by a lake, as was Yosemite Valley. (Matthes, *Paper 160*, 61–63, 98, 101, 104.)

Lois Lake (3,047 m.) *Devils Postpile, Mt. Ritter*
Origin unknown. The lake is about 1.2 miles south of Shadow Lake; it was first named on the *Devils Postpile* quad, 1953. It is in Inyo National Forest, but was within the park from 1890 to 1905.

Long Gulch *Hetch Hetchy Reservoir, Lake Eleanor*
An obvious descriptive name for a valley that was followed for about four miles by the route of the original Tioga Road; the stream in the gulch is part of the headwaters of the South Fork of the Tuolumne River. The namer is not known, but the name already existed when the road was being built. (*Mammoth City Times*, Nov. 8, 1879.) The name was on Lt. McClure's maps of 1895 and 1896.

Long Meadow *Tuolumne Meadows*
An obvious descriptive name for a meadow more than two miles long through which the Sunrise Trail runs. The namer is not known; the name first appeared on LeConte's 1893 map.

In 1872 Joseph LeConte named the meadow "Feldspar Valley" for the granite of the area, which is full of large feldspar crystals. (*American Journal of Science and Arts*, 3rd Series, v. 5, no. 29, May 1873: 325.) It became John Muir's custom to refer to the valley by that name. (Letter, Matthes to Farquhar, Dec. 11, 1925, in Farquhar files.)

Long: Mountain (11,502), **Creek** *Merced Peak*
Probably named by the USGS during the 1898–99 survey for the

Mt. Lyell 30′ map. Both names are on the first edition, 1901, but are not on McClure's maps of the 1890s.

Lost Arrow   *Yosemite Valley*

"The cliff east of the high fall, at the turn of Indian Cañon, was known as Ham-mo, meaning the lost arrow, as it marks the place of a pretended loss of an arrow that led to the death of Ten-ie-ya's son." (Bunnell, *Report*, 10–11.) Galen Clark said the formation was sometimes called "The Devil's Thumb." (Clark, 100.) A nineteenth century guidebook had it as the "Giant's Thumb." There is also a supposed Indian legend about what the name means and how it came about. (Hutchings, *In the Heart*, 370–74.) Although the name is an old one, it did not appear on the map until the eighth edition, 1958.

The *real* explanation of the origin of the formation called Lost Arrow is more prosaic. Upper Yosemite Fall has not carved a recess in its cliff because the cliff as a whole has receded by the scaling off of immense rock sheets. "The most remarkable remnant of such a sheet . . . is the gigantic tapering rock monument known as the Lost Arrow, which clings to the cliff east of the fall. It has a total height of about 1,500 feet, and its upper third stands detached, like a pinnacle, the parting behind it having been enlarged to an open cleft . . . as a result largely of the destructive action of the spray from the fall which freezes in it in winter." (Matthes, *Paper 160*, 111.)

Lost Bear Meadow   *Yosemite*

In June 1957 a small girl, Shirley Ann Miller, was lost for three and a half days. More than 100 men were involved in the search. When she was found, unharmed, she said, "I am not lost but the bear is lost. He went away and got lost." (YRL files; BGN decision, 1959.) The meadow is not named on the first edition of the *Yosemite* quad. It is near Bridalveil Creek, in sec. 30, T. 3 S., R. 22 E.

Lost Dog Lake   *Devils Postpile, Mammoth Mtn.*

Origin unknown. This tiny pond is two miles east of the Beck Lakes, and if you were ever there you certainly were a lost dog. It was first named on the *Devils Postpile* quad, 1953. It's in Inyo National Forest, but was within the park from 1890 to 1905.

Lost Lake (2,742 m.)   *Devils Postpile, Mt. Ritter*

Origin unknown, although because it is far off the beaten path you can understand how the name came about. The name first appeared on the

Devils Postpile quad, 1953. There are twenty-four lakes in California named "Lost Lake," and only one named "Found Lake"—whatever that means. This one is in Sierra National Forest, but was within the park from 1890 to 1905.

Lost Lakes   *Mono Craters*

Origin unknown, but possibly named by USGS topographers working on the *Mono Craters* quad, published in 1953. The lakes were "lost" since they were off the beaten path, but were "found" when seen on an aerial photo. The lakes are in Inyo National Forest, but were in the park from 1890 to 1905.

Lost Valley   *Merced Peak*

Before modern trails were built, "Lost Valley" was difficult of access from either direction on the Merced River, especially for people with stock—which is the way everyone traveled until well into the twentieth century. The present trail that follows the river, and climbs high up on the rocky slope east of Bunnell Point, was built in 1911. (YRL files.) The first use of the name in print is in *SCB* 5, no. 4, June 1905: 160; also J. N. LeConte's map, plate XXXIII. The name didn't appear on USGS maps until publication of the *Merced Peak* quad, 1953.

Lower Falls   *Devils Postpile, Crystal Crag*

The namer is unknown, but the reason for the name is obvious. It is half a mile downstream from the spectacular Rainbow Falls, and is less spectacular. The name appeared on the *Devils Postpile* quad, 1953. It is at the south boundary of Devils Postpile National Monument, and was within the park from 1890 to 1905.

Lukens Lake   *Hetch Hetchy Reservoir*

Theodore Parker Lukens, a conservationist and advocate of reforestation; mayor of Pasadena, 1890–95. The lake was named in 1894 by R. B. Marshall, USGS. Shirley Sargent characterized Lukens as "the John Muir of Southern California." (See Sargent, *Lukens*.)

In the earlier ice stages the Hoffmann Glacier filled the valley of Yosemite Creek. ". . . The ice overtopped the hills as well as the gaps of the northwesterly divide. . . . One of the largest diversions of ice took place through the pass now occupied by Lukens Lake, a body of water which owes its existence to the concentrated erosive action of the ice current in the defile." (Matthes, *Paper 160*, 83.)

Lundy (settlement); **Lundy: Canyon, Lake**   *Bodie*
Lundy Canyon; May Lundy Mine   *Matterhorn Peak*
Lundy Pass   *Tuolumne Meadows*

None of these places is in the park, but the pass, the mine, and the upper part of the canyon were within the park from 1890 to 1905. All of the names are included here because it makes more sense to do it that way than to arbitrarily exclude some because they have never been in Yosemite National Park.

William O. Lundy began operating a sawmill in the canyon sometime before 1879, which naturally gave rise to the name of **Mill Creek**. Indeed, according to George Montrose, an early resident of the town of Lundy, the town's original name was "Mill Creek." When the Homer Mining District was formed in 1879, Lundy became the mining recorder. The lake and the mine were named for Lundy's daughter. The messrs. Fox, Butterfield, Pike, and Kellogg filed on the "May Lundy Lode" in October 1881. The 1881 GLO plat shows "May Lundy Mine" and "Village of Lundy." (See *Eighth Annual Report of the State Mineralogist*, 1888: 367–71; DeDecker, 17–18; *SCB* 13, no. 1, Feb. 1928: 40–53.) William Lundy patented eighty acres in 1881: the north half of the northwest quarter of sec. 20, T. 2 N., R. 25 E.

The boosters of the Homer District had no fear for the future. "In many respects Homer District is a remarkable region. It abounds in 'big things.' Big mines, big mountains, big trees, big trout, and a sprinkling of big talkers. . . . Who knows but when, as the tide of years ebb and flow . . . Mill Creek millionaires shall spit tobacco juice on the polished floors of Parisian salons, or ride from Joppa to Jerusalem on the hurricane deck of Arab donkeys (no bigger than themselves) to weep, like Mark Twain, over the tomb of Adam (not caring A-dam for the expense, either), that Homer District may grow big men, with big hearts and big brains, and big girls, and big babies, and—and big dogs—and mayhap, some stalwart social tares, in the shape of big rascals? (Here the senior put his foot down and said this big fool business had to stop.)" (*Homer Mining Index*, vol. 1, no. 1, June 12, 1880.)

Lyell, Mount (13,114); **Lyell: Glacier, Fork** (of the Merced River)
                                                      Merced Peak
Lyell: Canyon, Fork (of the Tuolumne River)   *Tuolumne Meadows*

The mountain was named on July 2, 1863 by William H. Brewer and Charles F. Hoffmann of the California Geological Survey. "After seven hours of hard climbing we struck the last pinnacle of rock that rises through the snow and forms the summit—only to find it inaccessible, at least from that side. . . . As we had named the other mountain Mount

Dana, after the most eminent of *American* geologists, we named this Mount Lyell, after the most eminent of *English* geologists." (Brewer, *Up and Down*, 411.)

"Mount Lyell, from Sir Charles Lyell (1797–1875), whose admirable geological works have been well known to students of this branch of science, in this country, for the past thirty years." (Whitney, *Yosemite Guide-Book*, 1870: 100.)

Mount Lyell is the highest peak in Yosemite National Park. The first ascent was by John Boies Tileston of Boston, on August 29, 1871. "I was up early the next morning, toasted some bacon, boiled my tea, and was off at six. I climbed the mountain, and reached the top of the highest pinnacle ('inaccessible,' according to the State Geological Survey), before eight. I came down the mountain, and reached camp before one, pretty tired." (*SCB* 12, no. 3, 1926: 305.)

Lyell Glacier was first named on the fifth edition of the *Mt. Lyell* 30' map, 1922. On Lt. McClure's map of 1896 is "Mount Lyell Fork M. R." "Lyell Cañon" shows up on LeConte's map of 1900. What was designated as "No. Fork of Lyell Creek" was changed to "Hutching Creek" on the ninth edition of the map, 1948. The name "Lyell Glacier" probably was applied by Israel C. Russell in the early 1880s; he was the first to use the name. (Russell, *Quaternary*, 325, plates xxvii and xxviii.)

Maclure, Mount (over 12,960) *Merced Peak*
Maclure Creek *Tuolumne Meadows*

Named before 1868 by the Whitney Survey. "To the pioneer of American geology, William Maclure, one of the dominating peaks of the Sierra Nevada is very properly dedicated." (Whitney, *Yosemite Book*, 90.) Whitney neglected to mention that the survey had at first given this peak the name of "Mount Murchison," undoubtedly for Sir Roderick Impey Murchison (1792–1871), a prominent British geologist who was, at that time, director-general of the British geological survey. "To the east of us, and only twelve miles distant [from the top of Mount Clark], was the Mt. Lyell Group of peaks on the crest of the Sierra. The dark sharp pyramids of Mts. Murchison and Lyell side by side are probably the highest. . . ." (Journal of James T. Gardiner, July 12, 1866. Copy in Farquhar Papers, BL.) Having already named Mount Lyell for another British geologist, Whitney apparently had second thoughts and decided to give his naming of peaks some American balance.

Maclure (1763–1840) became known as "the father of American geology" because he produced, in 1809, the first geological map of the United States. The mountain is named on the Hoffmann and Gardiner map of 1863–67 as "Mt. Maclure." The Wheeler Survey atlas sheet 56D, 1878–79, had it misspelled as "McClure Pk.," a misspelling that was continued on later maps for more than fifty years. Willard D. Johnson had the incorrect spelling on his map in Russell, *Quaternary*, even though he cited *The Yosemite Book* where the spelling is correct. Theodore Solomons, Lt. McClure, and J. N. LeConte followed suit with the "McClure" spelling. Both the mountain and the creek, called "Fork," were spelled "McClure" on the first five editions of the *Mt. Lyell* 30' map, 1901–22. The BGN put out a decision in 1926 that corrected the spelling, and it was changed on the edition of 1927. The former "McClure Fork" (of the Merced River) was changed to "Lewis Creek" on the 30-minute map in 1944. The BGN in 1932 approved "Maclure Glacier" (on the north slope of Mount Maclure), and "Maclure Lake" (at the head of Maclure Creek). Neither name has thus far been on USGS maps, although W. D. Johnson used "McClure Glacier" in an illustration in Russell, *Quaternary*, plate xxvii, opp. p. 324.

Macomb Ridge   *Tower Peak*

Lieutenant Montgomery Meigs Macomb (1852–1924), Fourth Artillery, US Army, in charge of the Wheeler Survey field party in California, 1876, 1877, and 1878; mapped in the Yosemite region in 1878. (Wheeler Survey, *Reports*, 1877, 1878, 1879.) The name first appeared on the third edition of the *Dardanelles* 30' map, 1912, an indication that it may have been given by R. B. Marshall of the USGS.

Macomb had an adventurous career. He graduated from West Point in 1874; served in Alaska in 1875; with the Wheeler Survey from 1876 to 1883; involved with military explorations in Central America from 1891 to 1896; in the Spanish-American War in 1898; and was military attaché with Russian armies in Manchuria during the Russo-Japanese War in 1904 and 1905. From 1912 to 1916 he was a member of the US Board on Geographic Names. (Information from Donald J. Orth, Executive Secretary of the US Board on Geographic Names.)

There is a portrait of Macomb in *SCB* 12, no. 2, 1925: 138; also in Browning, *Place Names of the Sierra Nevada*.

Madera: Peak (10,509), **Creek, Lakes**   *Merced Peak*

In 1876 the California Lumber Company built a fifty-two-mile flume from the mountains above present-day Oakhurst to a sawmill in the San Joaquin Valley. The town that grew up around the mill was named *Madera*, the Spanish word for wood, or lumber. (Johnston, *Whistles*, 11, 87.) In 1893 the part of Fresno County north and west of the San Joaquin River was organized as a new county and named after the town. (Coy, 157.)

Madera Peak was originally named "Black Mt." by the Whitney Survey; it appears that way on the Hoffmann and Gardiner map of 1863–67. The Wheeler Survey revised that to "Black Pk." on atlas sheet 56D, 1878–79. That name and "Black Peak Fork"—beginning with McClure's map of 1896, for what is now Madera Creek—were on all maps through the first seven editions of the *Mt. Lyell* 30′ map, 1901–29. The Madera County commissioners wanted a prominent peak named for the county, and thus both the peak and the creek were given the name "Madera" by a BGN decision in 1926; the names appeared on the eighth edition of the 30-minute map, 1944. The lakes were first named on the *Merced Peak* quad, 1953. All these features are in Sierra National Forest, but they were in the park from 1890 to 1905.

Mahan: Peak (9,146), Lake   *Tower Peak*

There is strong circumstantial evidence to indicate that the peak was named by Col. William W. Forsyth, acting superintendent of the park from 1909 to 1912. During his tenure, Forsyth named a number of peaks and other features for army officers; e.g., "Kendrick," "Michie," and "Schofield." These names, and "Mahan Peak," appeared on the map at the same time: the third edition of the *Dardanelles* 30′ map, 1912.

Dennis H. Mahan was professor of military engineering at West Point prior to the Civil War, and was the author of a basic textbook on strategy and tactics. (Morison, 626; Heitman, 684.) He was the father of Adm. Alfred T. Mahan (1840–1914), the noted naval historian.

Mahan Lake was first named on the *Tower Peak* quad, 1956.

Mammoth Peak (12,117)   *Tuolumne Meadows*

The namer is unknown, but this was a favorite name in early mining days when everyone was thinking big. The peak is the high point of the Kuna Crest. The Whitney Survey gave this name to a peak east of Mount Lyell, but when the *Mt. Lyell* 30′ map was made it apparently was transferred to the present peak, which was first named on the third edition of the *Mt. Lyell* 30′ map, 1910. This should not be confused with Mammoth Mountain, some 20 miles to the southeast near Mammoth Lakes.

Many Island Lake   *Pinecrest*

The namer is unknown; the name is an obvious one. It first appeared on the *Pinecrest* quad, 1956.

Marie Lakes   *Merced Peak, Devils Postpile, Mt. Ritter*

Origin unknown. The lower, larger lake was named "Marie Lake" on the third edition of the *Mt. Lyell* 30' map, 1910—and thus may have been named by R. B. Marshall of the USGS who was naming many lakes for women at that time. The lakes are just east of Mount Lyell, in Inyo National Forest; they were in the park from 1890 to 1905.

Mariposa Grove Giant Sequoias *Yosemite*

The name *Mariposas* was given to an unknown location in the San Joaquin Valley in 1806. "This was called the place of the butterflies (*Llamose este Sitio de las Mariposas*), due to its great multitude especially at night and in the morning so unceasingly bothersome that they even reached the point of blocking the sun's rays, pursuing us everywhere so that one of the corporals of the expedition got one in his ear causing him much discomfort and no little trouble in extracting it." (Arch. MSB, vol. 4, Muñoz, Sept. 27, 1806.)

The name "Mariposa" was applied to two land grants and, eventually, to the town, the county, and the grove of sequoias. The grove was discovered in May 1857 by Galen Clark and Milton Mann. "As they were in Mariposa County, I named them the Mariposa Grove of Big Trees." (Clark, *Yosemite Souvenir and Guide*, 1901: 97.) But a brief newspaper item said that the grove was first seen by Clark and a man named Clayton in 1856. (*San Francisco Daily California Chronicle*, June 15, 1857.)

Yosemite Valley and the Mariposa Grove constituted the original Yosemite Grant, created in 1864 and administered by the state until the creation of Yosemite National Park in 1890.

Mary Lake *Tower Peak*

The lake was named about 1909 for Mary Forsyth, a daughter of Col. W. W. Forsyth, the acting superintendent of the park from 1909 to 1912. (Letter, Edith Nance Sisson to National Park Service, March 1979, in YRL files. See **Dorothy Lake** and the second **Helen, Lake**.) The namer was almost certainly Robert B. Marshall of the USGS. The name appeared on the third edition of the *Dardanelles* 30' map, 1912. The lake is at the headwaters of Tilden Creek, less than a mile from the park's northern boundary.

Mather (community) *Lake Eleanor*

An early sheepman pastured his flocks in the area. He painted a picture of an animal on a rock, intending to depict a sheep. His artistic talent was unequal to the task, and he admitted that the result looked more like a hog—and the area became known as "Hog Ranch." In October

1919 it was renamed "Mather," for Stephen Tyng Mather (1867–1930), first director of the National Park Service.

Courtesy Yosemite Research Library, NPS

Washington B. "Dusty" Lewis, superintendent of Yosemite from 1916 to 1928, and Stephen T. Mather, first director of the National Park Service.

Mather was a reporter on the *New York Sun* from 1887 to 1892. In 1893 he went to work for the Pacific Coast Borax Company; he was largely responsible for marketing packaged borax under the "Twenty-Mule Team Borax" trade name. In 1903 he formed an independent borax company, a business that in later years made him wealthy. He used his wealth to acquire privately owned lands within Sequoia National Park, and—with the help of friends—he purchased the Tioga Road in 1915 and donated it to the government. (*SCB* 16, no. 1, Feb. 1931: 55–59; see also *SCB* 15, no. 1, Feb. 1930: 98, 106–7.) "To him goes the everlasting thanks of the American people, for he fathered the National Park idea through its most trying period." (Horace M. Albright and Frank J. Taylor, *Oh, Ranger!*, 1946: 186.)

The locale was called "Hog Ranch" on Hoffmann and Gardiner's map, 1863–67, and retained that name on all maps through the final edition of the *Yosemite* 30' map, 1951. Mather is just outside the park's eastern boundary, but it was in the park from 1890 to 1905. Mather Pass in Kings Canyon National Park is named for the same man.

Matterhorn Peak (12,264)   *Matterhorn Peak*
Matterhorn Canyon   *Matterhorn Peak, Tuolumne Meadows*
The Wheeler Survey named both features in 1878; they are shown on atlas sheet 56D, 1878–79. In 1877 John Muir gave the name "Matterhorn" to what is now Banner Peak, or to some other summit near it. (Muir, "Snow Banners of the California Alps," *Harper's*, July 1877.)

"That the name is a poor one there can be no doubt, for . . . there is only the barest suggestion of resemblance to the wonderful Swiss mountain after which it is called." (Lincoln Hutchinson in *SCB* 3, no. 2, May 1900: 162–63.) Lt. McClure, in 1894, gave the name to what are now the "Finger Peaks" because of their striking resemblance to alpine peaks; his map of 1896 thus has "Matterhorn" misplaced, even though LeConte's map of 1893 had it in the right place. (Farquhar files, letter from McClure, Oct. 22, 1920.) Also in 1894 McClure gave "China Cañon" as an alternate name for Matterhorn Canyon, with no explanation. (*SCB* 1, no. 8, May 1896: 331.)

The first ascent of Matterhorn Peak was made on July 27, 1899 by Lincoln Hutchinson, C. A. Noble, M. R. Dempster, and J. S. Hutchinson, Jr. "The summit . . . is a great jagged tooth in what is known as the Sawtooth Ridge. . . . The intense exhilaration of the climb, the noble grandeur of the scene, and the wild exultation of standing on a spot which, so far as we were able to judge, had never before felt the pressure of human foot, combined to make up an experience never to be forgotten." (*SCB* 3, no. 2, May 1900: 162.)

Matthes: Crest (over 10,880), **Lake**   *Tuolumne Meadows*
François Emile Matthes (1874–1948), a USGS geologist for 51 years, made extensive studies in Yosemite and elsewhere in the Sierra Nevada. (See his USGS *Professional Paper 160, Professional Paper 329*, and *The Incomparable Valley*, ed. Fritiof Fryxell, published in 1950, two years after his death.) Among nearly one hundred published works, Matthes had fourteen articles in various issues of the *Sierra Club Bulletin*. Also see *SCB* 33, no. 7, July 1948: 8.

The names were first suggested for, and to, Matthes in 1946; the proposal was made more formally by Reid Moran, a YNP ranger, in 1949. "Dr. Matthes was a very modest and unassuming man and would have been the last to suggest that anything be named in his honor. However, he was greatly pleased at the suggestion that this ridge bear his name, saying he knew no other unnamed feature in the Sierra which he would rather have chosen." (*SCB* 34, no. 6, June 1949: 110–11.) Matthes Crest was known informally during the 1930s as "Echo Ridge" because of its proximity to Echo Peaks and Echo Lake.

Matthes Glaciers in Sierra National Forest, on the north side of Glacier Divide, were named for Matthes in 1972. (BGN decision.)

Mattie Lake   *Tuolumne Meadows*
Origin unknown, although this may be another one of the many features that were named by either Col. Forsyth or R. B. Marshall; the name appeared on the map at the same time—the third edition of the *Mt. Lyell* 30′ map, 1910. The lake is about a mile north of California Falls on the Tuolumne River.

Maul Lake   *Tuolumne Meadows*
Named in 1932 by Al Gardisky for a man who was a Forest Service supervisor around 1930–32. (Spuller.) Possibly this refers to William E. Maule, and is misspelled by Gardisky and Spuller, not the USGS. The lake is in Inyo National Forest at the headwaters of Lee Vining Creek; it was in the park from 1890 to 1905.

May Lake   *Tuolumne Meadows*
Charles F. Hoffmann of the Whitney Survey named the lake for Lucy Mayotta Browne, whom he married in 1870. She was the daughter of J. Ross Browne, a well-known pioneer, mining engineer, and writer. (Farquhar: Ross E. Browne.) May Lake is a mile due east of Mount Hoffmann, and is the location of one of the High Sierra Camps.

McCabe Lakes; Upper McCabe Lake   *Tuolumne Meadows*
McCabe Creek   *Matterhorn Peak*
Edward Raynsford Warner McCabe, a cavalry officer who had no association with the park—except that he married Polly Forsyth, daughter of Col. W. W. Forsyth, acting superintendent of the park from 1909 to 1912. The lakes were named during that period, probably by R. B. Marshall, a close friend of Forsyth. (Farquhar files; Heitman, 653.) "McCabe Lakes" appears on the fourth *Mt. Lyell* 30′ map, 1914. On the 1929 YNP map the creek was called "East Fork" (of Return Creek). In 1932 the

BGN approved "McCabe Creek" in order to eliminate the "East Fork" name. The new name first appeared on the *Matterhorn Peak* quad, 1956. "Upper McCabe Lake" was approved by the BGN in 1962 to ratify what had become local usage.

McClure Lake   *Merced Peak*

Nathaniel Fish McClure (1865–1942), Fifth Cavalry, US Army, stationed in the park in 1894 and 1895. (Heitman, 658.) He explored large parts of the park that were previously untraveled and unknown except by sheepmen, improved and constructed many trails, and compiled maps in 1895 and 1896. He wrote a superb, detailed account, including four sketch maps, of his 1894 travels in the northern part of the park. ("Explorations Among the Cañons North of the Tuolumne River," *SCB* 1, no. 6, May 1895: 168–86.)

McClure probably named the lake for himself; it first appears on his 1896 map. In the light of all that McClure did in and for the park, it is ironic that McClure Lake is in Sierra National Forest—although it was within the park from 1890 to 1905.

McGee Lake   *Tuolumne Meadows*

Origin unknown. The name appears on Lt. McClure's maps of 1895 and 1896, and therefore may be the name of an early sheepman. The lake is on the Tenaya Lake trail, 0.6 mile southwest of Glen Aulin.

McGurk Meadow   *Yosemite*

John J. McGurk was the third owner of this property. The original owner filed for 160 acres, but the description in the county records indicated a claim in the next township, six miles away. McGurk built a cabin here, but he was forced off the land by the US Army in 1897 when the invalid patent was discovered. (Robert F. Uhte, "Yosemite's Pioneer Cabins," *SCB* 36, no. 5, May 1951: 55–56.)

McSwain Meadows   *Hetch Hetchy Reservoir*

Origin unknown, although presumed to be named for the family that owned the land early in this century. (Snyder.) The land encompassing the meadows was patented by Timothy Carlon on October 11, 1888. Carlon ran horses on the meadow, and was a major supplier of horses to the US Cavalry during the 1890s. (Snyder.) The name did not appear on a map until publication of the *Hetch Hetchy Reservoir* quad, 1956.

Meadow Brook   *Yosemite Valley, Yosemite*

An old name, origin unknown. The stream drains a small area on the south side of Yosemite Valley; it flows over Silver Strand Falls and down Washburn Slide, about a mile west of Bridalveil Fall.

"There is another [fall], nearly opposite [Ribbon Fall], on a stream called Meadow Brook, which is well seen by those coming into the Valley on the Mariposa trail early in the season." (Whitney, *Yosemite Guide-Book*, 1870: 78.) Despite that early reference, the name did not appear on a map until the first *Yosemite Valley* map, 1907.

Medial Moraine   *Yosemite Valley*

The namer is unknown. The name appeared on the first *Yosemite Valley* map, 1907, and may actually be a misnomer. Rather than a medial moraine, it probably is a frontal moraine for either the Tenaya Glacier or the Merced Glacier. For a detailed, lucid explanation, see Matthes, *Paper 160*, 57–58.

Medlicott Dome   *Tuolumne Meadows*

Named for Harry P. Medlicott, who, with H. B. Carpenter, surveyed the route of the "Great Sierra Wagon Road"—the Tioga Road—in 1882. (Trexler; also *YNN* 27, no. 9: 109–12.)

Medlicott was a judge, US Deputy Mineral Surveyor, and prominent citizen of the new town of Lundy in the early 1880s. An early name for the dome was "Court House Rock." (*Mariposa Free Press*, Oct. 28, 1870.) Twelve years later it was called "Mount Medlicott. (*Homer Mining Index*, July 22, 1882; but on July 29, 1883 the same paper used its present name.) The name did not appear on a map until publication of the *Tuolumne Meadows* quad, 1956.

Merced River   *Merced Peak, Yosemite, Yosemite Valley, El Portal*

The expedition under Gabriel Moraga, including the diarist Fray Pedro Muñoz, crossed the river in the San Joaquin Valley and named it *El Rio de Nuestra Señora de la Merced* on September 29, 1806, five days after the feast day of Our Lady of Mercy. (Arch. MSB, vol. 4, Muñoz.) In 1844 Frémont referred to the river both as "Rio de la Merced" (*Expedition*, 360) and by an Indian name, "Aux-um-ne" (*Memoir*, 17). Preuss's 1848 map shows it as a plural: "R.d.l. Auxumnes," obviously referring to Indians living along the river.

The shortened version, "Merced River," was in use by the early 1850s. Hoffmann and Gardiner's map of 1863–67 has "So. Fork Merced River" as well. All the other "Merced" names derive from the river's name. These constitute classic examples of how a name is spread in a haphazard fashion by people who undoubtedly think they are doing something logical, but who almost certainly did not know the reason for the original name and may not even have known its English translation.

Merced Gorge   *Yosemite Valley, Yosemite*

An obvious name for the canyon of the Merced River from The Cascades to about two miles above El Portal. It was called "Merced Canyon" on *Yosemite Valley* maps from 1907 to 1922, and was changed to the present name on the edition of 1927.

Merced Grove   *El Portal*

This small grove of Big Trees probably was seen by the Joseph R. Walker party in 1833. (See **Tuolumne Grove.**) It was rediscovered in 1858. "The Mariposa *Gazette* is informed by Mr. Roney, of Coulterville, that a grove of big trees was discovered this past week . . . within one mile of the Coulterville and Yo-Semite trail. About forty trees were counted, largest of which was said to be thirty-six feet in diameter." (*Daily San Joaquin Republican*, May 21, 1858.)

Its first name was the "Crane Flat Grove," given by the Whitney Survey. (Whitney, *Yosemite Guide-Book*, 1870: 148.) It received its present name from Dr. John T. McLean, president of the Coulterville and Yosemite Turnpike Company, in 1871 or 1872. "While making the survey for this road a grove of big trees was discovered . . . which was named the Merced Grove by me because of its nearness to the Merced River." (Letter, McLean to Yosemite National Park Commission, 1899, in Russell, *100 Years*, 77.)

Merced Lake (7,216)   *Merced Peak*

"I first discovered this charming lake in the autumn of 1872, while on my way to the glaciers at the head of the river." (John Muir, "The Mountain Lakes of California," *Scribner's Monthly*, Jan. 1879: 416.) But Muir called it "Shadow Lake," a name he first used in a letter to Mrs. Carr, Oct. 7, 1874. (Badè, vol. II, 28.) The USGS showed it as "Merced Lake" on the first edition of the *Mt. Lyell* 30' map, 1901. The various maps of the 1890s did not even show a lake in that location.

Merced Pass; **Upper** and **Lower Merced Pass Lake**   *Merced Peak*

The pass was discovered by Corporal Ottoway while scouting for Lt. Benson in 1895, and was named by Benson. (Farquhar: Benson.) The name was on the first *Mt. Lyell* 30' map, 1901. The lakes were first named on the *Merced Peak* quad, 1953.

Merced Peak (11,726); **Merced Peak Fork**   *Merced Peak*
   The Clark Range was known as both the "Obelisk Group" and the "Merced Group" at the time of the Whitney Survey. (Whitney, *The Yosemite Book*, 97.) The present name for the peak first appeared on the Wheeler Survey atlas sheet 56D, 1878–79. The fork was named on the *Merced Peak* quad, 1953.

Mercur Peak (over 8,000)   *Pinecrest*
   James Mercur (1842–1896), professor of engineering at West Point from 1884 until his death. (Heitman, 703.) The peak, on the park's northwest boundary, was named in 1912 by Col. Forsyth. (Farquhar: Benson.) The name appeared on the third edition of the *Dardanelles* 30' map, 1912.

Michie Peak (10,365)   *Tower Peak*
   Named by Col. Forsyth for Peter Smith Michie (1839–1901), professor of engineering at West Point from 1871 until his death. (Farquhar: Forsyth; Heitman, 708.)

Middle Tuolumne River   *Hetch Hetchy Reservoir*
   This name was suggested in 1931 by Frank Bond, then the chairman of the US Board on Geographic Names, to replace "Middle Fork of Tuolumne River," which Bond thought was "misleading and improper." (BGN decision, 1932.) And when you think about it, Bond was right. This stream most certainly is *not* the middle fork of the Tuolumne. It doesn't flow into the Tuolumne, but rather into the South Fork of the Tuolumne.

Miguel: Meadow, Creek   *Lake Eleanor*
   "The ranch belongs to Mr. Miguel D. Errera, but his American friends have corrupted *Miguel* into *McGill* and by that name is his house known." (Lt. N. F. McClure in *SCB* 1, no. 5, Jan. 1895: 185.) But McClure on his 1896 map, and LeConte on his 1900 map, used "McGill" for both the meadow and the creek. The USGS continued the corruption, spelling the name "McGill" on the first five editions of the *Yosemite* 30' map, 1897–1911. A BGN decision in 1926 corrected it to "Miguel;" it appeared that way on the sixth edition, 1929.

Mildred Lake   *Tuolumne Meadows*
   Named for Mildred Sovulewski. The lake was first named on the *Tuolumne Meadows* quad, 1956.
   Her father, Gabriel Sovulewski, served as a ranger and supervisor in the park from 1906 to 1936. He came to Yosemite with the US Army in

1895 and served until 1899. When he returned seven years later as a civilian employee he at first worked on the trails, and eventually became a supervisor in charge of trail construction and road maintenance. For a brief life sketch and good sendoff, see *SCB* 24, no. 3, June 1939: 122.

Mill Creek   *Tuolumne Meadows, Matterhorn Peak*

William O. Lundy operated a sawmill on the creek in Lundy Canyon sometime before 1879. The name is on the Wheeler Survey atlas sheet 56D, 1878–79. The headwaters of the creek, now in Inyo National Forest, were within the park from 1890 to 1905.

Miller Lake   *Tuolumne Meadows*

"I returned to the lake, and imagine my surprise to find the detachment in camp, horses unsaddled, mules unpacked, and the cook-fire blazing merrily away. The man to whom I had spoken about camping had taken my remark about its being a good camping-place in real earnest, and had told the others that my orders were to stay there until next day. His name was Miller, and, naming the lake in honor of him, I decided to remain there until the next morning. (Lt. N. F. McClure in *SCB* 1, no. 5, Jan. 1895: 174.)

The name is correct, McClure's story undoubtedly is correct, but—the name is in the wrong place. It's even on the wrong topographic map. By my reading of McClure's account, the real "Miller Lake" is 3.5 miles north by east from the present Miller Lake, on the *Matterhorn Peak* quad. It's the tiny pond between Matterhorn and Spiller canyons, about 1.5 miles west-southwest from Spiller Lake. How the name migrated from this pond to its present location is unknown. LeConte's map of 1900 seemed to be showing the pond as "Lake Bell," and even showed the route taken by McClure in 1894—naming it "McClure's Pass." (The impetus for my recognition and understanding of this peculiar mixup comes entirely from Jim Snyder, trail foreman of Yosemite National Park.)

Minarets; Minaret: Lake, Mine   *Devils Postpile, Mt. Ritter*
Minaret Creek   *Devils Postpile, Mt. Ritter, Mammoth Mtn.*
Minaret: Falls, Summit   *Devils Postpile, Mammoth Mtn.*

"These granite spires in sharpness far surpass anything I have seen in the Sierra. King names them the Minarets." (Journal of James T. Gardiner, July 12, 1866. Copy in Farquhar Papers, BL. Gardiner and Clarence King of the Whitney Survey were on the summit of Mount Clark, having made the first ascent.)

Seventeen of the Minarets have been given unofficial names, for those who first climbed them. The first one climbed was "Michael Minaret," on September 6, 1923. "With nothingness on one side and a sheer wall on the other, I had a feeling as I crossed the ledge that the wall might give me a little shove on the shoulder and tip me into nothingness." (Charles W. Michael, *SCB* 12, no. 1, 1924: 31.)

Only "Minaret Creek" was on atlas sheet 56D, 1878–79. "Minarets" was on the Hoffmann and Gardiner map, 1863–67, and all other maps after sheet 56D. The other features first were named on the *Devils Postpile* quad, 1953.

The original claims to the Minaret Mine were staked shortly after 1906. The present claimant does the required annual assessment work, but no production has ever been recorded. (USGS, *Bulletin 1516 - A - D*, 138–40.) The Minarets are on the boundary between Sierra and Inyo national forests; the other features are in the latter. All of them were within the park from 1890 to 1905.

Mine Creek   *Tuolumne Meadows*

A tributary of Lee Vining Creek, heading in Spuller Lake. The namer is unknown, but the name plainly comes from the fact that the creek flows past the site of Bennettville and the mouth of the Great Sierra Mine tunnel. In the 1880s it was called "Slate Creek." (*Homer Mining Index*, Feb. 18, 1882.) The name first appeared on the *Tuolumne Meadows* quad, 1956. The creek is in Inyo National Forest, but the upper part of it was in the park from 1890 to 1905.

Minnow Lake   *Yosemite*

The reason for the name is obvious; the namer is unknown. The name appeared on the *Yosemite* quad, 1956.

Mirror Lake (4,094)   *Yosemite Valley, Yosemite*

"On our way down [Tenaya Creek], as we passed that looking-glass pond. . . ." (Bunnell, *Discovery*, 1911: 161. Bunnell's paraphrase of a narrative of Third Sergeant Alexander M. Cameron, Company B, Mariposa Battalion, May 1851.)

"This lake was so named by Mr. C. H. Spencer, of Utica, New York (one of my comrades). . . . The Indian name for the lake was Wai-ack, meaning the rock water, because of its nearness to Half Dome, and the perfect reflection of the rocks of peaks adjacent." (Bunnell, *Report*, 11.)

". . . We arrived at Lake *Ah-wi-yah*, so named and known by the Indians, but which has been newly christened by American visitors 'Lake Hiawatha,' 'Mirror Lake,' and several others, which, though pretty enough, are equally commonplace and unsuitable." (Hutchings *Illustrated* 4, no. 5, Nov. 1859: 196.) Later on, Hutchings seems to have forgotten what he wrote in 1859. ". . . Our explorations [in 1855] were limited to the valley, terminating at Mirror Lake—so named by our party." (Hutchings, *In the Heart*, 91.)

Whitney spelled the Indian name *Waiya*. (*Yosemite Guide-Book*, 1870: 17.) Powers has it as *A-wai'-a*. He said—in conjunction with Vernal and Nevada falls—that the word means, simply, a lake or body of water. (Powers, 365.) It is preserved in the name **Ahwiyah Point**.

". . . Lake Ah-wi-yah, known now, thanks to some American importer of looking-glasses, as Mirror Lake." (Jackson, 107.)

"Called by [the Indians] 'Ke-ko-too-yem,' or sleeping water, and 'Ah-wi-yah.' (Hutchings, *In the Heart*, 59.)

It was long assumed that Mirror Lake is of glacial origin, but later studies showed that it has no connection with the ice age. "It is impounded wholly by masses of rock débris that fell in avalanches from both walls of the canyon, principally from a place on the west wall, just back of the Washington Column." (Matthes, *Paper 160*, 105. See also p. 108.)

Mist Trail   *Yosemite Valley*

"Leaping from stone to stone, poising on slippery logs under water, clinging to Murphy's hand as to a life-preserver, blinded, choked, stifled, drenched, down into that canyon, through that steaming spray, we went. It was impossible to keep one's eyes open wide for more than half a second at a time. The spray drove and pelted, making great gusts of wind by its own weight as it fell. It seemed to whirl round and round, and wrap us, as if trying to draw us down into the black depths." (Jackson, 123.)

To assist hikers to reach Vernal Fall, ladders were placed at the upper part of the trail in 1857. These were eventually replaced by wooden stairs. The present steps were cut in the rock in 1897. (LeConte, *A Summer*, footnote p. 52.)

Although the name is an old one, it did not appear on the map until 1958.

Miwok Lake   *Tower Peak*

The origin of the name is unknown, although probably it is because there are Miwok sites at the lake. The name is a recent one; it appeared on the *Tower Peak* quad, 1956.

Moat Lake   *Matterhorn Peak*

Origin unknown. The name appeared on the first *Bridgeport* 30' map, 1911. Although in Inyo National Forest, the lake was within the park from 1890 to 1905.

Mono: Pass (10,604), **Lake, Craters, Dome** (10,614)   *Mono Craters*

". . . Lieut. Moore . . . found a pass at the head waters of the Merced, which they called the Mona Pass, from the Mona Indians who inhabit the country on the eastern slope of the Sierra Nevada. . . . About 120 miles east of Mariposa they found a lake, (not laid down in the maps), some 60 miles in length and 20 or 30 in breadth. This they called Mona Lake." (*San Joaquin Republican*, Aug. 25, 1852.) Lt. Tredwell Moore was in command of US troops in pursuit of Indians who had killed two white prospectors in Yosemite Valley in May of that year. He followed the old Mono Trail via Tenaya Lake, Mono Pass, and Bloody Canyon, a route that had long been used by Indians. (See **Mono Trail** in the Old Names section.)

"Mono County and Lake are named after a wide-spread division of Shoshonean Indians on both slopes of the Southern Sierra Nevada. . . . By their Yokuts neighbors they are called Monachi. . . . The Yokuts word for 'flies' was *monoi, monai,* or *monoyi.*" (Kroeber, 48–49.) "If we assume that this word forms the stem of *monachi*, it is quite certain that the name means 'fly-people' and is quite properly applied. On the shore of the otherwise barren lake are found countless millions of the pupae of a fly. . . These pupae were not only the favorite food of these Indians, but they used them for trading with the neighboring tribes. . . . The conclusion is forced upon us that the Yokuts called these Indians *Monachi* because their wealth consisted of flies." (*California Folklore Quarterly* 4, no. 1, Jan. 1945: 90 ff.)

"The worms are dried in the sun, the shell rubbed off, when a yellow-ish kernel remains, like a small yellow grain of rice. This is oily, very nutritious, and not unpleasant to the taste, and under the name of *koo-chah-bee* forms a very important article of food. The Indians gave me some; it does not taste bad, and if one were ignorant of its origin, it would make fine soup. Gulls, ducks, snipe, frogs, and Indians fatten on it." (Brewer, *Up and Down*, 417.)

The craters were named in the 1880s. "By far the grandest display of quaternary and post-quaternary volcanic action within the Mono Basin is furnished by the Mono Craters. I have given this name to the slightly crescent-shaped range of volcanic cones which commences at the southern margin of Lake Mono and extends about ten miles southward." (Russell, *Quaternary*, 378.) "Mono Dome" probably was named by the

USGS during the 1898–99 survey for the *Mt. Lyell* 30' map; it is on the first edition, 1901.

The pass is on the park's eastern boundary. The other "Mono" features are outside the park.

Mono Meadow   *Yosemite*

The Hoffmann and Gardiner map of 1863–67 shows "Old Mono Trail" passing through the meadow, which was first named on LeConte's 1893 map.

Monroe Meadows   *Yosemite*
Fort Monroe   *Yosemite Valley*

George F. Monroe was a black man who drove stage and worked as a guide for the Washburn brothers from 1868 to 1886. The "fort" was a stage station on the old Wawona Road; it had no military connection. "It is reported that George Monroe had a flair for army life and was always talking about it, hence the name *Fort*." (*YNN* 34, no. 1, Jan. 1955: 6.)

The site had the name of "Fort Monroe" on Solomons' 1896 map and on all the *Yosemite* 30' maps, 1897–1951. It is not named on the *Yosemite* 15-minute quad. It was named on the *Yosemite Valley* maps, 1907–70, but is not on the latest edition, 1977. It is located above the west end of the Wawona Tunnel where the Pohono Trail changes direction from southwest to east, just a short distance outside the boundary of the original Yosemite Grant. Monroe Meadows was first named on the *Yosemite* quad, 1956.

"Our driver was a colored man, raised in the country, had never been outside of the State and had been with the Yosemite Stage Co. some twelve years. His gentleness and kindness were only exceeded by his skill, of which we soon became both proud and grateful." (Bailey, 43–44.) Monroe's employers said of him that "he never met with any accident, never failed to be on time and never cost the company a quarter of a dollar for damages to passengers, horses, or vehicles. Whenever George was on the box and held the lines, we knew everything was all right. He always did his duty." ("Death of George F. Monroe," *Mariposa Gazette*, Nov. 27, 1886.)

Monument Lake   *Merced Peak*

Origin unknown; the name appeared on the *Merced Peak* quad, 1953. The lake is in Sierra National Forest, about 1.4 miles east-southeast of Fernandez Pass. It was in the park from 1890 to 1905.

Courtesy Yosemite Research Library, NPS

George F. Monroe, stage driver *par excellence.*

Moraine Dome (8,055)   *Yosemite Valley, Merced Peak*

The "high dome, alt. 8050, north of Little Yosemite Valley; named it 'Moraine Pt.' this day." (Matthes, v. 9, Sept. 5, 1905.)

". . . A massive tree-grown embankment wound in a long, smooth curve up the bulging south side of the dome. . . . It was manifestly a 'moraine' of the ancient Merced Glacier, a ridge of ice-transported debris, deposited along the margin of the 'mer-de-glace' that once filled the Little Yosemite." (Matthes, "Little Studies in the Yosemite Region: The Story of Moraine Dome," manuscript in Matthes Papers, Carton 1, BL. See also Matthes, *Paper 160.*)

Matthes was in Yosemite in the summers of 1905 and 1906 surveying for the first USGS map of Yosemite Valley, which was published in 1907.

Moraine Flat   *Tuolumne Meadows*

This broad, gently-sloping area is north of the Tioga Road, about mid-way between Tuolumne Meadows and Gaylor Lakes. It undoubtedly was given this name for its glacial rock deposits, probably by the USGS during the 1898–99 survey for the *Mt. Lyell* 30' map; it is on the first edition, 1901.

Moraine: Mountain (9,754), Meadow   *Merced Peak*

The mountain possibly was named by Lt. McClure; it appears on his 1896 map as "Mt. Moraine." The meadow was first named on the third edition of the *Mt. Lyell* 30' map, 1910.

Moraine Ridge   *Tower Peak, Pinecrest*

The namer is unknown. It was not yet named when Lt. McClure described it in 1894. (*SCB* 1, no. 5, Jan. 1895: 182–83.) A trail along the top of this southwest-northeast ridge provides access to the park's north country from Lake Eleanor and Hetch Hetchy, but the ridge is a considerable barrier to those trying to travel at right angles to it. It was first named on the third *Dardanelles* 30' map, 1912.

Moran Point   *Yosemite Valley, Yosemite*

Thomas Moran (1837–1926), born in England, came to the US in 1844 with his parents. His first foray into the West was with the Hayden expedition to Yellowstone in 1871. He became famous for his large paintings of Yellowstone and the Grand Canyon. The point is on the old Four-Mile Trail, just east of Union Point. The name first appeared on the *Yosemite Valley* map, 1929, but it was in use at least as early as the 1880s (Hutchings, *In the Heart*, 468), and probably before that.

Morrison Creek   *Hetch Hetchy Reservoir*

This creek is presumed to be named for J. M. Morrison, who was on the State Board of Fish Commissioners from about 1892 to 1906. It flows into the Grand Canyon of the Tuolumne two miles east of the east end of Hetch Hetchy Reservoir. The name appeared on the first *Yosemite* 30' map, 1897.

Moss Creek   *Lake Eleanor*
Moss: Creek, Canyon   *El Portal*

The creek flows south from the divide west of Crane Flat to the Merced River two miles below El Portal. The namer is unknown; the name first appeared on the Wheeler Survey atlas sheet 56D, 1878–79. Although it probably is a descriptive name, it should be noted that partners named

Leonard and Moss ran a saddle train between Yosemite Valley and Lundy in the early 1880s. (*Mariposa Gazette*, Aug. 26, 1882.)

Moss Spring   *Yosemite Valley, Yosemite*

". . . The many-voiced, plant-garnished Moss Springs, and Fern Springs, gushing out at our side, temptingly invite us to drink of their transparent and ice-tempered waters." (Hutchings, *In the Heart*, 402.) The name is on the Wheeler Survey map of 1883.

Muir Gorge   *Hetch Hetchy Reservoir*

The gorge, in the canyon of the Tuolumne River, was named in 1894. "We named this gorge Muir Gorge, after Mr. John Muir, the first man to go through the cañon." (R. M. Price in *SCB* 1, no. 6, May 1895: 206.)

John Muir (1838–1914), "born in Scotland, reared in the University of Wisconsin, by final choice a Californian, widely traveled observer of the world we dwell in, man of science and of letters, friend and protector of Nature, uniquely gifted to interpret unto other men her mind and ways." (Benjamin Ide Wheeler, President of the University of California, conferring the degree of Doctor of Laws on Muir, May 14, 1913.)

Muir was one of the four founders of the Sierra Club, and its first president, 1892–1914. He was the foremost conservationist of his time, a mountain explorer and exponent of the outdoor life. "John Muir was not a 'dreamer,' but a practical man, a faithful citizen, a scientific observer, a writer of enduring power, with vision, poetry, courage in a contest, a heart of gold, and a spirit pure and fine." (Robert Underwood Johnson in *SCB* 10, no. 1, Jan. 1916: 15. Also see that issue of *SCB*, 1–77.)

Murdock Lake   *Tower Peak*

Named by Lt. McClure in 1895 for William C. Murdock of the California State Board of Fish Commissioners. (Farquhar: McClure.) The name was on McClure's map of 1896 (misspelled "Murdoch") and on Benson's 1896 map and LeConte's 1900 map—but it was not on subsequent maps. The Sierra Club submitted the name to the BGN in 1926, and it reappeared on the fifth edition of the *Dardanelles* 30' map, 1939.

Murphy Creek   *Tuolumne Meadows*

"J. L. Murphy, an intelligent gentleman and a pioneer thoroughly familiar with every foot of country in this part of the range, settled upon the beautiful meadow along the western shore of Lake Tenaya on the 1st day of August 1878." ("Across the Sierra," *Homer Mining Index*, July 22, 1882.)

Murphy built a cabin on the north shore of the lake—before the construction of the original Tioga Road—and catered to travelers and campers in summer. (Robert F. Uhte, "Yosemite's Pioneer Cabins," *SCB* 36, no. 5, May 1951: 56–57.) On the 1883 GLO plat there is a "house" marked midway along the north shore of the lake, and at the west end is written "Murphy's Enclosure." Murphy patented 160 acres in secs. 20 and 21, T. 1 S., R. 23 E. in 1890.

"But one may wish that Mr. Watkins had been denied his mountain, and Mr. Murphy his dome if it were only for the sake of poets yet to be. What will they do with such monsters." (Chase, 31.) Murphy did not have a nearby dome named for him—that is now **Pywiack Dome**—but wound up with a creek. LeConte's 1893 map has "Murphy's Cabin." Lt. McClure's 1896 map is the first one to have the creek named on it.

Naked Lady Meadow   *Devils Postpile, Cattle Mtn.*
Origin unknown; the name first appeared on the *Cattle Mtn.* quad, 1983. To locate it on the *Devils Postpile* quad: it is on the trail, about 2.6 miles west-southwest of Iron Mountain. It's in Sierra National Forest, but was within the park from 1890 to 1905. A bit of advice to men: don't go there and lounge around, expecting that something will happen.

Nance Peak (over 8,400)   *Pinecrest*
Named in 1910 by Major William W. Forsyth for Col. John Torrence Nance, professor of military science at the University of California, 1904–27. (Farquhar; Heitman, 740.) The peak overlooks **Edyth Lake**, named by Forsyth for Nance's daughter. "Nance Peak" appeared on the third edition of the *Dardanelles* 30' map, 1912.

Neall Lake   *Hetch Hetchy Reservoir*
Named by H. C. Benson for John Mitchell Neall, a first lieutenant on duty with the Fourth Cavalry in the park from 1892 to 1897. (Farquhar: Benson; Heitman, 741.) The lake was named "Rodgers Lake" (for Capt. Alexander Rodgers) on the first two editions of the *Yosemite* 30' map, 1897–1900. It was changed to its present name on the 1903 edition because there was already a lake in another part of the park named for Rodgers.

Ned Gulch   *Lake Eleanor, El Portal*
There is no hard and fast information on the origin of the name of this stream that flows south into the Merced River about seven miles west of El Portal. As a possibility, Edward R. Rowland patented 160 acres in the northwest corner of sec. 26, T. 2 S., R. 19 E. in 1889. Ned Gulch runs along

the west side of that property. The gulch is in Stanislaus National Forest, but it was within the park from 1890 to 1905.

Nelson Lake (9,636)   *Tuolumne Meadows*

William Henry (Billy) Nelson (1873–1952), a colorful early-day ranger. He served from 1917 to 1936, and 1943 to 1945. He escorted many celebrated visitors, including King Albert of Belgium. In July 1934 he accompanied Eleanor Roosevelt on a pack trip to the Young Lakes, and provided her with a hot-water bottle to keep her warm during the cold nights at 10,000 feet. (Bingaman, *Guardians*, 96. See **Roosevelt Lake**.)

Nevada Fall   *Yosemite Valley, Yosemite*

Lafayette H. Bunnell suggested the name when the fall was discovered by members of the Mariposa Battalion in 1851. "The Nevada Fall was so called because it was the nearest to the Sierra Nevada, and because the name was sufficiently indicative of a wintry companion for our spring [Vernal Fall]. The white, foaming water, as it dashed down Yo-wy-we from the snowy mountains, represented to my mind a vast avalanche of snow." (Bunnell, *Discovery*, 1880: 205.)

"Yo-wai-yi, Nevada Fall. In this word also we detect the root of *awaia*"—meaning a lake, or body of water. (Powers, 364.)

"A literal interpretation of the Indian name, Yo-wi-we, could not be tolerated, Yo-wi-we meaning the 'Squirming or Worm Fall,' from a twist given the water by a curving rock upon which the water strikes during its descent." (Bunnell, *Report*, 11.) When Bunnell says "could not be tolerated" he seems to imply that the Indian name had a sexual connotation—medicine that was too strong for the delicate sensibilities of his nineteenth-century audience. He could tolerate it so little that he never told us what it was. But surely your imagination is as good as that of an Indian. Give it a whirl—or a twist.

In its natural state at the time of its discovery by the Mariposa Battalion, a small part of the Merced River flowed down the gulch just north of Nevada Fall—the place where the "Zig Zag Trail" comes up to Little Yosemite Valley. Albert Snow, the proprietor of "La Casa Nevada," a hotel he operated from 1870 to the 1890s on the flat between Vernal and Nevada falls, apparently considered this to be an aberration of nature. He dammed the smaller stream, forcing the water into the main river, an action he termed "fixing the falls."

Noname Lake   *Devils Postpile, Mt. Ritter*

Origin unknown—but obviously someone gave it that name because it didn't have a name. It is a very small lake next to the trail on the way to Holcomb Lake, and was first named on the *Devils Postpile* quad, 1953. It's in Inyo National Forest, but was in the park from 1890 to 1905.

North Dome (7,542)   *Yosemite Valley, Hetch Hetchy Reservoir*
    Named by the Mariposa Battalion in 1851; it was across the valley from "South Dome," an early name for Half Dome. "The dome was known as To-co-yah, meaning a round basket used in gathering acorns." (Bunnell, *Report*, 11.)
    "To-ko-ye, North Dome. This rock represents Tisseyak's (Half Dome) husband. On one side of him is a huge conical rock, which the Indians call the acorn-basket that his wife threw at him in anger." (Powers, 364. See **Basket Dome** and **Half Dome**.) The name is on the King and Gardiner map of 1865.
    Some of the early tourists were unaware that North Dome had already been named. "After passing up the north fork of the river [Tenaya Creek], a very fine view of the peaks is to be seen. The most prominent object at this point is Capitol Rock. It is a large bluff surmounted by a dome. . . ." (*San Joaquin Republican*, Oct. 16, 1856.) Thus they had "Capitol Rock" looming above what would soon be named "Washington Column." Nothing wrong with that.

North Peak (12,242)   *Tuolumne Meadows*
    Probably named by the USGS during the 1898–99 survey for the *Mt. Lyell* 30' map; the name is on the first edition, 1901. The peak is on the park's eastern boundary, about a mile north by east from Mount Conness.

Nydiver Lakes   *Devils Postpile, Mt. Ritter*
    For David *Nidever*, a prospector in the early 1900s. (INF archives. See **Cabin Lake**.) The lakes are in Inyo National Forest, but were within the park from 1890 to 1905.

Obelisk Lake   *Merced Peak*
    Mount Clark was originally named the "Obelisk" by the Whitney Survey, and the Clark Range was sometimes called the "Obelisk Group." (Whitney, *Yosemite Guide-Book*, 1870: 108.) "Obelisk Lake," less than a mile northeast of Mount Clark, is the only remaining use in Yosemite of the early name. It was ratified by the BGN in 1932, and first appeared on the *Merced Peak* quad, 1953.

Odell Lake   *Tuolumne Meadows*

Al Gardisky named the lake in 1932 for a friend. (Spuller.) The lake, at the headwaters of Mill Creek, is in Inyo National Forest, but was in the park from 1890 to 1905.

Olaine Lake   *Devils Postpile, Mammoth Mtn.*

Origin unknown. It is 0.7 mile east of Shadow Lake, and was first named on the *Devils Postpile* quad, 1953. The lake is in Inyo National Forest, but was in the park from 1890 to 1905.

Old Inspiration Point   *Yosemite Valley, Yosemite*

This viewpoint was originally known as "Mount Beatitude." The *real* old point was at an altitude of 6,802 feet, a few feet off the Pohono Trail at the top of the hill coming west from Meadow Brook. It was the first view of Yosemite Valley from the Mann Brothers trail. (YRL files.)

"Almost before the gratifying fact is realized, you have reached 'Inspiration Point,' and are standing out upon a bold promontory of rock. . . . In all my life, let it lead me where it may . . . I think I shall see nothing else so sublime and beautiful, till, happily, I stand within the gates of the Heavenly City." (Hutchings, *Scenes*, 1871: 85–86; see also **Beatitude, Mount** and **Inspiration Point.**)

Olmsted Point   *Tuolumne Meadows*

A viewpoint on the Tioga Road named for Frederick Law Olmsted and for his son, Frederick Law Olmsted, Jr. The senior Olmsted was a conservationist and the "father of American landscape architecture." He designed New York City's Central Park, a work done so well that he went on to plan similar parks in other American cities. He came to California in 1863. When the Yosemite Grant was created in 1864, Olmsted directed the survey and took charge of the property for the state of California. He was also the chairman of the first Board of Yosemite Valley Commissioners, appointed to administer the grant.

The junior Olmsted followed his father as a leader in environmental design and city planning. He was connected with Yosemite as a National Park Service planner, and was appointed a member of the Yosemite Advisory Board in 1928. (Russell, *100 Years*, 14.)

The name was proposed in January 1961 by John B. Preston, the park superintendent at the time. (YRL files.) It is not on the *Tuolumne Meadows* quad, but is on present Yosemite National Park maps. The point is about 1.5 miles southwest of Tenaya Lake.

Onion Lake (over 10,400)   *Matterhorn Peak*

Origin unknown, although probably named for the wild onion. The lake is near the park's northeast boundary, about five miles north of Mount Conness. The name appeared on the first *Bridgeport* 30′ map, 1911.

O'Shaughnessy Dam   *Lake Eleanor*

Michael M. O'Shaughnessy was the city engineer of San Francisco and chief of the Hetch Hetchy construction project. The dam was built between 1919 and 1923, and the entire project of tunnels and pipelines was completed in 1934. O'Shaughnessy died sixteen days before the project was dedicated. Between 1935 and 1938 the dam was raised another eighty-five feet. (See Ted Wurm, *Hetch Hetchy and its Dam Railroad*.)

Ostrander: Rocks, Lake   *Yosemite*

The rocks were named by the Whitney Survey for Harvey J. Ostrander, who came to California during the gold rush. In the early 1860s he settled at the junction of the Glacier Point and Old Mono trails. (YRL files.) Ostrander was a sheepman; his cabin was near Bridalveil Creek. The King and Gardiner map of 1865 and the Hoffmann and Gardiner map of 1863–67 show "Ostrander's Rocks," and the latter has "Ostrander's"—the cabin.

The lake was originally called "Pohono Lake," since it was at the headwaters of Bridalveil (Pohono) Creek. (Clark, 96.) The present name appeared on McClure's maps of 1895 and 1896. Hutchings described the lake in the 1880s but did not use a name. (Hutchings, *In the Heart*, 407.) Thus it may have been McClure himself who decided on the name.

Otter Lake; Little Otter Lake   *Tower Peak*

Origin unknown, but doubtless because someone saw an otter at the lake. The "Little" lake may only be a derivative name. Both names first appeared on the *Tower Peak* quad, 1956.

Ottoway: Peak (over 11,440), **Creek; Upper** and **Lower Ottoway Lake**
                                                                Merced Peak

The peak was named in 1895 by Lt. N. F. McClure for a corporal in his detachment. (Farquhar: McClure.) The peak and the creek were named on the first *Mt. Lyell* 30′ map, 1901. The names for the lakes were ratified by the BGN in 1932, and appeared on the *Merced Peak* quad, 1953.

Panorama: Cliff, Point (6,224)   *Yosemite Valley, Yosemite*

The namer is unknown, but the features undoubtedly were named for the panoramic view. The names first appeared on the *Yosemite Valley* map of 1907, but the name for the cliff dates from the early days. The photographer Eadweard Muybridge used it to identify one of his pictures in 1867. (*CHSQ* 42, no. 1, March 1963: 9.) When the trail was constructed in 1886 it was called the "Echo Wall Trail." (*YNN* 34, no. 1, Jan. 1955: 14.) In 1905 Matthes used the name "Panorama Wall." (Matthes, v. 9, Aug. 10, 1905.)

The altitude of 5,224 feet for Panorama Point that is shown on the 1958 edition of the *Yosemite Valley* map is wrong by 1,000 feet. All other editions of the map, before and since 1958, have the correct altitude. It is quite possible that Matthes named the point, although he doesn't claim to have done so. He used the name in his diary, and also entered the correct altitude of 6,224. (Matthes, v. 9, Oct. 10, 1905.)

Parker: Pass, Creek, Lake, Peak (12,861); **Parker Pass Lake**   *Mono Craters*
Parker Pass Creek   *Mono Craters, Tuolumne Meadows*

"The creek was named for an early settler of Mono County." (Farquhar: W. L. Huber.) The name for the creek was used by Israel C. Russell in 1883. (Russell, *Quaternary*, 325 et. seq.; also map, plate XVII.) The name "Parker Canyon" is in the *Homer Mining Index*, Oct. 1, 1881, and "Parker Pass" is in the same paper, Aug. 23, 1884.

It has also been suggested that the source of all these "Parker" names was Edward A. Parker, a student of Professor Joseph LeConte. J. N. LeConte reported on the records he found on the summit of Mount Lyell in 1889. The oldest was that of Parker and another man in 1875. The next after that was Russell and Grove Karl Gilbert of the USGS in 1883, implying that those two began the use of the Parker name. (*SCB* 11, no. 3, 1922: 247.)

All the Parker names except the creek and the lake west of the pass were on the first *Mt. Lyell* 30' map, 1901. Those features were first named on the *Mono Craters* quad, 1953. They are in the park, the pass is on the park's eastern boundary, and although the others are in Inyo National Forest they were within the park from 1890 to 1905.

Parsons: Peak (over 12,080), **Memorial Lodge**   *Tuolumne Meadows*

Edward Taylor Parsons (1861–1914), a director of the Sierra Club for nine years; member of the outing committee for thirteen years; photographer of many of the club's early trips. The peak was named by R. B. Marshall of the USGS about 1909; the name is on the third edition of the

Mt. Lyell 30′ map, 1910. It was first climbed by Parsons' widow, Marion Randall Parsons, sometime before 1931. In 1915 the Sierra Club built the lodge on the club's Soda Springs property on the north side of Tuolumne Meadows. (*SCB* 10, no. 1, Jan. 1916: 84–85.) The lodge was sold to the National Park Service in 1973.

There are memorials to Parsons by John Muir and William E. Colby in *SCB* 9, no. 4, Jan. 1915: 219–24.

Pate Valley   *Hetch Hetchy Reservoir*
An old name of uncertain origin. It may possibly have been named for Francis M. Pate, a resident of Indian Gulch in 1867. (YRL files.) Pate was a member of Company C of the Mariposa Battalion, discoverers of Yosemite Valley in 1851. (Eccleston, 141.) But also: "Pate was a sheepman from Merced Falls who ran his sheep in Pate Valley." (Homer Robinson notebook, YRL files.) R. M. Price and Theodore S. Solomons spelled the name "Pait." (*SCB* 1, no. 6, May 1895: 207–8.) Lt. McClure had "Pait" on his 1895 map, and the present name on his 1896 map.

Peninsula Lake; Upper Peninsula Lake   *Tower Peak*
The namer is unknown, but the reason for the name is obvious. Peninsula Lake has a half-mile-long peninsula running down the middle of the lake. And Upper Peninsula Lake, which has no peninsula, is upstream from Peninsula Lake. What could be simpler? Both names appeared on the *Tower Peak* quad, 1956.

Peregoy Meadow   *Yosemite*
Charles E. Peregoy had a cattle camp on the trail between Wawona and Yosemite Valley. In 1869–70 he enlarged his log cabin into a hotel for sixteen, named it the "Mountain View House," and with his wife operated it until 1878. (Sargent, *Innkeepers*, 15–16; and *Pioneers*, 20–21.)

The King and Gardiner map of 1865 shows "Trail from Peregoy's." The 1884 GLO plat has "Old Peregoy House." McClure's 1895 map had "Old Hotel;" his 1896 map had "Paragor's Mdw." The first two editions of the *Yosemite* 30′ map, 1897 and 1900, converted it to "Paragon Meadow." It was corrected on the edition of 1903.

Pettit Peak (10,788)   *Tuolumne Meadows*
Named by Col. Forsyth, acting superintendent of the park, 1909–12, for Col. James Sumner Pettit, commander of the US Fourth Volunteer Infantry in the Spanish-American War. (Farquhar: Forsyth. Heitman, 787.)

The name appeared on the third edition of the *Mt. Lyell* 30' map, 1910. It was misspelled "Petit" on the Mono National Forest map, 1928.

Pinnacles (9,512 and 9,432)   *Yosemite Valley, Tuolumne Meadows*
Two sharp peaks, half a mile southwest of Clouds Rest and just above the trail. The name was recommended by E. M. Douglas, a geographer with the USGS, on March 1, 1907, and was approved at once by the BGN.

Piute Mountain (10,541)   *Tower Peak*
Piute Creek   *Matterhorn Peak, Tower Peak, Hetch Hetchy Reservoir*
The Piutes (or Paiutes) are a division of Shoshonean Indians. The name has been widely used in California, often indiscriminately. The names are old, but it is not known who gave them or when. The name "Piute Cañon" apparently was used, or given, by the USGS, according to Lt. McClure. (*SCB* 1, no. 8, May 1896: 331.) The USGS survey for the *Dardanelles* 30' map was conducted from 1891 to 1896; both these names appear on the first edition, 1898. McClure called the creek "Cascade Creek" on his 1895 map, but on his 1896 map it was "Piute or Slide C."

Pleasant Valley   *Hetch Hetchy Reservoir*
Named by the Bright family, who ran stock in this area before the national park was created. (Snyder. See **Irwin Bright Lake**.) The valley is about four miles north of Pate Valley. The name appeared on the fifth *Yosemite* 30' map, 1911. No doubt it is a pleasant valley, but the name lacks originality: there are fourteen places in California with this name.

Pohono Trail   *Yosemite Valley, Yosemite*
"*Pohono*. The Bridal Veil Fall, explained to signify a blast of wind, or the night-wind . . . or possibly with reference to the constant swaying of the sheet of water from one side to the other under the influence of the wind. Mr. Hutchings, more poetically, says that 'Pohono' is an evil spirit, whose breath is a blighting and fatal wind, and consequently to be dreaded and shunned." (Whitney, *Yosemite Guide-Book*, 1870: 16.)
"The whole basin drained, as well as the meadows adjacent, was known to us of the battalion, as the Pohono branch and meadows. . . . I have recently learned that Po-ho-no means a daily puffing wind, and when applied to fall, stream, or meadow, means simply the fall, stream, or meadow of the puffing wind, and when applied to the tribe of Po-ho-no-chees, who occupied the meadows in summer, indicated that they dwelled on the meadows of that stream. . . . Mr. Hutchings' interpretation

is entirely fanciful, as are most of his Indian translations." (Bunnell, *Discovery*, 1911: 212–13.)

Courtesy The Bancroft Library

"Pohono," or Bridalveil Fall. From a photograph by Charles L. Weed, taken in 1859.

Polly Dome (9,810); **Polly Dome Lakes**   *Tuolumne Meadows*

The dome was named by R. B. Marshall, USGS, for Mrs. Polly McCabe, a daughter of Col. W. W. Forsyth and the wife of Lt. McCabe. (Farquhar: Forsyth. See **McCabe Lakes**.) The name was later applied to the lakes because it was in common use. (USGS.) Although the dome was named about 1910—a name that was ratified by the BGN in 1932—neither name appeared on a map until the *Tuolumne Meadows* quad, 1953.

Pond Lily Lake   *Devils Postpile, Crystal Crag*

"Famous for the mass of yellow pond lilies, usually in full bloom in late July, that cover the surface of the water near its outlet." (Smith, 14.) The name first appeared on the *Devils Postpile* quad, 1953. The lake is in Sierra National Forest, but was in the park from 1890 to 1905.

Poopenaut Valley *Lake Eleanor*

The truth is that the origin of this name is a mystery, even though various authorities seem to be making a stab at explaining it.

"Named after an early settler by that name of German extraction." (Lt. McClure.) "Name applied in 1889 by Frank Elwell, who homesteaded the property." (Col. Benson.) Both those quotes are in Farquhar's files, from Chester Versteeg. The name is spelled "Poopenant" on LeConte's map of 1893 and McClure's maps of 1895 and 1896, "Poopino" in the Report of the Acting Superintendent of Yosemite National Park in 1901, and "Poopeno" on LeConte's 1900 map. And now you know.

Porcupine: Flat, Creek *Hetch Hetchy Reservoir*

The name existed when the Brewer party of the Whitney Survey camped at the flat on June 23, 1863, but there is no indication that they named it. "We camped at Porcupine Flat, a pretty, grassy flat, at an elevation of 8,550 feet, surrounded by scrubby pines, and tormented by myriads of mosquitoes." (Brewer, *Up and Down*, 401.) The flat is named on the Hoffmann and Gardiner map, 1863–67. The creek was first named on the *Hetch Hetchy Reservoir* quad, 1956.

Porphyry Lake *Merced Peak*

Origin unknown, but presumably named because there is porphyry— a dark reddish rock with feldspar crystals in it—at the lake. The name first appeared on the *Merced Peak* quad, 1953. This tiny lake is next to the Post Peak Pass trail, in Sierra National Forest, just outside the park's southeast boundary. It was within the park from 1890 to 1905.

Post: Peak (11,009), Creek, Lakes; Post Peak Pass *Merced Peak*

The peak and the creek were named for William S. Post of the USGS during the 1898–99 survey for the *Mt. Lyell* 30′ map. (Farquhar: R. B. Marshall.) The names are on the first edition, 1901, and are also on LeConte's map of 1900. The pass and the lakes were first named on the *Merced Peak* quad, 1953. The pass is on the park's southeast boundary, and although the peak, the creek, and the lakes are in Sierra National Forest, they were within the park from 1890 to 1905.

Pothole Meadows   *Yosemite Valley, Yosemite*

Named for bowl-shaped depressions about five feet in diameter. The area is three miles south of Glacier Point, east of the road. Since this locale was not glaciated, these potholes are the result of either running water or local weathering. (See Matthes, *Paper 160*, 63–64.) Matthes didn't claim to have named the meadows, but the earliest use of the name that I have seen was in his diary (v. 9, July 9, 1905), and the name first appeared on the *Yosemite Valley* map, 1907, for which he was the topographer.

Potter Point (10,728)   *Tuolumne Meadows*

Named in 1909 by R. B. Marshall, USGS, for Dr. Charles Potter of Boston. (Farquhar: Marshall.) Potter was an army doctor. (Heitman, 801.)

Price Peak (10,716)   *Tower Peak*

Named for George Ehler Price, who entered the US Cavalry as a private in 1896 and retired as a lieutenant in 1912. (Farquhar: Marshall. Heitman, 806.) The namer may have been Col. Forsyth, acting superintendent of the park from 1909 to 1912. The name appeared on the third *Dardanelles* 30' map, 1912.

Profile Cliff   *Yosemite Valley, Yosemite*

The cliff is below the fissures at Taft Point on the south rim of Yosemite Valley. For that reason it was sometimes referred to in the early literature as "Fissure Mountain." (*YNN* 34, no. 1, Jan. 1955: 14.) "The . . . appellation comes from the many faces that can be distinctly traced upon its northeastern edge at almost any hour of the day." (Hutchings, *In the Heart*, 412.) The name first appeared on the Wheeler Survey map of 1883.

"The streamlet that descends through the asymmetric gorge east of Profile Cliff cuts not vertically but obliquely downward, sliding sidewise, so to speak, along the plane of an inclined master joint. The overhang of Profile Cliff and of the entire west wall of the gorge is due to the undercutting action of the streamlet." (Matthes, *Paper 160*, 110.)

Pulpit Rock   *Yosemite Valley, Yosemite*

A rock formation that looks like a raised pulpit. It is on the south wall of the valley, between the Wawona Tunnel and the Merced River. The origin of the name is unknown. It appeared on the first *Yosemite Valley* map, 1907.

Pumice Butte (9,533–2,912 m.)   *Devils Postpile, Crystal Crag*

The namer is unknown. It was called "Pumice Ridge" as early as 1893.

(*Eleventh Report*, 219.) The butte is in Inyo National Forest. It was in the park from 1890 to 1905.

Pumice Flat   *Devils Postpile, Mammoth Mtn.*

"Dr. Randall arrived at old Monoville in the spring of 1861. He engaged men to accompany him to what was called Pumice Flat, now said to be eight miles north of Mammoth Canyon." (Chalfant, *Gold*, 35.) Although the name wasn't used, the area was described as "pumice-covered flats" in 1893. (*Eleventh Report*, 220.) The name is on the first *Mt. Lyell* 30' map, 1901. The area is along the road a mile to two miles north of Devils Postpile. It is in Inyo National Forest, but was within the park from 1890 to 1905.

"It will readily be seen how Pumice Flat . . . got its name. It is simply a broad level space in the canyon of the Middle Fork, into which the loose pumice from the surrounding hillsides has been washed by the rain." (Matthes, unpublished manuscript in Matthes Papers, Carton 1, BL.)

Pywiack: Cascade, Dome (over 8,800)   *Tuolumne Meadows*

"The north or Ten-ie-ya branch of the Merced, which comes down the North Cañon from the glistening rocks at its source, was called Py-we-ack, 'the river of glistening rocks,' or more literally, perhaps, 'the river-smoothed rocks.'" (Bunnell, *Discovery*, 1911: 207.) Both the creek and Tenaya Lake were called "Py-we-ack" by the Indians. (See **Tenaya Lake**, etc.) The cascade also had an early name of "Slide Fall." In 1932 the BGN revoked that name and approved "Pywiack." "Glistening rocks" is a well-taken name, since there is an abundance of glacier polish in the upper Tenaya basin. Matthes referred to the cascade as "Tenaya Cascade." "It glides down a steeply inclined, marvelously smooth cliff of undivided granite and has a height of about 600 feet. It is strictly a ribbon cascade, but it is the most voluminous and most impressive of its kind; indeed, it is to be counted among the major waterfalls of the Yosemite region." (Matthes, *Paper 160*, 20.) The name "Pywiack Cascade" was recommended by the Park Service (BGN); it appeared on the ninth edition of the *Mt. Lyell* 30' map, 1948.

The dome was remarked on by the Whitney Survey in 1863. "At the head of Lake Tenaya is a very conspicuous conical knob of bare granite, about 800 feet high, the sides of which are everywhere finely polished and grooved by former glaciers." (Whitney, *Geology*, 425.) Various names were given to the dome, among them "Murphy's Dome" (see **Murphy Creek**), "Teapot Dome," "Matthes Dome," "Ten-ieya Dome," and "Turtle Rock."

David Brower recommended "Pywiack Dome" in the early 1950s; the name first appeared on the *Tuolumne Meadows* quad, 1956.

Quarry Peak (11,161)   *Matterhorn Peak*
Seemingly a descriptive name for this peak on the west side of Matterhorn Canyon. Rock slides on the peak's northeastern side may have struck the namer as having been quarried out. Probably named by the USGS during the 1905–9 survey for the *Bridgeport* 30' map; the name is on the first edition, 1911.

Quarter Domes (highest, 8,318)   *Yosemite Valley, Hetch Hetchy Reservoir*
The name was recommended by E. M. Douglas, geographer with the USGS, on March 1, 1907. (BGN.) "Each dome doubtless had, at the end of the El Portal glaciation [200,000 or more years ago], a fairly sharp point and angular edges, but through exfoliation these points and angles have been blunted and rounded off." (Matthes, *Paper 160*, 115.) The El Portal glaciation is now termed the Sherwin glaciation. (Huber, 46.)

Quartzite Peak (10,440)   *Merced Peak*
This easy summit at the north end of the Clark Range was named by François Matthes, probably in 1913 when he was doing geological studies in the park. The name appeared on the ninth edition of the *Mt. Lyell* 30' map, 1948, as "Quartz Peak," even though it had been verified as "Quartzite Peak" by the BGN in 1932.

Rafferty: Peak (over 11,120), **Creek**   *Tuolumne Meadows*
Captain Ogden Rafferty (1860–1922), US Army Medical Corps. (Heitman, 812.) The names were given in 1895 by Lt. McClure when he was accompanied by Rafferty on a patrol of the park. The creek is along the route of the trail from Tuolumne Meadows to the Vogelsang High Sierra Camp, and the peak is 1.5 miles north of the camp. McClure had only the creek named on his 1896 map. Both features were named on the first *Mt. Lyell* 30' map, 1901.

Ragged Peak (10,912)   *Tuolumne Meadows*
"July 6 [1863] Hoffmann and I visited a peak about four miles north of camp [at Tuolumne Meadows], to complete our bearing for this region. It is a naked granite ridge, about 10,500 feet high, and like all the rest commands a sublime view." (Brewer, *Up and Down*, 415.) The peak's descriptive name probably was given by the Wheeler Survey; it appears on atlas sheet 56D, 1878–79.

Rainbow Falls   *Devils Postpile, Crystal Crag*

Probably named by the USGS during the 1898–99 survey for the *Mt. Lyell* 30' map; the name is on the first edition, 1901. The Middle Fork of the San Joaquin River falls over a cliff and into a sunlit pool where rainbows form. ". . . the most beautiful in the Sierra outside of Yosemite." (*Starr's Guide*, 47.) The falls was seen by an adventurous tourist party in 1878. It had no name then, nor did they name it, but they gave the first written description and may have been the first whites other than sheepmen to have seen it. (George B. Bayley, "Eleven Days in the High Sierra," *The Argonaut* 3, no. 24, Dec. 21, 1878.) The falls is in Devils Postpile National Monument, but was within the park from 1890 to 1905.

Rainbow Lake   *Merced Peak*

Origin unknown. The name first appeared on the *Merced Peak* quad, 1953. The lake is in Sierra National Forest, 1.2 miles southeast of Fernandez Pass on the park's southeastern boundary. It was within the park from 1890 to 1905.

Rainbow View   *Yosemite Valley, Yosemite*

A viewpoint on the Old Big Oak Flat Road opposite the east end of the Wawona Tunnel. It got its name from the rainbow that sometimes may be seen in Bridalveil Fall during summer midafternoons. (*YNN* 34, no. 1, Jan. 1955: 14.) The name appeared on the fourth edition of the *Yosemite Valley* map, 1927.

Rancheria Creek   *Hetch Hetchy Reservoir, Tower Peak, Matterhorn Peak*
Rancheria: Mountain (8,995), **Falls**   *Hetch Hetchy Reservoir*

The Spanish word "rancheria" originally meant a collection of crude dwellings, but in Spanish California it was used to mean Indian villages in general. Several sites have been located on the slopes of Rancheria Mountain. (YRL files.) However, what seems a more likely explanation for the existence of the name in this locale is that sheepmen were using it to indicate their summer home or range. ". . . the other [trail], leading out at the east end of the valley [Hetch Hetchy] to a meadow known as 'Rancheria' and to numerous other meadows used as sheep ranges." (Macomb, *Report*, 1879: 260.)

The name "Rancheria Creek" is on atlas sheet 56D, 1878–79. The mountain was named on the first edition of the *Yosemite* 30' map, 1897, and the falls was named on the fifth edition, 1911.

Red Cones (9,015 and 8,985)   *Devils Postpile, Crystal Crag*
   An obvious name for two reddish volcanic cones, although the namer
is not known. The route of the John Muir and Pacific Crest trails passes
between the two cones. It may well be that the cones were named during
construction of the John Muir Trail; the name appeared on the fifth edition
of the *Mt. Lyell* 30' map, 1922. The cones are in Inyo National Forest, but
were within the park from 1890 to 1905.

Red: Peak (11,699), **Creek; Red Peak Fork; Red Devil Lake**   *Merced Peak*
   The peak was named "Red Mountain" by the Whitney Survey for the
predominate color of its upper portion. (Whitney, *The Yosemite Book*, 97.)
The present name first appeared on the Wheeler Survey's atlas sheet 56D,
1878–79. The other names derive from the peak. "Red Peak Fork" was on
McClure's 1896 map. Red Creek was named on the first *Mt. Lyell* 30' map,
1901, while Red Devil Lake was not named until publication of the *Merced
Peak* quad, 1953.

Red Top (9,977)   *Merced Peak*
   The descriptive name for this peak on the park's southern boundary
probably was provided by the USGS during the 1898–99 survey for the
Mt. Lyell 30' map; it is on all editions of the map, 1901–1950, as "Redtop."

Red Top Mountain (10,532–3,203 m.)   *Devils Postpile, Mt. Ritter*
   The first use of this name was by H. D. Erwin in 1934. ("Geology and
Mineral Resources of Northeastern Madera County, California," *California
Journal of Mines and Geology* 30, no. 1: 7–78.) The information is from N.
King Huber, a geologist with the USGS, who officially proposed the name
in 1976; it was approved that same year by the BGN. The entire upper part
of the mountain is of a dark reddish hue.
   The peak is not named on the *Devils Postpile* quad. It is 1.9 miles
southeast of the outlet of Minaret Lake, marked "10532." On the *Mt. Ritter*
quad, provisional edition 1983, the name is on the wrong peak. It should
be on the next summit to the southwest, marked "3203." The mountain is
in Inyo National Forest, but it was within the park from 1890 to 1905.

Reds: Meadow, Creek   *Devils Postpile, Crystal Crag*
Reds Lake   *Devils Postpile, Mammoth Mtn.*
   Named for "Red" Sotcher, who came to the area in 1879 as a sheep-
herder. (Smith, *Mammoth*, 14.) A stockman with a red beard. (Farquhar.)
An earlier name for the meadow was "Potts Meadow." (*San Francisco
Mining and Scientific Press*, Aug. 16, 1879: 98.) "Reds Meadows" was

named on Lt. McClure's 1895 map, and the name of the creek was added to his 1896 map. The lake was first named on the *Devils Postpile* quad, 1953. On that map the creek flows west from near the lake. On the *Crystal Crag* quad the name "Reds Creek" has been placed on the creek heading on the southwest side of Mammoth Mountain and flowing into Reds Meadow. Although presently in Inyo National Forest, all these features were within the park from 1890 to 1905.

Register Creek   *Tuolumne Meadows, Hetch Hetchy Reservoir*
    The origin of the name is unknown, "but possibly because of some sort of registration book along the creek." (YRL files.) The creek joins the Tuolumne River at the lower end of Muir Gorge.
    The name was not used by travelers down the Grand Canyon of the Tuolumne River in 1894 and 1897, but it appears on the first edition of the *Mt. Lyell* 30' map, 1901. Thus one must assume that it was named either by army patrols or by USGS surveyors in the late 1890s.

Regulation: Peak (over 10,560), **Creek**   *Tuolumne Meadows*
    In 1895 Lt. Harry C. Benson and a trumpeter named McBride placed copies of Yosemite National Park regulations on trees throughout the park. McBride suggested the name "Regulation Peak" for a mountain between Smedberg Lake and Rodgers Lake. Benson put the name on his 1896 map. Lt. McClure, on his 1896 map, put the name in an ambiguous position. When the USGS 30-minute maps were published, the name was put on the wrong peak. The true "Regulation Peak" was given the name "Volunteer Peak" on the first *Bridgeport* 30' map, a name it has had ever since. (Farquhar: Benson.)
    On the first *Mt. Lyell* 30' map, 1901, "Regulation Peak" was on a summit a mile south of Rodgers Lake. On the 1905 edition the name had disappeared. The 1910 edition moved it north to its present position, and gave the name "West Peak" to the former "Regulation Peak."
    Regulation Creek was named "West Fork Return Creek" on the *Mt. Lyell* 30' maps, 1901–29. It acquired its present name on the eighth edition, 1944.

Return Creek   *Matterhorn Peak, Tuolumne Meadows*
    A large stream flowing down through Virginia Canyon, draining much of the northeastern part of the park. The origin of the name is unknown. However, since it appears on the Wheeler Survey atlas sheet 56D, 1878–79, one might speculate that it was named by the survey's field party of 1879 under Lt. Macomb. Perhaps they attempted to follow the

creek down to the Tuolumne River, but were forced by the rough terrain to turn back.

Reymann Lake   *Tuolumne Meadows*

Named for William M. Reymann (1883–1938), a park ranger in 1927. (Bingaman, *Guardians*, 115.) The lake is at the head of a branch of Echo Creek, just northwest of Rafferty Peak in the Cathedral Range.

Ribbon: Fall, Meadow   *Yosemite Valley, Yosemite*
Ribbon Creek   *Hetch Hetchy Reservoir, Yosemite, Yosemite Valley*

"The Indians call this Lung-oo-too-koo-yah, or the graceful and slender one; while a lady, whose name shall be nameless, once christened it 'Virgin's Tears.'" (Hutchings, *In the Heart*, 398.)

"The name for the little fall to which the name of 'Virgin's Tears' has been applied, was known to us [the Mariposa Battalion] as 'Pigeon Creek Fall.' The Indian name is 'Lung-yo-to-co-ya;' its literal meaning is 'Pigeon Basket,' probably signifying to them 'Pigeon Nests,' or *Roost*. In explanation of the name for the creek, I was told that west of El Capitan, in the valley of the stream, and upon the southern slopes, pigeons were at times quite numerous." (Bunnell, *Discovery*, 1911: 213–14.) "Mr. Hutchings has named the fall 'The Ribbon Fall,' as an English name was desirable." (Bunnell, *Report*, 9–10.)

The Hoffmann and Gardiner map, 1863–67, has "Virgin Tear Cr." King and Gardiner's map of 1865 has "Virgin Tears Creek" and "Virgin Tear's Fall." Lt. McClure's 1896 map has "Ribbon Falls." The name "Ribbon Meadow" was submitted in March 1905 by E. M. Douglas, a geographer with the USGS; it was approved by the BGN that same month. Douglas described the meadow as a "swamp or marsh on a tributary of Ribbon Creek." The meadow and the creek were named on the first USGS *Yosemite Valley* map, 1907.

Richardson Peak (9,884)   *Tower Peak*

Named in June 1879 by Lt. Macomb of the Wheeler Survey. "I was accompanied by Mr. Thomas Richardson, who has a sheep range in Cherry Valley and vicinity, and who is perfectly familiar with the rugged country south of the Relief trail." (Macomb, *Report*, 1879: 257.) The name is on atlas sheet 56D as "Richardson's Pk." It became "Richardson Peak" on the first *Dardanelles* 30' map, 1898.

Ritter, Mount (13,157–4,006 m.); **Ritter: Lakes, Pass**

Devils Postpile, Mt. Ritter

Ritter Range   *Devils Postpile, Mt. Ritter, Cattle Mtn.*

The mountain was named by the Whitney Survey in 1864. "Ritter is the name of the great German geographer, the founder of the science of modern comparative geography." (Whitney, *Yosemite Guide-Book*, 1870: 101.) Karl Ritter (1779–1859) was professor of history at the University of Berlin when Whitney was a student there during the 1840s.

John Muir made the first ascent in October 1872. "I was suddenly brought to a dead stop, with arms outspread, clinging close to the face of the rock, unable to move hand or foot either up or down. My doom appeared fixed. I *must* fall. There would be a moment of bewilderment, and then a lifeless rumble down the one general precipice to the glacier below. When this final danger flashed upon me, I became nerve-shaken for the first time since setting foot on the mountain, and my mind seemed to fill with a stifling smoke. But . . . life blazed forth again with preternatural clearness. I seemed suddenly to become possessed of a new sense. . . . Then my trembling muscles became firm again, every rift and flaw in the rock was seen as through a microscope, and my limbs moved with a positiveness and precision with which I seemed to have nothing to do at all. Had I been borne aloft upon wings, my deliverance could not have been more complete. . . . I found a way without effort, and soon stood upon the topmost crag in the blessed light." (Muir, *Mountains*, 64–65.)

The mountain is named on Hoffmann and Gardiner's map, 1863–67. "Ritter Range" appears on the fifth edition of the *Mt. Lyell* 30' map, 1922. Neither the lakes nor the pass are named on the *Devils Postpile* quad. There are four lakes, two large and two small, west of Mount Ritter and south of Lake Catherine. The pass is across the range 1.2 miles south-southeast of Mount Ritter. The mountain, the pass, and the range are on the boundary between Inyo and Sierra national forests; the lakes are in the latter. All the features were within the park from 1890 to 1905.

Rock Island: Lake, Pass; Rock: Canyon, Creek   *Matterhorn Peak*

"I named the stream Rock Creek, and the lake Rock Island Lake, from a large granite island that was visible near the northern end." (Lt. N. F. McClure in *SCB* 1, no. 5, Jan. 1895: 178.) In the same article McClure also used "Rock Cañon." The canyon and the lake are named on McClure's maps of 1895 and 1896, and the pass is marked simply with the word "Pass" on the 1896 map. All three names are on the first *Bridgeport* 30' map, 1911, but the creek name doesn't appear until the *Matterhorn Peak* quad, 1956.

Rockbound Lake   *Merced Peak*

Obviously a descriptive name, but the namer is unknown. The lake is in Sierra National Forest at the headwaters of Long Creek, about a mile east of Long Mountain on the park's southeast boundary, and was first named on the *Merced Peak* quad, 1953. It was within the park from 1890 to 1905.

Rockslides   *Yosemite Valley, Yosemite*

An early BGN decision designated the area "Rockslides Slope," but that name was never on the maps. The present name was submitted in March 1907 by E. M. Douglas, a geographer with the USGS. It appeared on the first USGS *Yosemite Valley* map, 1907.

"The lower Yosemite chamber doubtless owes its great width to the ease with which the glacier quarried in the large bodies of well-jointed gabbro and diorite which extend throughout most of its length. . . . Their unstable masonry, crisscrossed by numerous joints, has not remained standing in the form of a sheer wall but has broken down completely, producing the immense talus known as the Rock Slides, over which the Big Oak Flat Road is built." (Matthes, *Paper 160*, 92.) In October 1942, rockslides wiped out the "Zigzags" on the Old Big Oak Flat Road, converting it in an instant from a road to a little-used trail.

Rocky Point   *Yosemite Valley, Yosemite*

"Rocky Point . . . is just under the lowest shoulder of the 'Three Brothers,' and is formed by large blocks of rocky talus that once peeled from its side." (Hutchings, *In the Heart*, 394.)

"The obstructing rocks on the old north side trail were known as 'Weäck,' 'The Rocks,' and understood to mean the 'fallen rocks,' because, according to traditions they had fallen *upon* the old trail." (Bunnell, *Discovery*, 1911: 151.)

Rodgers: Canyon, Meadow   *Hetch Hetchy Reservoir*
Rodgers Lake   *Tuolumne Meadows*
Rodgers Peak (12,978)   *Merced Peak*
Rodgers Lakes   *Devils Postpile, Mt. Ritter*

All these features are named for Capt. Alexander Rodgers, Fourth Cavalry, US Army, acting superintendent of the park in 1895 and 1897. (Heitman, 841.)

The peak was originally named "Mount Guyot" by the Whitney Survey in the 1860s. Arnold Henri Guyot (1807–1884) was born in Switzerland, came to America 1n 1848, and was professor of physical geography and geology at Princeton, 1854–84. The name did not appear on any maps, although it was used by Gardiner in 1866. (Journal of James T. Gardiner, July 12, 1866. Copy in Farquhar Papers, BL.) In 1881 a mountain in the southern part of Sequoia National Park was successfully named for Guyot.

In 1895 Lt. McClure gave the peak its present name. That same year, Lt. Benson gave Rodgers' name to the lake and to the peak just south of it. On his 1896 map Lt. McClure had the canyon, the lake, and the peak he had named—the one just south of Mount Lyell, on the park's eastern boundary. On his 1896 map Benson had the lake, the meadow, and the peak he had named. To avoid duplication, the USGS gave the name "Regulation Peak" to the second "Rodgers Peak." (Farquhar: McClure, Benson. See **Regulation: Peak, Creek.**)

The first edition of the *Yosemite* 30' map had "Rodgers Canyon" and "Rodgers Lake." This lake (which is not the present one) had its name changed to "Neall Lake" on the third edition of the map, 1903. The present Rodgers Lake was named on the first *Mt. Lyell* 30' map, 1901. After being on Benson's map, the meadow was not named on a map again until the *Hetch Hetchy Reservoir* quad, 1956.

At about the time that Lt. McClure named Rodgers Peak, J. N. LeConte named it "Mount Kellogg," for Vernon L. Kellogg, professor of entomology at Stanford. (LeConte, *Alpina*, 10.) He had the name on his 1896 and 1900 maps. Neither name was on the *Mt. Lyell* 30' map until "Rodgers Peak" appeared on the final edition, 1950, even though the name had been ratified by the BGN in 1932. On early editions of the *Merced Peak* quad, 1953 through 1972, it was misspelled "Rodger."

Rodgers Lakes, at the headwaters of Rush Creek, were first named on the *Devils Postpile* quad, 1953. The lakes are in Inyo National Forest, but were in the park from 1890 to 1905.

Roosevelt Lake (10,184)   *Tuolumne Meadows*
Near the park's northeast boundary, half a mile west of Mount Conness, the lake was named for Eleanor Roosevelt, to commemorate a visit she made to the park in July 1934. (Bingaman, *Guardians*, 40.) The name was suggested by Douglass Hubbard, the park's naturalist at the time. (USGS.) Bingaman and a ranger named Eastman had suggested the name "My Day Lake," from the title of a syndicated newspaper column that Mrs. Roosevelt wrote for many years.

Rosalie Lake   *Devils Postpile, Mammoth Mtn.*
Origin unknown. It's the next lake south of Shadow Lake, on the John

Muir Trail. The name first appeared on the *Devils Postpile* quad, 1953. The lake is in Inyo National Forest, but was within the park from 1890 to 1905.

Rostrum, The   *Yosemite Valley*

A descriptive name for a cliff on the south side of the Merced River. The name appeared on the 1970 edition of the map. It is north of Turtleback Dome—just north by east of "BM 4873" on the Wawona Road.

Royal Arches; Royal Arch Cascade   *Yosemite Valley, Yosemite*
Royal Arch Creek   *Hetch Hetchy Reservoir, Yosemite, Yosemite Valley*

"The name given to the rocks now known as 'The Royal Arches' is Scho-ko-ya when alluding to the fall, and means 'Basket Fall,' as coming from To-ko-ya, and when referring to the rock itself was called Scho-ko-ni, meaning the movable shade to a cradle, which, when in position, formed an arched shade over the infant's head. The name of 'The Royal Arch' was given to it [in 1851] by a comrade who was a member of the Masonic Fraternity, and it has since been called 'The Royal Arches.'" (Bunnell, *Discovery*, 1880: 212.)

"Cho-ko-nip'-o-deh (baby basket), Royal Arches. This curved and overhanging canopy-rock bears no little resemblance to an Indian baby-basket. Another form is *cho-ko'-ni*; and either one means literally 'dog-place' or 'dog-house.'" (Powers, 364.)

There has also been a contention that the Indian name was "Hunto." "From an Indian word for eye." (Sanchez, 278.) *Huntu* is "eye" in Southern Sierra Miwok. (Kroeber, 43.) "Shun'-ta, Hun'-ta (the eye), the Watching Eye." (Powers, 365.)

"Owing to the curve of these wing-like arches, stretching as they do from a kind of lion-like head . . . a gentleman resident of Philadelphia suggested that 'The Winged Lion' (one of the sculptures found by Layard in the ruined cities of the Euphrates Valley) would be a more expressive and suitable name for it than 'Royal Arches.'" (Hutchings, *In the Heart*, 383. Layard was the excavator of Nineveh.)

"Royal Arches" appears on the King and Gardiner map, 1865. In 1872 John Muir referred to the cascade as "Arch Falls," doubtless the common name at the time. (Muir, "Yosemite Valley in Flood," *Overland Monthly* 8, no. 4, April 1872: 348–49.) The cascade and the creek were first named on the fourth *Yosemite Valley* map, 1927.

". . . Such arches originate through the calving off of the lower portions of shells. The remaining portion of each shell naturally tends to assume the shape of an arch, because the arch is . . . the form of structure best adapted to bearing a heavy distributed load. The finest example is afforded by the Royal Arches. . . . The Yosemite Glacier was the principal sculptor; during the last stage of glaciation it plucked away the lower portions of the shells, which had previously been loosened by exfoliation from a partial, low-set dome that bulged out into the valley. A short distance west of the Royal Arches is another set of arches. . . . They receive little attention, yet they are a good average example of the type as it occurs in different parts of the Sierra Nevada." (Matthes, *Paper 160*, 116.)

Royal Arch Lake *Yosemite*
The namer is unknown. It's a small lake on the Buena Vista Trail, south by east from Buena Vista Peak. The name was in use at least as early as 1921 (Matthes, v. 25, July 20, 1921), and first appeared on the sixth edition of the *Yosemite* 30' map, 1929.

Ruby Lake (3,021 m.) *Devils Postpile, Mt. Ritter*
Origin unknown. The lake is on the John Muir Trail between Thousand Island Lake and Garnet Lake; it was first named on the *Devils Postpile* quad, 1953. Although in Inyo National Forest, the lake was in the park from 1890 to 1905.

Rush Creek *Mono Craters, Devils Postpile, Mt. Ritter*
This is one of the older names on the east side of the Sierra, yet its origin is unknown. It appears on the Hoffmann and Gardiner map of 1863–67 and in Whitney's *Yosemite Book*, 1868. On A. W. Von Schmidt's plat of 1857 it is called "Lake Creek," possibly because it was the major stream flowing into Mono Lake. That name was still used on GLO plats as late as 1895, even though the Wheeler Survey used the name "Rush Creek" on atlas sheet 56D, 1878–79.

Rush Creek *Yosemite*
Origin unknown, but probably named because it rushes downhill at a great rate in the spring. It may have been named by the Whitney Survey; the name is on Hoffmann and Gardiner's map of 1863–67. Heading near Devil Peak, the creek flows east and north to join the South Fork of the Merced River in the Wawona Campground.

Ruth Lake *Merced Peak*
Origin unknown. The lake is in Sierra National Forest about a mile southeast of Fernandez Pass on the park's southestern boundary, and was first named on the *Merced Peak* quad, 1953. It was within the park from 1890 to 1905.

Rutherford Lake   *Merced Peak*

Named for Lt. Samuel McPherson Rutherford, Fourth Cavalry, US Army, on duty in the park in 1896. (Farquhar; Heitman, 854.) The name appeared on the first *Mt. Lyell* 30' map, 1901. The lake is in Sierra National Forest, just beyond the park's southeastern boundary. It was within the park from 1890 to 1905.

Saddle Horse Lake   *Hetch Hetchy Reservoir*

Named by the Bright family, who ran stock in this area before the national park was created. The lake was where they pastured their saddle horses. (Snyder.) This lake and "Irwin Bright Lake" switched names due to a BGN decision in 1960. The lake discharges into Piute Creek, which flows into the Tuolumne River at Pate Valley.

Saddlebag Lake (10,087)   *Tuolumne Meadows*

Undoubtedly named for its shape—two partly rounded ends with a narrowing in the middle—at the time of the mining activity in the early 1880s. The name "Saddlebags Lake" was used in the *Homer Mining Index* as early as Jan. 28, 1882.

On the 1895 GLO plat (surveyed in 1883), the lake was called "Lee Vinings Lake," since it is at the head of Lee Vining Creek. The first two editions of the *Mt. Lyell* 30' map, 1901 and 1905, called it "Saddleback Lake." It was changed to "Saddlebag Lake" beginning with the edition of 1910. Although in Inyo National Forest, the lake was within the park from 1890 to 1905.

Sadler: Peak (10,567), **Lake** (9,345)   *Merced Peak*

Both features were named in 1895 by Lt. McClure for a corporal in his detachment. (Farquhar: McClure; see also *SCB* 1, no. 8, May 1896: 334.) The name was mistakenly spelled "Sadlier" on McClure's map of 1896, and on the first four editions of the *Mt. Lyell* 30' map, 1901–14. It was corrected beginning with the fifth edition, 1922. LeConte's 1900 map had both names misspelled as "Saddler." Although presently in Sierra National Forest, both features were within the park from 1890 to 1905.

San Joaquin River
San Joaquin Mountain (11,600–3535.7 m.) *Devils Postpile, Mammoth Mtn.*

Gabriel Moraga named the river in 1805 or 1806 for San Joaquin (Saint Joachim), the father of the Virgin Mary. (Arch. MSB, vol. 4, Muñoz, Sept. 24, 1806.) The name spread up the river into the mountains, where it became North, Middle, and South forks.

The mountain probably was named by the USGS during the 1898–99 survey for the *Mt. Lyell* 30' map, simply because it was a convenient name to borrow for a triangulation point. The name is on the first edition, 1901.

The North Fork drains the region between the park's southeast boundary and the west side of the Ritter Range, while the Middle Fork drains the east side of the Ritter Range. This area is in Sierra and Inyo national forests, but it was almost entirely within the park from 1890 to 1905.

Sardine Lake, Lower and **Upper**   *Mono Craters*
In the spring of 1860, Judge Michael M. Magee, Justice of the Peace at Big Oak Flat, along with Allen S. Crocker and two other men, went on an exploring trip to the headwaters of the Tuolumne River. North of Tenaya Lake they met a party of men with a train of wornout and nearly starved pack mules attempting to cross the canyons north of the Tuolumne to get to the Monoville diggings. Magee led the train to Mono Pass, at the head of Bloody Canyon, and sent it on its way.

"In descending a precipitous slope to a seemingly bottomless lake, situated about one mile below the head of the canyon proper, one of the pack mules, heavily laden with kegs of whisky, fell and rolled into the lake, carrying with him in his descent another mule loaded with cases of sardines, no trace of either mules or packs ever being seen afterward— and to this day that beautiful sheet of water is known as Sardine Lake." (*Homer Mining Index*, Jan. 5, 1884.)

"Sardine Lake" (the lower one) was first named on Lt. McClure's map of 1896. That lake was called "Red Lake" by John Muir in 1869. (*Overland Monthly*, Sept. 1874.) The lake is about a mile outside the park's eastern boundary, but was within the park from 1890 to 1905.

Saurian Crest (11,095)   *Tower Peak*
Named in 1911 by William E. Colby because of its resemblance to an ancient monster. (Farquhar: Colby. See also *SCB* 8, no. 3, Jan. 1912: photo opp. 157.) Colby submitted the name to the BGN in 1920, and it was approved that same year. It appeared on the fourth *Dardanelles* 30' map, 1924.

Savage, Mount (5,745)   *Yosemite*
Named for Major James D. Savage, leader of the Mariposa Battalion whose members were the first white men to enter and explore Yosemite Valley and who named many of the features, in 1851. The name was suggested by Chester Versteeg in the early 1950s. The mountain formerly

was known in the Wawona area as "Twin Peaks" and "Mt. Adeline." (YRL files.)

Sawtooth Ridge   *Matterhorn Peak*

A descriptive name, in use since about 1880. It first appeared on McClure's map of 1896. The ridge is on the park's boundary just northwest of Matterhorn Peak. It is also known locally as "The Crags."

Schofield Peak (9,935)   *Tower Peak*

General John McAllister Schofield (1831–1906), secretary of war, 1868–69; superintendent at West Point, 1876–81; commander-in-chief of the US Army, 1888–95. (Heitman, 865.) The peak was named by Major W. W. Forsyth, acting superintendent of the park from 1909 to 1912. (Farquhar: H. C. Benson.) The name appeared on the third edition of the *Dardanelles* 30' map, 1912.

Seavey Pass   *Tower Peak*

Named by R. B. Marshall of the USGS for Clyde L. Seavey, a member— at different times—of the State Board of Control, the State Civil Service Commission, the State Railroad Commission, and the Federal Power Commission. (Farquhar: Marshall.)

"That was a mighty snippy letter you sent me in acknowledgment of my wonderful efforts to record the Seavey family to fame on the Yosemite Administrative Map." (Letter, Marshall to Seavey, June 16, 1910, in Marshall Papers, Part I, Box I, BL.) The pass is on the trail between Benson Lake and Kerrick Canyon. It was first named on the third *Dardanelles* 30' map, 1912.

Sentinel: Rock (7,038), Dome (8,122), Creek, Fall

Yosemite Valley, Yosemite

"Opposite the Three Brothers is a prominent point, which . . . from its fancied likeness to a gigantic watch-tower, is called 'Sentinel Rock.'" (Whitney, *Geology*, 412.) This was the first "Sentinel" feature named; the others derive from it. Probably the earliest name for the rock, which never got onto a map, was "Pyramid Rock," used by the Mariposa County surveyor in 1856. (*San Joaquin Republican*, Nov. 26, 1856.)

"The present 'Sentinel' they [mission Indian guides] called 'Loya,' a corruption of Olla (oya), Spanish for an earthen water-pot." (Bunnell, *Discovery*, 1880: 212.) "If the name comes from the Spanish word Ho-yas, holes in rocks, the sentinel designated the place of the acorn mortar mills; or, perhaps, the obelisk form was supposed to resemble the stone pestle for pulverizing the acorns used by the Indians as food." (Bunnell, *Report*, 12.) "The peak called by us the 'South Dome' has since been given the name of 'Sentinel Dome.'" (Bunnell, *Discovery*, 1880: 212.)

The rock and the dome were named on the King and Gardiner map of 1865. The Wheeler Survey map of 1883 had the dome named, and showed Sentinel Rock as "The Sentinel;" and it also had the creek named "Lola Brook." The creek acquired its present name on the first USGS *Yosemite Valley* map, 1907, and the fall was named on the fourth edition, 1927. Earlier the fall had been referred to as the "Sentinel Cascades." (Hutchings, *In the Heart*, 413–14.)

VIEW OF NORTH AND SOUTH DOMES, "TO-COY-Æ" AND "TIS-SA-ACK," FROM THE VALLEY.

Courtesy The Bancroft Library

North Dome and Half Dome, from a photograph
by Charles L. Weed, 1859.

77 Corral   *Devils Postpile, Cattle Mtn.*

Named for a corral constructed here in 1877. (See **Corral Meadow**.) The name is on Lt. McClure's 1895 map as "77 Camp," and on his 1896 map with the present name. It was on all editions of the *Mt. Lyell* 30' map from 1901 to 1950, but is not shown on the *Devils Postpile* 15-minute map. It is at Corral Meadow, in the lower left quadrant of the map, just north of the trail where the letters 'BM' appear. This is in Sierra National Forest, but was within the park from 1890 to 1905.

Shadow: Lake, Creek   *Devils Postpile, Mt. Ritter*

The name probably originated with miners at the time of the Mammoth mining boom. It was an accepted name, and was on a newspaper map in 1879. One might speculate that the name is because the cliffs at the lake's eastern end cast long shadows across the lake until the sun is high in the sky. On McClure's maps, Solomons' 1896 map, and LeConte's 1900 map the lake is called "Garnet Lake," and the name "Shadow Lake" is on what is now Rosalie Lake. The lake and the creek are in Inyo National Forest, but were in the park from 1890 to 1905.

Shamrock Lake   *Matterhorn Peak*

On the map the lake appears to have three lobes—like a shamrock. It probably was named by the USGS during the 1905–9 survey for the *Bridgeport* 30' map; it is on the first edition, 1911. The lake is about 1.5 miles east-northeast of Smedberg Lake.

Shamrock Lake   *Tuolumne Meadows*

Al Gardisky named the lake in 1932 because of its shape. (Spuller.) It is in Inyo National Forest, but was within the park from 1890 to 1905.

Sheep Crossing   *Devils Postpile, Cattle Mtn.*

An old name, dating from the 1890s when sheep in large numbers were driven into the Sierra—and when the US Cavalry was making a concerted effort to drive them out of the recently-created Yosemite National Park. This is a major crossing point of the North Fork of the San Joaquin River. On LeConte's map of 1893 it is simply marked "Bridge," on what was then called the "Mammoth City Trail." Lt. McClure's 1895 map had it as "Sheep Bridge;" his 1896 map had the present name. Although in Sierra National Forest, the crossing was within the park from 1890 to 1905.

Sheep Peak (over 11,840)   *Tuolumne Meadows*

Origin unknown, but probably named by or for the sheepmen who brought their flocks into this region from the 1880s into the early 1900s. The peak, which is 1.5 miles northwest of Mount Conness, was named on the first edition of the *Mt. Lyell* 30' map, 1901.

Shellenbarger Lake (2,993 m.)   *Devils Postpile, Mt. Ritter*

Origin unknown, but possibly named for a USGS field man. The lake is at the head of a tributary of Dike Creek, about 3.3 miles south of Mount Ritter. It was first named on the *Devils Postpile* quad, 1953. Although in Sierra National Forest, it was within the park from 1890 to 1905.

Shepherd: Crest, Lake   *Matterhorn Peak*

Origin uncertain, but probably named after the sheepherders of the late nineteenth and early twentieth centuries. (YRL files.) The crest was named on the first *Bridgeport* 30' map, 1911, and the creek on the *Matterhorn Peak* quad, 1956. François Matthes described the upland valley near the crest as a "fragment of the ancient landscape." ("The Little 'Lost Valley' on Shepherd's Crest," *SCB* 18, no. 1, Feb. 1933: 68–80.)

Shirley: Creek, Lake   *Merced Peak*

Origin unknown. These features are in Sierra National Forest, east-southeast of Gale Peak on the park's southeastern boundary, and were first named on the *Merced Peak* quad, 1953. They were within the park from 1890 to 1905.

Sierra Nevada

Spanish for "snowy mountain range." *Sierra* is the word for "saw," and when used in this way means a jagged range of mountains—the teeth of the saw being similar to a row of mountain peaks. The Spanish used the name *Sierra Nevada* with abandon—any time they saw a mountain range with snow on it. As early as 1542, Juan Rodriguez Cabrillo gave that name to what we now know as the "Santa Lucia Range," south of Big Sur. The present Sierra Nevada received its name from Fray Pedro Font, who saw it from a hill east of the contemporary town of Antioch in April 1776.

"If we looked to the east we saw on the other side of the plain at a distance of some thirty leagues a great Sierra Nevada, white from the summit to the skirts, and running diagonally almost from south-southeast to north-northwest." (Bolton, 386; see also Farquhar, *History*, 15–20.)

John Muir favored a name he thought more appropriate. "Then it seemed to me the Sierra should be called, not the Nevada or Snowy Range, but the Range of Light." ("The Treasures of the Yosemite," *Century Magazine*, August 1890: 483.)

The US Board on Geographic Names has defined the Sierra Nevada as extending from Tehachapi Pass on the south to the gap south of Lassen Peak on the north. Thus, Yosemite National Park is in the Sierra Nevada.

Sierra Point   *Yosemite Valley, Yosemite*

A point sought for, and discovered, by Charles A. Bailey, from where one can see Illilouette, Vernal, Nevada, and Upper and Lower Yosemite falls. "That this point might no longer remain incognito, but be known to all lovers of Yosemite, on June 14, 1897, accompanied by Walter E. Magee and Warren Cheney, of Berkeley . . . I deposited thereon Register Box of the Sierra Club No. 15, and took the liberty of naming it Sierra Point, in honor of the Sierra Club, and raised a flag bearing the name." (*SCB* 2, no. 4, June 1898: 217.) The name appeared on the second *Yosemite Valley* map, 1918.

Because of dangerous hiking conditions that resulted in injuries, the former trail to the point has been eliminated.

Siesta Lake   *Hetch Hetchy Reservoir*
Origin unknown; a small lake on the Tioga Road 1.5 miles south of White Wolf.

Silver Apron   *Yosemite Valley*
The name originated in the nineteenth century; the namer is unknown. It was called the "Silver Chain" in one early guidebook. (*YNN* 34, no. 1, Jan. 1955: 16.) ". . . the whole river is scurrying over smooth, bare granite, at the rate of a fast express train on the best of railroads." (Hutchings, *In the Heart*, 450.) This is the stretch of the Merced from below Nevada Fall to the bridge above Emerald Pool. Although this is an old name it did not appear on any map until the eighth edition of the *Yosemite Valley* sheet, 1958.

Silver Strand Falls   *Yosemite Valley, Yosemite*
The falls is on Meadow Brook, which drains a small area and thus quickly runs dry once the snow has melted. Its earlier name was "Widow's Tears Falls," because—as early stage drivers told tourists—it lasted only two weeks. (*YNN* 34, no. 1, Jan. 1955: 16.) It appeared with that name on the Wheeler Survey map of 1883 and on the *Yosemite Valley* maps from 1907 to 1922. The present name was given at the suggestion of François E. Matthes, and appeared on the 1927 edition of the map.

Simmons Peak (12,503)   *Tuolumne Meadows*
Named in 1909 by R. B. Marshall, USGS, for Dr. Samuel E. Simmons of Sacramento. (Farquhar: Marshall.) The name appeared on the third edition of the *Mt. Lyell* 30' map, 1910.

Sing Peak (10,552)   *Merced Peak*
Named in 1899 by R. B. Marshall, USGS, for Tie Sing, a Chinese cook with the Geological Survey from 1888 until 1918, when he was killed in an accident in the field. (Farquhar: Marshall.) The peak, on the park's southeast boundary, was named on the first *Mt. Lyell* 30' map, 1901.

Sister Lake   *Matterhorn Peak*

The lake, which is 0.6 mile northeast of Smedberg Lake, possibly was named by Lt. H. C. Benson in 1895. All the named features in the vicinity appeared on the first *Bridgeport* 30' map, 1911; several of them are known to have been named by Benson.

Skelton Lakes   *Tuolumne Meadows*

Henry A. Skelton (1869–1955). He was hired in June 1898 as a forest agent to protect the north end of the park during the absence that summer of the army troops, due to the Spanish American War. After that he worked for the General Land Office, and was a park ranger from 1916 to 1932. (YRL files; Bingaman, *Guardians*, 92–93.)

Slab Lakes   *Merced Peak*

Origin unknown; perhaps there are distinctive slabs of rock at the lake. The name first appeared on the *Merced Peak* quad, 1953. The lakes are about 1.2 miles southeast of Triple Divide Peak, in Sierra National Forest. They were within the park from 1890 to 1905.

Slide: Canyon, Mountain (northern), **Mountain** (southern, 10,479);
The Slide   *Matterhorn Peak*

Lt. N. F. McClure used the name "Slide Cañon" in 1894, but in such a way that it seems the name already existed—perhaps applied by sheep-herders after its salient feature. "I came to the most wonderful natural object that I ever beheld. A vast granite cliff, two thousand feet in height, had literally tumbled from the bluff on the right-hand side of the stream across the cañon, but many large stones had rolled far up on the opposite side." (McClure in *SCB* 1, no. 5, Jan. 1895: 175–76.)

The canyon and the "Great Slide" were named on McClure's maps of 1895 and 1896. The northern Slide Mountain, on the park's northern boundary at the head of The Slide, was named on the first *Bridgeport* 30' map, 1911. The southern Slide Mountain, four miles to the south and with a more modest slide on its northern side, was first named on the *Matterhorn Peak* quad, 1956.

Slide Creek   *Devils Postpile, Mt. Ritter*

A tributary of the North Fork of the San Joaquin, flowing down from the west side of the Ritter Range. It plunges down a steep cliff for a third of a mile, which probably is what gave rise to the name. The name was added to the *Devils Postpile* quad, 1953, at the request of the US Forest

Service. (USGS.) The creek is in Sierra National Forest, but was in the park from 1890 to 1905.

Smedberg Lake *Matterhorn Peak*

Lt. H. C. Benson named the lake in 1895 for Lt. William Renwick Smedberg, Jr., Fourth Cavalry, US Army, who was on duty in the park that year. (Farquhar: Benson. Heitman, 893.) Lt. McClure had the name on his 1896 map.

Smith Meadow *Lake Eleanor, Hetch Hetchy Reservoir*
Smith Peak (7,751) *Hetch Hetchy Reservoir*

"Hetch-Hetchy is claimed by a sheep-owner, named Smith, who drives stock into it every summer, by a trail which was built by Joseph Screech. It is often called Smith's Valley." (John Muir in *Overland Monthly*, July 1873: 49–50.) Cyril C. Smith, originally from Maine, built a cabin in the meadow in 1885. (*SCB* 36, no. 5, May 1951: 64.)

Charles F. Hoffmann wrote that he traveled up the Tuolumne River via Hardin's Rancho to Cottonwood Creek and "ascended the highest peak from which I had an unobstructed view up the Tuolumne Cañon." He called the peak "Cottonwood Peak." (Hoffmann letter to J. D. Whitney, Sept. 10, 1873, in Hoffmann correspondence, BL.) That name appeared on the Wheeler Survey atlas sheet 56D, 1878–79, and on LeConte's, McClure's, and Benson's maps from 1893 to 1896. In 1896 a BGN decision changed the name to Smith Peak, and it appeared that way on the first *Yosemite* 30' map, 1897. The name "Smiths Meadow" first appeared on McClure's 1895 map.

Smith did quite well for himself. He wound up owning 500 acres in and adjacent to the floor of Hetch Hetchy Valley, and another 800 acres in Tiltill Valley, at Hog Ranch, and at two other nearby locations. In 1908, during San Francisco's political drive to get control of Hetch Hetchy for a reservoir, Smith sold all of his property to the city of San Francisco for $150,000. (YRL files.)

Smoky Jack Campground *Hetch Hetchy Reservoir*

John Muir encountered Smoky Jack in the spring of 1869. ". . . one of the sheep-men of the neighborhood, Mr. John Connell, nicknamed Smoky Jack, begged me to take care of one of his bands of sheep . . . . Smoky Jack was known far and wide, and I soon learned that he was a queer character. . . . He lived mostly on beans. In the morning after his bean breakfast he filled his pockets from the pot with dripping beans for luncheon, which he ate in handfuls as he followed the flock. His overalls and boots soon . . . became thoroughly saturated, and instead of wearing thin, wore thicker and stouter, and by sitting down to rest from time to time, parts of all the vegetation, leaves, petals, etc., were embedded in them, together with wool fibers, butterfly wings, mica crystals, fragments of nearly everything that the world contained—rubbed in, embedded and coarsely stratified, so that these wonderful garments grew to have a rich geological and biological significance . . . ." (Badè, vol. 1, 195–96.)

Snake Meadow *Devils Postpile, Cattle Mtn.*

Origin unknown, but it doesn't sound like a place for rolling around in the grass. The name first appeared on the *Devils Postpile* quad, 1953. The meadow is in Sierra National Forest, a mile east of Sheep Crossing; it was within the park from 1890 to 1905.

Snow Canyon *Devils Postpile, Cattle Mtn., Crystal Crag*

An old name, origin unknown. It was called "Snow Cañon" as early as 1893. (*Eleventh Report*, 219.) The canyon is in Inyo National Forest, but it was within the park from 1890 to 1905.

Snow Creek *Hetch Hetchy Reservoir, Tuolumne Meadows*
Snow Creek Falls *Hetch Hetchy Reservoir*
Snow Flat *Tuolumne Meadows*

The creek was called "Glacier Brook" on the King and Gardiner map of 1865. "This stream was called Glacier Brook, from the abundant traces of former glacial action in its vicinity." (Whitney, *The Yosemite Guide-Book*, 1870: 117.) John Muir called it "Dome Creek" in 1869. (Muir, *First Summer*, 200.) It was "Glacier Brook" on the Wheeler Survey atlas sheet 56D, 1878–79, and on the map of Yosemite Valley, 1883. On Lt. McClure's 1896 map it was called "Hoffman Creek," since it flows out of May Lake, just southeast of Mount Hoffmann. Its present name was ratified by a BGN decision in 1896. It appeared on the first *Yosemite* 30' map, 1897, but the name apparently was in common use before that. (*Homer Mining Index*, July 28, 1883; Hutchings, *In the Heart*, 480.)

The name "Snow's Flat" was on LeConte's 1893 map; it became "Snow Flat" on McClure's 1895 map and all subsequent maps. The name for the falls was ratified by the BGN in 1932, and first appeared on the *Hetch Hetchy Reservoir* quad, 1956.

Snow Peak (10,950) *Tower Peak*

An old, obvious name; the namer is unknown. The name was on the first *Dardanelles* 30' map, 1898.

Snyder: Gulch, Ridge   *El Portal*

John W. Snyder homesteaded 160 acres in sec. 15, T. 4 S., R. 19 E. in 1885. The area is in Sierra National Forest; it was within the park from 1890 to 1905.

Soda Springs   *Tuolumne Meadows*

"The Soda Springs cover quite an extensive area, and have a copious flow of water, which, at the time of our visit, July, 1863, had a temperature of 46° to 47°, resembling in taste that of the 'Congress Spring,' at Saratoga." (Whitney, *Geology*, 428.)

Hoffmann and Gardiner's map of 1863–67 showed "Soda Spr." McClure's maps of 1895 and 1896 had it as "Lamberts Soda Spring." The name was omitted from the last two editions of the *Mt. Lyell* 30′ map, 1948 and 1950, but was reinstated with publication of the *Tuolumne Meadows* quad, 1956.

Soda Springs   *Devils Postpile, Mammoth Mtn.*

". . . Soda Springs Meadows, so named from several very strong alkaline springs, containing a large percentage of gas." (*Eleventh Report*, 219.)

The springs are about 0.3 mile north of Devils Postpile. The name has been on maps since Lt. McClure's map of 1895. It was omitted from the *Devils Postpile* quad, but reappeared on the *Mammoth Mtn.* quad, 1984. The springs are in Devils Postpile National Monument; they were within the park from 1890 to 1905.

Soldier Lake (10,624)   *Matterhorn Peak*

The origin is uncertain, but probably named for soldiers of the US Army, which administered Yosemite National Park from 1890 until creation of the National Park Service in 1916. The name is on the first *Bridgeport* 30′ map, 1911, which was surveyed between 1905 and 1909.

Soldier Meadow   *Merced Peak, Devils Postpile, Cattle Mtn.*

The meadow was the site of a patrol camp during the years when the US Army administered Yosemite National Park. (YRL files.) It was called "Little Jackass Meadow" on the first four editions of the *Mt. Lyell* 30′ map, 1901 to 1914, and was changed to the present name on the 1922 edition. McClure's maps and LeConte's 1900 map had the older name. The meadow is in Sierra National Forest, but was within the park from 1890 to 1905.

Sotcher Lake (7,616)   *Devils Postpile, Mammoth Mtn., Crystal Crag*

Named for "Red" Sotcher. (See **Reds Meadow**, etc.) The name was spelled as it is now on McClure's map of 1896, LeConte's map of 1900, and the first five editions of the *Mt. Lyell* 30′ map, 1901–1922. It was changed to "Satcher" from 1927 to 1950, and back again to "Sotcher" on the *Devils Postpile* quad, 1953. The change to "Satcher" apparently was due to that spelling being used in Farquhar's *Place Names* (1926) on the authority of W. A. Chalfant. The USGS investigated further, and stated that "Sotcher" is correct. (USGS quad report, 1953.)

Spano Meadow   *Devils Postpile, Cattle Mtn.*

Origin unknown. The name appeared on the *Cattle Mtn.* quad, 1983. To locate it on the *Devils Postpile* quad: it is 1.4 miles south-southwest of Iron Mountain, just west of the trail. The meadow is in Sierra National Forest, but was within the park from 1890 to 1905.

Spiller: Creek, Lake (10,696)   *Matterhorn Peak*

J. Calvert Spiller was a topographical assistant with Lt. Macomb's field party of the Wheeler Survey in 1878 and 1879. (In *SCB* 10, no. 3, Jan. 1918, there is a photo opposite p. 369 of the record of an ascent of Mount Conness made by Macomb, Spiller, and J. H. Morgan, the party's meteorologist.) The name "Spiller's Cañon" is on atlas sheet 56D. "Spiller Creek" is on Lt. McClure's sketch map of 1894. (*SCB* 1, no. 5, Jan. 1895: 173.) On his 1896 map McClure has "Spiller or Randall Canon." (Randall is not identified, but may have been a sheepman. McClure also used the name in *SCB* 1, no. 8, May 1896: 330.) Both the creek and the lake were named on the first *Bridgeport* 30′ map, 1911.

Spillway Lake   *Mono Craters*

Origin unknown, but one might hazard a guess that the lake's inlet stream from Helen Lake resembles a spillway—or that early season runoff from melting snow coming down steep cliffs south of the lake is what occasioned the name, which first appeared on this quad, in 1953.

Split Pinnacle   *Yosemite Valley, Yosemite*

The name came into use among Sierra Club climbers in the 1930s. (USGS.) It appeared on the *Yosemite* quad, 1956. Split Pinnacle is on the north side of the valley, between the Three Brothers and El Capitan.

Spotted Fawn Lake *Pinecrest*

Obviously someone spotted a spotted fawn here, but the namer is not known. The name first shows up on the *Pinecrest* quad, 1956.

Spotted Lakes *Merced Peak*

A cluster of five small lakes at the headwaters of the South Fork of the Merced River, possibly named because of their spotty appearance on the map. (YRL files.) The name was ratified by the BGN in 1932, and appeared on the ninth edition of the *Mt. Lyell* 30' map, 1948.

Spuller Lake *Tuolumne Meadows*

Everett Spuller named it for himself in 1932. "Al [Gardisky] did not know a lake was there, and I was the first one ever to plant it." (Spuller.) The lake is in Inyo National Forest a mile east of the park's boundary; it was in the park from 1890 to 1905.

Squirrel Creek *Yosemite*

A very short creek flowing into the South Fork of the Merced River about two miles below Wawona. Origin unknown, although we can be certain that no squirrel named it for himself. The name was not on any map prior to publication of the *Yosemite* quad, 1956.

Staircase Falls *Yosemite Valley, Yosemite*

A series of small falls on the south valley wall back of Curry Village. The falls have a total drop of 1,300 feet down a succession of rock ledges, giving the appearance of a large staircase. The namer is unknown; the name is first seen on the fourth edition of the *Yosemite Valley* map, 1927.

Stairway: Creek, Meadow *Devils Postpile, Cattle Mtn.*

These features obviously were named from the Granite Stairway, which was named in the early 1890s or before. The creek, a tributary of the Middle Fork of the San Joaquin, was named on the first *Mt. Lyell* 30' map, 1901. The name for the meadow appeared on the *Devils Postpile* quad, 1953. Although in Sierra National Forest, both features were within the park from 1890 to 1905.

Stanford Lakes *Merced Peak*

A misspelled name. The lakes were named in the late teens or early twenties by Billy Brown, a local packer, for the Kenneth J. *Staniford* family of Fresno. (Letter from Barton A. Brown, M.D., November 7, 1983.)

Although now in Sierra National Forest, the lakes were in the park from 1890 to 1905.

Stanford Point   *Yosemite Valley, Yosemite Valley,*
Named for Leland Stanford (1824–1893), one of the "Big Four" who built the Central Pacific Railroad; governor of California, 1862–63; US Senator, 1885–93; founder of Stanford University, 1891. The name appeared on the first USGS *Yosemite Valley* map, 1907.

Stanton Peak (11,695)   *Matterhorn Peak*
Origin unknown, but it may have been named for an army officer by Major W. W. Forsyth, acting superintendent of the park from 1909 to 1912. A possibility is William Stanton (1843–1927), who was a colonel in the Sixth Cavalry when Forsyth was a captain. (Heitman, 916.) The name is on the first *Bridgeport* 30' map, 1911. The peak is in the northeast part of the park at the headwaters of Return Creek.

Starkweather Lake   *Devils Postpile, Mammoth Mtn.*
Along the road to Devils Postpile; named for a prospector who had claims on the slopes above the lake. He was referred to by some as "the human gopher." (Smith, 13.) The name was first used on the *Devils Postpile* quad, 1953. The lake is in Inyo National Forest, but was within the park from 1890 to 1905.

Starr King, Mount (9,092)   *Yosemite Valley, Yosemite*
Starr King Meadow   *Yosemite Valley, Yosemite, Merced Peak*
Starr King Lake   *Yosemite*
Thomas Starr King (1824–1864), famous preacher and lecturer; pastor of the Hollis Street Unitarian Church in Boston at age twenty-four; came to San Francisco Unitarian Church, 1860; visited Yosemite, the Big Trees, and Lake Tahoe; orator for the Union cause during the Civil War. The dome-shaped mountain was named "King's Peak" in 1862. (*Mariposa Gazette*, Sept. 17, 1864.) The present form of the name was on Hoffmann and Gardiner's map, 1863–67.
In May 1862 the Brewer party of the Whitney Survey gave the name "Mount King" to the northeast peak of Mount Diablo, in Contra Costa County; it is now simply named "North Peak." Brewer characterized King as "the most eloquent divine and, at the same time, one of the best fellows in the state." (Brewer, *Up and Down*, 263, 267.)
The meadow was named on the first USGS *Yosemite Valley* map, 1907.

François Matthes used the name two years before that, and quite likely was the namer. (Matthes, v. 9, Oct. 8, 1905.)

John Muir used the name "Starr King Lake" long before the lake was named on maps. (*Scribner's Monthly*, Jan. 1879: 418.) The lake was named "Helen Lake" on the *Yosemite Valley* map from 1918 to 1929, "Starr King Lake" in 1938 and 1947, no name at all on the editions of 1949 and 1958, and back to its present name again beginning with the 1970 edition. "A former lake, now a mosquito-infested swamp." (YRL files.)

Steelhead Lake   *Tuolumne Meadows*
Al Gardisky planted steelhead trout in the lake in 1929 and 1930, and named it in 1932. (Spuller.) The lake is in Inyo National Forest, but was within the park from 1890 to 1905.

Stevenson Meadow   *Devils Postpile, Mt. Ritter*
Origin unknown; at the headwaters of the North Fork of the San Joaquin. The name appeared on the *Devils Postpile* quad, 1953. The meadow is in Sierra National Forest, but was in the park from 1890 to 1905.

Stoneman: Meadow, Bridge   *Yosemite Valley*
The Stoneman House, a four-story hotel built by the state of California in 1885, was named for the then-governor, George Stoneman, and was located at the east end of the meadow. It burned in 1896. (*YNN* 34, no. 1, Jan. 1955: 17.) The meadow was first named on the third *Yosemite Valley* map, 1922.

Straube Lake   *Devils Postpile, Cattle Mtn.*
Origin unknown. The name appeared on the *Cattle Mtn.* quad, 1983. It is a small lake at the headwaters of Cargyle Creek, 1.6 miles southwest of Iron Mountain. Although in Sierra National Forest, it was in the park from 1890 to 1905.

Strawberry Creek   *Yosemite*
A short tributary of the South Fork of the Merced, crossed by the Wawona Road about two miles south of Chinquapin. The origin of the name is unknown, but undoubtedly it is for wild strawberries in the vicinity. The name first appeared on the *Yosemite* quad, 1956.

Stubblefield Canyon   *Tower Peak*
The name was first used by Lt. McClure on his explorations in 1894, and is probably the name of an early sheepman. (*SCB* 1, no. 5, Jan. 1895:

179, sketch map; also *SCB* 1, no. 8, May 1896: 330–32.) The name has been on all maps since that time.

Suicide Ridge   *Matterhorn Peak*

Origin unknown. Lt. McClure crossed the ridge in 1894, but used no name for it. The name appeared on the first *Bridgeport* 30′ map, 1911.

Sullivan Lake   *Devils Postpile, Mt. Ritter*

Origin unknown. The name appeared on the *Devils Postpile* quad, 1953. The lake is in Inyo National Forest, but was in the park from 1890 to 1905.

Summit Lake   *Matterhorn Peak*

"Summit Lake" is one of the more obvious and overused of names. Any time there is a lake at or near the summit of something, that's the name the unimaginative will bestow. There are twenty-three Summit Lakes in California. This one was referred to as "Castle Lake" by Lt. McClure in 1894. (*SCB* 1, no. 5, Jan. 1895: 171.) That name may have been given by sheepmen, and perhaps was derived from "Castle Peak," an early name for nearby Dunderberg Peak.

The lake is at the headwaters of Green Creek, which flows northeast. The present name was on the first *Bridgeport* 30′ map, 1911. Although just outside the park boundary, the lake was within the park from 1890 to 1905.

Summit Lake   *Mono Craters*

At the summit of Mono Pass, on the long-used route of the Mono Trail across the Sierra. The namer is unknown; the name appeared on the *Mono Craters* quad, 1953.

Summit Meadow (9,020)   *Devils Postpile, Crystal Crag*

The namer of this meadow is unknown. It is at the summit northeast of Granite Stairway on the trail from Soldier Meadow to Devils Postpile. The name is first used on the *Devils Postpile* quad, 1953. Although in Sierra National Forest, the meadow was in the park from 1890 to 1905.

Sunrise: Mountain (9,974), Lakes   *Tuolumne Meadows*
Sunrise Creek   *Tuolumne Meadows, Yosemite, Merced Peak*

The origin of this name is unknown, and one can only guess that the namer may have been going up the creek toward the sunrise or saw the rising sun strike the mountaintop. Circumstantial evidence indicates that the name arose in the 1890s. None of the names is on LeConte's 1893 map.

But the mountain is named on Lt. McClure's 1895 map, and both the mountain and the creek are on his 1896 map. The lakes were first named on the *Tuolumne Meadows* quad, 1956.

Superior Lake (2,852 m.)   *Devils Postpile, Mt. Ritter*
Origin unknown. The name appeared on the *Devils Postpile* quad, 1953. It is about 2.7 miles west of Devils Postpile National Monument on the trail to Beck Lakes. Although in Inyo National Forest, it was in the park from 1890 to 1905.

Surprise Lake   *Matterhorn Peak*
Just half a mile north of Smedberg Lake, this lake will indeed surprise you: it is well hidden by the terrain, and you can't tell it's there until you arrive at it. Undoubtedly the first to be surprised were those who surveyed the *Bridgeport* 30' map from 1905 to 1909; the name is on the first edition, 1911. No maps prior to that even show a lake existing in this spot.

Swamp Lake   *Lake Eleanor*
Origin unknown. A small lake about two miles west of Hetch Hetchy Reservoir. The name was ratified by the BGN in 1932, but it was not on a map until publication of the *Lake Eleanor* quad, 1956.

Swamp Lake   *Merced Peak*
Origin unknown. A tiny lake 0.2 mile west of the Chiquito Trail crossing of the South Fork of the Merced River at Gravelly Ford. Since the name first appeared on Lt. McClure's 1895 map, it may well have been given that year by McClure's exploring party.

Table Lake   *Hetch Hetchy Reservoir*
Named by the Bright family, who ran cattle in this vicinity in the 1880s —before the national park was created. (Snyder.) The lake is in a flat area, and I assume that that accounts for the name. It first appeared on Lt. McClure's 1895 map.

Taft Point   *Yosemite Valley, Yosemite*
Named by R. B. Marshall, USGS, for William Howard Taft (1857–1930), twenty-seventh president of the United States, 1909–13, and chief justice of the Supreme Court, 1921–30. (Farquhar: Marshall.) Taft visited the park in the fall of 1909. The point is on the south rim of the valley near Profile Cliff and The Fissures. It is reached by an easy trail from the Glacier Point Road. The name appeared on the *Yosemite Valley* map in 1918.

Tallulah Lake   *Matterhorn Peak*

David Brower speculated that the lake may have been named for Tallulah LeConte. (Gudde, *Place Names*, 330.) Several of the features in this area were named in 1895 by Lt. H. C. Benson; one would like to know the names of his female relatives. The lake is named on the first *Bridgeport 30'* map, 1911.

Tamarack Flat   *Hetch Hetchy Reservoir*
Tamarack Creek   *Hetch Hetchy Reservoir, Yosemite*

The flat was named by Lafayette H. Bunnell in 1856 when he and others were blazing a trail from Coulterville to Yosemite Valley. "Going from this camp [Crane Flat], we came to what I finally called 'Tamarack Flat,' although the appealing looks of the grizzlies we met on their way through this pass to the Tuolumne, caused me to hesitate before deciding upon the final baptism . . . ." (Bunnell, *Discovery*, 1911: 321.) Bunnell used the common but incorrect name for the lodgepole pine, *Pinus contorta* var. *latifolia*.

"The flat is named after the two-leaved pine, common here, especially around the cool margin of the meadow." (Muir, *First Summer*, 131.) "Tamarack Creek is icy cold, delicious, exhilarating champagne water. It is flowing bank full in the meadow with silent speed. . . ." (Ibid., 133.)

"Dense, dark, desolate; trees with black-seamed bark, straight and branchless, unloving and grim, up to the very tops; and even the tops did not seem to blend, though they shut out the sky. A strange ancient odor filled the air, as from centuries of distilling essence of resins, and mouldering dust of spices." (Jackson, 167.)

Ten Lakes   *Hetch Hetchy Reservoir*

"A glacier basin with ten glassy lakes set all near together like eggs in a nest." (John Muir, letter to Mrs. Carr, October 8, 1872, in Badè, vol. 1, 344.) The name first appears on a small map in Whitney, *Yosemite Guide-Book*, pocket edition, 1874. The name "Ten Lakes Pass"—for where the Ten Lakes Trail crosses the ridge and the county line south of Colby Mountain —was ratified by the BGN in 1932, but it is not on the maps.

Tenaya: Lake (8,149), **Peak** (10,301)   *Tuolumne Meadows*
Tenaya Creek
        Tuolumne Meadows, Hetch Hetchy Reservoir, Yosemite, Yosemite Valley
Tenaya Canyon   *Yosemite Valley*

Lafayette H. Bunnell of the Mariposa Battalion named the lake on May 22, 1851. "Looking back to the lovely little lake, where we had been encamped during the night, and watching Ten-ie-ya as he ascended to our group, I suggested . . . that we name the lake after the old chief, and call it 'Lake Ten-ie-ya'. . . . At first, he seemed unable to comprehend our purpose, and pointing to the group of glistening peaks, near the head of the lake, said: 'It already has a name; we call it Py-we-ack.' Upon my telling him that we had named it Ten-ie-ya, because it was upon the shores of the lake that we had found his people, who would never return to it to live, his countenance fell and he at once left our group and joined his own family circle. His countenance as he left us indicated that he thought the naming of the lake no equivalent for the loss of his territory." (Bunnell, *Discovery*, 1880: 236–37.) In 1855 the guide of one of Yosemite's first tourist parties, knowing of the lake's existence but not its name, referred to it as "Yo-Semity Lake." (*San Joaquin Republican*, Oct. 16, 1855.)

"The Ten-ie-ya Cañon was known as Py-we-ack, meaning the stream of the glistening rocks, from the dazzling brightness of the glacial ground peaks at Lake Ten-ie-ya, its source." (Bunnell, *Report*, 11. See **Pywiack: Cascade, Dome**.) The name "Tenaya Cañon" was used as early as *Bancroft's Tourist Guide*, 1871: 41.

In 1870 Joseph LeConte put an 'eternal' name on Tenaya Peak—but it didn't last long. "Looking back from the trail soon after leaving the lake, we saw a conspicuous and very picturesque peak with a vast amphitheater, with precipitous sides, to the north, filled with a grand mass of snow . . . . We called this *Coliseum Peak*. So let it be called hereafter, to the end of time." (LeConte, *Ramblings*, 76–77.) That name did not appear on maps. The Wheeler Survey atlas sheet 56D, 1878–79, had the name "Tenaiya Cliff" for the peak. J. N. LeConte had "Tenaya Pk." on his 1893 map, as did Solomons on his 1896 map. The name didn't appear again after that until the fifth edition of the *Mt. Lyell* 30' map, 1922.

The Hoffmann and Gardiner map of 1863–67 had "L. Tenaya" and "Tenaya Fork." The Wheeler Survey map of the valley, 1883, used the name "Ten-ai-ya Creek."

Thompson Canyon   *Tower Peak, Matterhorn Peak*
Apparently named by Lt. McClure in 1894, but he didn't say for whom; perhaps a sheepman, or someone in his command. (*SCB* 1, no. 5, Jan. 1895: 186.) A possibility is that the name is for John Taliaferro Thompson, a West Point classmate of Lt. H. C. Benson. (Heitman, 957.)

Thousand Island Lake (9,834)   *Devils Postpile, Mt. Ritter*
Almost, but not quite, named by Theodore S. Solomons in 1892. "Next morning we passed down the slope of the mountain to the lake, with its

hundred islets . . . ." (*SCB* 1, no. 2, Jan. 1894: 70.) John Muir called it "Islet Lake" in 1872. (*Scribner's Monthly*, July 1880: 350.)

The name first appears on Lt. McClure's 1895 map. The lake is in Inyo National Forest, but was in the park from 1890 to 1905.

Courtesy The Bancroft Library

The Three Brothers. "Mountains Playing Leap Frog."
Photograph by Muybridge.

Three Brothers; Middle Brother; Lower Brother

Yosemite Valley, Yosemite

"These remarkable peaks were so named by the writer from their number coinciding with the three brothers captured by us while hidden among the rocks of the peaks. Young Ten-ie-ya, a son of the chief, was subsequently killed while attempting to escape." (Bunnell, *Report*, 10.)

"I soon learned that they were called by the Indians 'Kom-po-pai-zes,' from a fancied resemblance of the peaks to the heads of frogs when sitting up *ready to leap*. A fanciful interpretation has been given the Indian name as meaning 'mountains playing leap-frog,' but a literal translation is not desirable." (Bunnell, *Discovery*, 1911: 152.) What Bunnell is trying to say, without offending delicate sensibilities, is that the Indian name had a sexual meaning. Take a look at the Three Brothers again, and you'll get the idea.

". . . three points which the Indians know as 'Eleacha,' named after a plant much used for food, but which some lackadaisical person has given the commonplace name of 'The Three Brothers.'" (Hutchings, *Scenes*, 1860: 94.)

"The common idea is that the Indians imagined the mountains to be playing 'Leap Frog.' It would remain, in that case, to show that the Indians practiced that, to us, familiar game; we have never caught them at it." (Whitney, *The Yosemite Book*, 17.)

A third Indian name was also advanced. "*Wawhawke*. The Three Brothers; said to mean 'falling rocks.'" (Whitney, *Yosemite Guide-Book*, 1870: 16. See also **Rocky Point**.) The name "Three Brothers" is on King and Gardiner's map of 1865.

"The finest example of asymmetric sculpture called forth by oblique master joints is presented by the massif of the Three Brothers. Its three successive roofs slant with architectural regularity, all at a uniform angle, because they are determined by joint planes having the same westerly dip." (Matthes, *Paper 160*, 110.)

Tilden: Lake, Creek, Canyon, Canyon Creek   *Tower Peak*

The origin of the "Tilden" name is not known. It was first used by Lt. McClure in 1894. (*SCB* 1, no. 5, Jan. 1895: 179, 182.) On his 1895 map he had the lake named, and also "Tilden Cañon" for the creek above and below the lake. The latter was what is now Tilden Creek. The present Tilden Canyon is on a different stream: Tilden Canyon Creek, which originates half a mile south of Tilden Lake, has no connection with the lake or with Tilden Creek, and flows south into Rancheria Creek. These four names were ratified by the BGN, in their present positions, in 1932. The names of the two creeks appeared on the sixth edition of the *Dardanelles* 30' map, 1947.

On Hoffmann's map of 1873 the lake is called "Lake Nina," a name probably given by Hoffmann and Alfred Craven in 1870 when they made the first ascent of Tower Peak. Nina Florence Browne, Hoffmann's sister-in-law, married Craven in 1871.

Tiltill Valley   *Hetch Hetchy Reservoir*
Tiltill Creek   *Tower Peak, Hetch Hetchy Reservoir*
Tiltill Mountain (9,005)   *Tower Peak*

Eugene M. Elwell homesteaded 160 acres in sections. 5 and 6, T. 1 N., R. 21 E. in 1887—all of Tiltill Valley. The valley was said to have been named by Elwell. (Farquhar files: Versteeg from Col. Benson.) The meaning of the name is unknown. Lt. McClure had the valley named on his 1895 map, and added the creek's name to his 1896 map. The mountain's name was ratified by the BGN in 1932; it is first seen on the *Tower Peak* quad, 1956.

Timber: Knob (9,945), **Creek**   *Merced Peak*

A descriptive name for—guess what—a timbered knob, apparently given by Lt. McClure in 1895. (*SCB* 1, no. 8, May 1896: 333.) It was on his map of 1896. The creek's name, obviously derived from the knob, appeared on the first *Mt. Lyell* 30' map, 1901. These features are in Sierra National Forest, but were in the park from 1890 to 1905.

Tioga: Pass (9,945), **Crest**   *Tuolumne Meadows*
Tioga Peak (11,513)   *Mono Craters*
Tioga Lake (9,651)   *Tuolumne Meadows, Mono Craters*

Tioga is an Iroquois name meaning "where it forks" (Farquhar), "at the forks," "swift current," or "a gate." (Gannett, 253). The name has been preserved in counties, towns, and a river in Pennsylvania and New York.

The Tioga Mining District was organized in 1878, and one can only assume that one or more of the promoters was from Pennsylvania or New York. The Tioga Mine was known as "The Sheepherder" when it was located in 1860. The site marked "Bennettville" on the *Tuolumne Meadows* quad was briefly called "Tioga," and had a post office under that name from May 1880 to June 1881. (*Post Offices*, 222.)

Before the "Tioga" name became rampant, the pass was called "MacLane's Pass" (Whitney, *Geology*, 434), and also "McLean Pass" (*Homer Mining Index*, Jan. 12, 1884. See **McLean Pass** in the Old Names section.) Tioga Lake was originally named "Lake Jessie," for Jessie Montrose of Lundy. (YRL files.) Both the pass and the lake had their present names on Lt. McClure's 1895 map.

Tioga Crest had an early name of "Mount Warren Ridge." (Russell, *100 Years*, 131; also *SCB* 13, no. 1, Feb. 1928: 45.) The crest was the route of the "summer trail" between Tioga (Bennettville) and Lundy. (*Homer Mining Index*, Dec. 10, 1881.) The name "Tioga Hill" was once used for Gaylor Peak and, in general, the ridge west of Bennettville and the Great Sierra

Mine tunnel. (Ibid., Oct. 1, 1881.) And lastly, "Tioga Meadows" was an early name for Dana Meadows—the long meadows running south from Tioga Pass.

The Tioga Road, first known as "The Great Sierra Wagon Road," was built in 1882 and 1883. Tioga Pass is on the park's eastern boundary. The other "Tioga" features are in Inyo National Forest.

Tower Peak (11,755)   *Tower Peak*

"I recognized also several other well known peaks, one of which was a lofty castellated peak south of the Sonora and Walker River Immigrant Road, named the Castle Peak, and whose position I had determined when on the Railway Exploration under Lieut. Moore, U.S.A., in 1853." (Goddard, *Report*, 101.)

"The grand mass of Tower Peak is a prominent and most remarkably picturesque object. This is one of the three points in the Sierra to which the name of 'Castle Peak' has been given, and is the first and original one of that name, having been called so by Mr. G. H. Goddard. . . . By some unaccountable mistake the name was transferred to a rounded, and not at all castellated, mass about eighteen miles a little south of east from the original 'Castle Peak,' where it has become firmly fixed. Hence we have been obliged to give a new name to Mr. Goddard's peak, which we now call 'Tower Peak.'" (Whitney, *Yosemite Guide-Book*, 1874: 131–32.) The Wheeler Survey atlas sheet 56D, 1878–79, had the peak correctly located and named with the one word "Tower."

Townsley Lake   *Tuolumne Meadows*

Forest Sanford Townsley (1882–1943), chief ranger in the park from 1916 until his death. The lake was named for him when he planted golden trout in it. Before then it was called "Upper Fletcher Lake," a name now applied to the next lake downstream from Townsley Lake. (Bingaman, *Guardians*, 88–89; obituary in *YNN* 22, no. 9, Sept. 1943: 75.)

Tressider Peak (over 10,560)   *Tuolumne Meadows*

Donald B. Tressider, husband of Mary Curry Tressider, was president of the Yosemite Park & Curry Co., 1925–48, and president of Stanford University, 1943–48. During Tressider's reign as head of the Curry Company, he built the Ahwahnee Hotel, the cafeteria and dining room at Camp Curry, and the Big Trees Lodge in the Mariposa Grove. He was also responsible for beginning a skiing program in Yosemite and for constructing the High Sierra Camps. The peak was named in 1958, ten years after his death. (BGN decision, 1959.) The peak is not named on the first edition of the *Tuolumne Meadows* quad, 1956. It is one half mile southwest of Cathedral Pass, in section 23.

Trinity Lakes   *Devils Postpile, Mammoth Mtn.*
Origin unknown; the name appeared on the *Devils Postpile* quad, 1953. There are six small lakes just east of the John Muir Trail, about halfway between Devils Postpile and Shadow Lake. Although in Inyo National Forest, the lakes were in the park from 1890 to 1905.

Triple Divide Peak (11,607); **Triple Peak Fork**   *Merced Peak*
The peak, which was named in 1895 by Lt. McClure, indeed marks the headwaters of three streams: the Merced River, the South Fork of the Merced, and the North Fork of the San Joaquin. (*SCB* 1, no. 8, May 1896: 334.) The name appears on McClure's 1896 map. The fork probably was named by the USGS during the 1898–99 survey for the *Mt. Lyell* 30′ map; the name is on the first edition, 1901. A 1978 BGN decision altered the fork's official name to "Triple Peak Fork Merced River."

Trumbull Peak (5,004)   *El Portal*
"Known earlier as 'Cranberry Mountain,' it was named after a Senator Trumbull at an undisclosed date when he and his party visited Yosemite National Park." (Hartesveldt, YRL files.) This probably refers to Lyman Trumbull (1813–1896), US Senator from Illinois, 1855–73. The name was submitted by the USGS to the BGN in 1896, and approved in 1897. Lt. McClure had the name on his maps of 1895 and 1896. Although in Stanislaus National Forest, it was in the park from 1890 to 1905.

Tueeulala Falls   *Lake Eleanor*
"Its Indian name is *Tu-ee-u-lá-la.* . . . From the brow of the cliff it leaps, clear and free, for a thousand feet; then half disappears in a rage of spattering cascades among the bowlders of an earthquake talus." (John Muir, "Hetch-Hetchy Valley," *Overland Monthly*, July 1873: 46.) There is no explanation of what the name means. Despite its early use by Muir, the name did not get onto a map until publication of the *Lake Eleanor* quad in 1956. Perhaps it is a generic name. See **Timalula** in the Indian Names list.

Tuolumne River   *Tuolumne Meadows, Hetch Hetchy Reservoir, Lake Eleanor*
Tuolumne: Meadows, Peak (10,845), **Falls, Pass**   *Tuolumne Meadows*
Tuolumne Grove   *Lake Eleanor*
The name is from a tribe of Indians that lived on the banks of the lower Tuolumne and Stanislaus rivers, in the vicinity of Knights Ferry.

(Kroeber, 64.) The tribe was called *Taulámne*—and also *Tahualamne*—by Padre Muñoz. (Arch. MSB, vol. 4, Oct. 3, 1906, ff.) The Moraga-Muñoz party named the Tuolumne River the *Dolores,* from the time of its discovery, October 1, the "Dolores of September," but that name did not prevail.

Frémont and Preuss, on their 1845 map, mistakenly called the Tuolumne River the "Rio de los Merced." On their 1848 map, they corrected it to "R. d. l. Towalumnes." The modern spelling is on Derby's 1849 map. It is said that the Indians pronounced the word *Tu-ah-lum'-ne.* (Sanchez, 222.)

The Whitney Survey named Tuolumne Meadows; the name is on Hoffmann and Gardiner's map, 1863–67. The falls was initially called "Lower Virginia Falls" by the Whitney Survey (Whitney, *Yosemite Guide-Book,* 1874: 155), but had its present name on Hoffmann's 1873 map. The peak was first named on the Wheeler Survey atlas sheet 56D, 1878–79, and the pass on Lt. McClure's 1896 map. The grove had its name at least as early as the mid-1880s. (Hutchings, *In the Heart,* 327.) LeConte's map of 1900 had the name "Tuolumne Big Trees" for Tuolumne Grove. The present name was ratified by the BGN in 1932, but did not appear on a USGS map until the *Lake Eleanor* quad, 1956.

Turner Lake   *Merced Peak*

Named for Henry Ward Turner (1857–1937), USGS, who pioneered some of the early geologic studies and mapping in the Sierra Nevada, in the 1890s, with especial reference to the origin of Yosemite Valley—which he erroneously believed to be mainly a stream-cut canyon rather than glacially formed. (Matthes, *Paper 160,* 5, 65.) The name was approved by the BGN in 1963.

Turner: Meadows, Ridge   *Yosemite*

Will Turner, grandfather of Arthur L. Gallison. (See **Gallison Lake**. Gallison was a park ranger for thirty-seven years.) Turner ran cattle in the area in the 1880s, before the creation of Yosemite National Park. (Bingaman, *Guardians,* 93.) The meadows was named on Lt. McClure's 1896 map, but after that, neither "Turner" name was on a map until publication of the *Yosemite* quad, 1956.

Turtleback Dome   *Yosemite Valley, Yosemite*

A descriptive name, probably given by either François E. Matthes or E. M. Douglas, the topographer and geographer of the first USGS *Yosemite Valley* map, published in 1907.

"Turtleback Dome is composed of sparsely and imperfectly jointed granite. The overriding Yosemite Glacier consequently found but few blocks that it could quarry away and confined itself to grinding and smoothing the rock mass. The sharp hackled edge is controlled wholly by vertical joints." (Matthes, *Paper 160*, plate 43; also p. 110.)

Twin Island Lakes (2,991 m. and 2,943 m.)   *Devils Postpile, Mt. Ritter*
The namer of these two distinctive—and appropriately named—lakes is unknown. Each lake has a single island. The lakes are two miles west of Mount Ritter, near the head of the North Fork of the San Joaquin. The name first appeared on the *Devils Postpile* quad, 1953. Although in Sierra National Forest, they were within the park from 1890 to 1905.

Twin Lake   *Tuolumne Meadows*
The correct name should be "Twin Lakes." These two ponds at the head of Mill Creek were named in 1932 by Al Gardisky. (Spuller.) The lakes are in Inyo National Forest, but were in the park from 1890 to 1905.

Twin Lakes   *Tower Peak*
The lakes are at the headwaters of Kendrick Creek, just inside the park's north boundary. The name probably was given by the USGS during the 1891–96 survey for the *Dardanelles* 30' map; it is on the first edition, 1898.

Twin Lakes   *Merced Peak*
The namer of these two small lakes is unknown. The name appeared on the *Merced Peak* quad, 1953. An abandoned trail passes between the lakes. Although in Sierra National Forest, they were in the park from 1890 to 1905.

Twin Peaks   *Matterhorn Peak*
Two adjacent, similar peaks on the park's northeast boundary about 1.5 miles southeast of Matterhorn Peak. The name probably was given by the Wheeler Survey; it is on atlas sheet 56D, 1878–79.

Two Teats (11,387)   *Devils Postpile, Mammoth Mtn.*
A descriptive name. Although it first appears on Lt. McClure's 1896 map, I would guess that it originates with early sheepmen or miners; it isn't the sort of naming that McClure did. The peaks are about three miles east of Garnet Lake, in Inyo National Forest; they were within the park from 1890 to 1905.

Unicorn: Peak (over 10,880), **Creek**   *Tuolumne Meadows*

The peak was named by the Whitney Survey in 1863. "A very prominent peak, with a peculiar horn-shaped outline, was called 'Unicorn Peak.'" (Whitney, *Geology*, 427.) But then Whitney added an apologetic footnote for the romantic/mythical name. "Names are frequently given to prominent objects, by parties like ours, for convenience; as where peaks are used for topographical stations. If not named, they would have to be numbered, which would be both awkward and inconvenient."

The creek was first named on Lt. McClure's 1895 map.

Union Point   *Yosemite Valley, Yosemite*

A viewpoint on the Four-Mile Trail, probably named when the trail was built, in 1871, or shortly thereafter. "Union" was a frequently used patriotic name during and after the Civil War. The present name was on the Wheeler Survey map of Yosemite Valley, 1883.

"On our way down we stopped for a few moments to rest on Union Point, half way between Glacier Point and the valley. Here we found an Irishman living in a sort of pine-plank wigwam, from the top of which waved the United States flag." (Jackson, 133.) The name was on *Yosemite Valley* maps from 1907 through 1970, but was deleted from the 1977 edition.

Valley View   *Yosemite Valley, Yosemite*

When coming up the valley from the west, this is the first place from which most of the valley can be seen. "Turning to the left . . . we find the magnificent Valley View from 'Enchantment Point'—Too-nu-yah. . . . There opens up before us one of the most charmingly impressive scenes that human eyes can look upon." (Hutchings, *In the Heart*, 400.)

The spot was called "River View" on the Wheeler Survey map of the valley, 1883. Although the present name is an old one, it did not appear on a map until the seventh edition of the *Yosemite Valley* sheet, 1947.

Vandeburg Lake   *Merced Peak*

Probably named by packer Billy Brown in the 1930s, for a Fresno physician whom he packed in to this area and whose name actually might have been Chester M. *Vanderburgh*. (Letters from Barton A. Brown, M.D., November 7, 1983, and November 11, 1987; *Fresno and Fresno County Directory*, 1925.) The name appeared on the *Merced Peak* quad, 1953. Although in Sierra National Forest, the lake was in the park from 1890 to 1905.

Courtesy The Bancroft Library

Vernal Fall. Photograph by Muybridge.

Vernal Fall   *Yosemite Valley, Yosemite*
   Named in 1851 by Lafayette Bunnell. "The Vernal Fall I so named because of the cool, vernal spray in contrast at midday with summer heat,

reminding me of an April shower, and because of the blue grass curiously growing among dark rocks and gay, dripping flowers, making it an eternal April to the ground. The Indian name is Yan-o-pah, meaning a little cloud, because of the spray through which the old trail passed, and because of the circular rainbow, nowhere else seen in the mountains." (Bunnell, *Report*, 12.)

"While gazing at its beauties, let us, now and forever, earnestly protest against the perpetuation of any other nomenclature to this wonder than *Pi-wy-ack*, the name which is given to it by the Indians, and means *a shower of sparkling crystals. . . .*" (Hutchings *Illustrated* 4, no. 6, Dec. 1859: 249.)

"Mr. Hutchings . . . has misstated the Indian name for this fall, furnished him by myself. . . . The name given by the Yosemites to the Ten-ie-ya branch of the Merced was unmistakably Py-we-ack. This name has been transferred from its original locality by some *romantic* preserver of Indian names. . . . It is indeed a laughable idea for me to even suppose a worm- and acorn-eating Indian would ever attempt to construct a name to mean *'a shower of sparkling crystals;'* his diet must have been improved by *modern* intelligent culture." (Bunnell, *Discovery*, 1911: 211.)

Vernon, Lake   *Tower Peak*

The lake was named sometime before 1879 by sheepmen, for one of their own. "After getting out of the cañon [Hetch Hetchy] on this route, by following a trail forking abruptly to the right, we reach in a few miles a very pretty sheet of water on Hetch-Hetchy Creek, called Lake Vernon by the sheep-owners, on whose range it is; this is the principal reservoir for the Hetch-Hetchy Fall." (Macomb, *Report*, 1879: 260.) Lt. McClure's sketch map of 1894 showed a cabin in the meadow just north of the lake. (*SCB* 1, no. 5, Jan. 1895: 182–86.) The lake was named on atlas sheet 56D, 1878–79.

Virginia Canyon   *Matterhorn Peak, Tuolumne Meadows*
Virginia: Pass, Peak (12,001)   *Matterhorn Peak*
Virginia Lake (9,230)   *Tuolumne Meadows*

The "Virginia" name probably originated among early miners from Virginia. Virginia Creek, in Inyo National Forest, was named on Hoffmann's map of 1873. The name then seems to have been carried across the ridge into what is now the national park; the Wheeler Survey atlas sheet 56D, 1878–79, has "Virginia Creek Trail" running up what is now named Cold Canyon.

The name obviously had a nice ring to surveyors, who were generous in its use. Lt. McClure had "Return or Virginia Canon" on his 1896 map, no doubt since this was the route to the Virginia Creek on the other side of the ridge. He also had the name "Vir. Pass," but placed it just east of Summit Lake rather than where it is now.

The name "Virginia Lake" appeared on the third edition of the *Mt. Lyell* 30' map, 1910. Virginia Peak was called "Red Peak" on the *Bridgeport* 30' maps. The Park Service recommended changing the name to "Virginia Peak," since there already was another "Red Peak" (in the Clark Range) within the park. (BGN decision, 1932.)

Vogelsang: Peak (11,516), **Lake** (10,341)   *Tuolumne Meadows*

Farquhar (*Place Names*, 99) stated that Col. Benson named these features for Alexander Theodore Vogelsang, president of the California State Board of Fish and Game Commissioners, 1896–1901. However, Charles Adolphus Vogelsang (a brother) wrote Farquhar that Benson named the peak for him, in 1907. He was the executive officer of Fish and Game, 1901–10, 1919–22. (Letter, Oct. 20, 1930, in Farquhar files.) "My recollection is that Col. Benson gave the name for ATV, but CAV may be right." (Farquhar files.) In 1932 the BGN ratified these names and also "Vogelsang Pass," which is generally known by that name but is not named on the map. It is half a mile south of Vogelsang Lake. Lt. McClure marked the pass "Real Pass" on his 1896 map. It should be noted that LeConte's map of 1900 has Vogelsang Lake named, which seems to be conclusive evidence that the features were named for Alexander.

"Although named for a man, the name is singularly fitting to the beautiful place; it means in older German 'a meadow in which birds sing.'" (Gudde, *Place Names*, 356.)

But it all depends on *which* bird sings. "My mind was exercising itself with conjectures as to the reason for the name of this peak and the lake lying under it,—Vogelsang. I was on the point of giving up the riddle when the strident voice of the Clarke crow, almost the only bird that inhabits these highest solitudes, gave me a clue, and I perceived that a spirit of irony had suggested the name." (Chase, 339.) Chase was referring to Clark's Nutcracker (*Nucifraga columbiána*), a bird with a raucous call, first described by William Clark of the Lewis and Clark Expedition. One wishes that this were the true origin of the name rather than that it had been named for a Fish and Game personage, no matter how worthy.

Volcanic Ridge   *Devils Postpile, Mt. Ritter*

A descriptive name, probably given by the USGS during the 1898–99 survey for the *Mt. Lyell* 30' map; it is on the first edition, 1901.

Volunteer Peak (10,479)   *Matterhorn Peak*
    See **Regulation Peak**.

Walker: Lake (7,935), **Creek**   *Mono Craters*
    William J. Walker patented 159 acres in secs. 6 and 7, T. 1 S., R. 26 E. in 1883—the land just east of the lake outlet. In 1869 John Muir called the lake "Moraine Lake," from "the large lateral moraines which extend out into the desert." (Muir, *First Summer*, 301.) But fifteen years later the name "Walker's Lake" was in common use. (*Homer Mining Index*, Aug. 23, 1884.) Muir also named the creek "Cañon Creek," because it flowed down through Bloody Canyon, which was already named. (*Overland Monthly*, Sept. 1874, 272–73.) The lake had its present name on LeConte's map of 1893, and the creek's name appeared on the first *Mt. Lyell* 30' map, 1901.
    The two features are in Inyo National Forest, but were within the park from 1890 to 1905.

Walton Lake   *Merced Peak*
    Charles K. Fisher of the DFG reported in 1948 that the name was given in 1940 by John Handley, formerly at the DFG's Madera hatchery. (DFG survey.) No reason was given for the name, but one might guess it was for Izaak Walton, author of *The Compleat Angler*. The lake is in Sierra National Forest, 0.7 mile southeast of Triple Divide Peak on the park's southeast boundary; it was in the park from 1890 to 1905.

Wapama Falls   *Lake Eleanor*
    An Indian name whose meaning is unknown. The falls has often been described as Hetch Hetchy's counterpart of Yosemite Falls. "These falls which pour over the north wall of the valley at about its middle are in an angle formed by a great buttress just to the west, which recalls the El Capitan of the Yosemite. While this water-fall is similar in position and effect to the Yosemite it has not the same sheer plunge which is the remarkable feature of that fall. But to make up for this it has a far larger drainage basin . . . so that in volume and constancy at least it is far superior." (Macomb, *Report*, 1879: 260.)
    The Whitney Survey apparently named it "Hetch Hetchy Fall," which is how it appears on Hoffmann and Gardiner's map, 1863–67. On Benson's 1896 map it is called "Macomb Falls," obviously for Lt. Macomb of the Wheeler Survey; but Macomb himself did not use any name for the falls, nor is the falls named on atlas sheet 56D. The present name appeared on the fifth edition of the *Yosemite* 30' map, 1911.

Ward Lakes   *Merced Peak*
Origin unknown; the name first appeared on the *Merced Peak* quad, 1953. The two lakes are in Sierra National Forest just outside the park's southeast boundary, near Isberg Pass and Post Peak Pass. They were within the park from 1890 to 1905.

Wasco Lake   *Tuolumne Meadows*
Named by Al Gardisky in 1932 after the town in which a close friend of his lived. (Spuller.) The lake is in Inyo National Forest, but was within the park from 1890 to 1905.

Washburn Lake   *Merced Peak*
Washburn: Point, Slide   *Yosemite Valley, Yosemite*
Albert Henry Washburn operated the Yosemite Stage & Turnpike Co. in the 1870s and later. In December 1874 he and two partners bought Clark and Moore's Station on the South Fork of the Merced, and developed the Wawona Hotel Company. (Sargent, *Wawona*, 22 ff.)
The lake was named in 1895 by Lt. McClure. (Farquhar: McClure.) On his 1896 map he called it "Lake A. H. Washburn." Washburn Point is a viewpoint on the road half a mile south of Glacier Point. The name appeared on the seventh edition of the *Yosemite Valley* map, 1947, but it was in use at least as early as 1914. (Williams, 68.) Washburn Slide is a talus slide below Silver Strand Falls, half a mile east of the east end of the Wawona Tunnel. The name showed up on the fourth edition of the map, 1927.

Washington Column   *Yosemite Valley, Yosemite*
The name dates from the early days in Yosemite, but the namer is unknown; it is on King and Gardiner's map of 1865. From the right place on the south rim of the valley, the rock formation is said to look like a gigantic sculpture of George Washington. It has also been called "Washington Tower." (Hutchings, *In the Heart*, 383–84.)

Waterwheel Falls   *Tuolumne Meadows*
"The lowest set of cascades in this group we called the 'Rocket Cascades,' because the water, striking the edges of the great plates of granite . . . was continually thrown off in great arches. . . ." (Whitney, *The Yosemite Guide-Book*, pocket edition, 1874: 155–56.) This name did not appear on any map.
"The water dashes 600 or 700 feet down a surface inclined at an angle of 50 to 55 degrees, a mass of foam and spray. At intervals . . . the water is

thrown out in columns fifteen to twenty feet high, and in huge water-wheels of fantastic forms." (R. M. Price, "Through the Tuolumne Canyon," *SCB* 1, no. 6, May 1895: 204.) But Price named it "Le Conte Falls," the name now applied to the group of cascades above Waterwheel Falls. (See **Le Conte Falls** and **California Falls**.)

In 1904 William F. Badè suggested the name "Fountain Cascade" for this spectacular granite slope down which the Tuolumne River runs. But at the same time he came close to giving it its present name. ". . . a pall of misty smoke through which bombs of spray and fantastic water-wheels are hurled with titanic energy." (*SCB* 5, no. 4, June 1905: 292.) The name "Waterwheel Falls" was in use in 1911. (*SCB* 8, no. 3, Jan. 1912: opp. 224.) It was not on the first two editions of the *Mt. Lyell* 30' map, 1901 and 1905; it appeared on the edition of 1910.

Courtesy The Bancroft Library

Mount Watkins reflected in Mirror Lake.
Photograph by Muybridge.

Watkins, Mount (8,500)   *Yosemite Valley, Hetch Hetchy Reservoir*
Watkins Pinnacles   *Yosemite Valley*

". . . a noble overhanging mass of rock, to which the name of Mount Watkins has been given, as a compliment to the photographer who has done so much to attract attention to this region." (Whitney, *The Yosemite Book*, 63.)

Carleton E. Watkins (1829–1916), one of the early photographers of Yosemite. He provided illustrations for the publications of the Whitney Survey, thus earning himself a place on their maps. His view of Mirror Lake, with "Mount Watkins" reflected in it, is doubtless what led to his name being affixed to the peak.

Watkins visited the Mariposa Grove in 1858 or 1859, and took the first picture of a Sequoia—the "Grizzly Giant," with Galen Clark standing beside it. In 1861 he went to Yosemite Valley and made the first 18 x 22 landscape photographs in California. (*News Notes of California Libraries* 13, no. 1, Jan. 1918: 29–37.)

The mountain had an Indian name, but there was a small difference of opinion about what it was and what it meant. "*Waijau*. Mount Watkins; meaning the Pine Mountain." (Whitney, *The Yosemite Guide-Book*, 1870: 17.) "*Wei-yow*', meaning 'Juniper Mountain.'" (Clark, 108.)

The pinnacles were first named on the eighth edition of the *Yosemite Valley* map, 1958. The name does not appear on the *Hetch Hetchy Reservoir* quad.

Waugh Lake (9,424)   *Mono Craters, Devils Postpile, Mt. Ritter*
An artificial lake, created in 1918 and named for E. J. Waugh, the engineer in charge of constructing the dam. (Farquhar: W. L. Huber.) The lake is a reservoir for Southern California Edison. Although the lake is in Inyo National Forest, it was within the park from 1890 to 1905.

Wawona (community); **Wawona: Dome** (6,903), **Point** (6,810), **Tunnel**
                                                                 Yosemite
The large meadow at Wawona had an earlier name. ". . . Crane Flat—so named by us, as one of our party shot a large crane there while going over, but it is now known as Wawona." (Stephen F. Grover's narrative, May 1852, in Russell, *100 Years*, 57.)

"The Indians' name for the area was *Pallahchun* (a good place to stop)." (Sargent, *Wawona*, 11.)

Galen Clark built a cabin in the meadow on the South Fork of the Merced in April 1857. This became known as "Clark's Station." When Edwin Moore acquired a half interest in 1869 it got the name of "Clark and Moore's." The Washburn brothers purchased the property in December 1874, and renamed it "Big Tree Station." In 1882 Jean Bruce Washburn suggested a more appropriate name—*Wah-wo-nah*. (Sargent, *Wawona*, 12–16, 39.)

Galen Clark said that the word meant "Big Tree." (Clark, 109.) Stephen Powers was of the same opinion. "The California big tree is also in a manner sacred to them, and they call it *woh-woh'-nau*, a word formed in imitation of the hoot of the owl, which is the guardian spirit and deity of this great monarch of the forest." (Powers, 398.)

"Wawona Meadows themselves might be called the Sleepy Hollow of the West. It is the most peaceful place that I know in America, and comes near being the most idyllic spot I have seen anywhere (which is a considerable admission for an Englishman to make)." (Chase, 165.)

Wawona Point was first named on Lt. McClure's map of 1895, but it was in use at least as early as the middle 1880s. (Hutchings, *In the Heart*, 262.) Wawona Dome was named on McClure's 1896 map.

There were six stage stations on the old Wawona Road between Wawona and Yosemite Valley: Four Mile, Eight Mile, Eleven Mile, Chinquapin, Grouse Creek, and Fort Monroe. The Wawona Tunnel, completed in 1933, replaced a portion of the old road that climbed high across the shoulder of the hill above Turtleback Dome.

Weber Lake   *Devils Postpile, Mt. Ritter*
Origin unknown. The name appeared on the *Devils Postpile* quad, 1953. The lake, about a mile north of Thousand Island Lake, is in Inyo National Forest, but was within the park from 1890 to 1905.

Wegner Lake   *Hetch Hetchy Reservoir*
Named for John H. Wegner, a Yosemite ranger from the beginning of the National Park Service in 1916 until 1944, and chief ranger at Sequoia National Park, 1944–49. (Bingaman, *Guardians*, 94–95.)

Wells Peak (11,118)   *Tower Peak*
Named by R. B. Marshall, USGS, for Rush Spencer Wells, a lieutenant in the US Cavalry in the early 1900s. (Farquhar: Marshall. Heitman, 1,018.) The name appeared on the third *Dardanelles* 30' map, 1912.

West Peak (over 10,480)   *Tuolumne Meadows*
The name appeared on the third edition of the *Mt. Lyell* 30' map, 1910. On the 1905 map it was unnamed. On the 1901 map it was called "Regulation Peak." The origin of the present name is unknown, but I think it a distinct possibility that it is for Barrington King West, a lieutenant in the Sixth Cavalry in the early 1890s and a classmate of Lt. H. C. Benson at West Point. (Heitman, 1,019. See **Regulation Peak**.)

Westfall Meadows   *Yosemite*

Joel J. Westfall was born in Virginia in 1819, and came to Mariposa County in 1854. He had 160 acres of land on the old trail between Wawona and Yosemite Valley, near its junction with the southern branch of the old Mono Trail. ". . . follow along Alder Creek to its source in a large meadow, known as Westfall's. . . . Here are two houses, Westfall's and Ostrander's, sometimes occupied during the summer by herders of sheep, and which have often afforded a kind of shelter, poor, but better than none, to persons overtaken by night, or too much fatigued to go farther. Usually, however, this is the lunch place, or half-way house between Clark's and the valley, as will be easily recognized from the number of empty tin cans lying about." (Whitney, *The Yosemite Book*, 53–54.) Hoffmann and Gardiner's map of 1863–67 has "Westfall's," and shows a building. After that the name was not on a map again until publication of the *Yosemite* quad in 1956.

Westfall had a butcher shop in Yosemite Valley from about 1875 to about 1905. (YRL files.)

Wheeler Peak (9,001)   *Tower Peak*

Probably named about 1910 for an army officer. Col. W. W. Forsyth, acting superintendent of the park, 1909–12, named a number of features in the northern part of the park for army officers. The names all appeared on the third *Dardanelles* 30' map, 1912. There are two Wheelers who might fit the bill: Charles Brewster Wheeler, a West Point classmate of Lt. N. F. McClure; and Homer Webster Wheeler, a cavalry officer from 1875 to the early 1900s. The peak is on the park's northwest boundary.

White Cascade   *Tuolumne Meadows*

Named by the Whitney Survey in 1866. "Just at the crossing is a charming group of shelving rapids, in which the Tuolumne River falls about 80 feet perpendicular, in a mass of white foam; to this we gave the name of the 'White Cascades.'" (Whitney, *The Yosemite Guide-Book*, 1874: 155.) The name first appeared on the Wheeler Survey atlas sheet 56D, 1878–79, and was on LeConte's maps of 1893 and 1900, but not on Lt. McClure's maps. It showed up again on the third edition of the *Mt. Lyell* 30' map, 1910.

White Mountain (over 12,000)   *Tuolumne Meadows*

Probably named by the USGS during the 1898–99 survey for the *Mt. Lyell* 30' map; it is on the first edition, 1901. The peak is on the park's eastern boundary, about 1.6 miles south-southeast of Mount Conness.

White Wolf   *Hetch Hetchy Reservoir*

Said to have been named by John Meyer, a native of Germany, who, with his two brothers, had a cattle ranch near Groveland. While chasing Indians who had stolen some of their horses, they came to a temporary Indian camp in an alpine meadow, and called it White Wolf, for the Indian chief. (Paden, 153.)

Meyer later patented the land, and soon found himself on the route of the Great Sierra Wagon Road—the Old Tioga Road. The place became a summer resort, remaining in private hands until 1952. The government purchased the land that year, and the resort is now operated by the Yosemite Park and Curry Co. (Trexler, 42.) The name first appears on Lt. McClure's 1895 map.

Whorl Mountain (12,029)   *Matterhorn Peak*

Probably named by the USGS during the 1905–9 survey for the *Bridgeport* 30′ map; it is on the first edition, 1911. It has been suggested that the name "Whorl" is meant in its botanical sense: several leaves or branches growing out of the same place. (YRL files.) The mountain, which is 1.2 miles south of Matterhorn Peak, has three closely associated peaks. The name applies to the middle one.

Wildcat: Creek, Falls   *Yosemite Valley, Yosemite*

Probably named for the local species of bobcat. (*YNN* 34, no. 1, Jan. 1955: 20.) Both names appeared on the fourth edition of the *Yosemite Valley* map, 1927, but were in use before then. (Hall, 15.) Wildcat Creek flows down through a "hanging gulch," which ends at the brink of the Merced Gorge at a height of 700 feet. (Matthes, *Paper 160*, 41.)

Wildcat Point (9,455)   *Tuolumne Meadows*

Origin unknown, but possibly named by the USGS during the 1898–99 survey for the *Mt. Lyell* 30′ map; it is on the first edition, 1901. The point, which overlooks the Tuolumne River at Le Conte Falls, may be the feature referred to as "Tuolumne El Capitan" by Jennie Price in 1897. (*SCB* 2, no. 3, Jan. 1898: 176.)

Wilma Lake   *Tower Peak*

Named by R. B. Marshall, USGS, for Wilma Seavey, daughter of Clyde L. Seavey. (Farquhar: Marshall. See **Seavey Pass**.) The name was mistakenly given as "Wilmer" on the *Dardanelles* 30′ maps, 1912–47, and in Farquhar's *Place Names*. It was changed to "Wilma" on the *Tower Peak* quad, published in 1956. That spelling was ratified by a BGN decision in 1964. The lake is in Jack Main Canyon in the northern part of the park.

Courtesy Yosemite Research Library, NPS

The first drawing ever made of the Yosemite Falls,
by Thomas Ayres, 1855.

Wilson Creek   *Matterhorn Peak*

Named by Lt. H. C. Benson for his friend Mountford Wilson, a San Francisco attorney. (Farquhar: Benson.) The creek is a western tributary of the creek in Matterhorn Canyon. Lt. McClure's maps of 1895 and 1896, and LeConte's map of 1900, called it "West Fork." The present name appeared on the first *Bridgeport* 30' map, 1911.

Wilson Meadow   *Lake Eleanor*

William B. Wilson patented 159 acres in this vicinity in 1892. The name was not on any maps prior to publication of the *Lake Eleanor* quad, 1956. The meadow is about 1.5 miles southwest of Lake Eleanor. It is in Stanislaus National Forest, but was within the park from 1890 to 1905.

Wood, Mount (12,637)   *Mono Craters*

Named in 1894 by Lt. McClure for Capt. Abram Epperson Wood, acting superintendent of the park from 1891 to 1893. (Farquhar: McClure. Heitman, 1,054.) Wood commanded the first troops assigned to protect Yosemite National Park after its creation in 1890: companies I and K of the Fourth Cavalry. They arrived on May 19, 1891, and set up camp at Wawona in a place that later came to be known as Camp A. E. Wood. (Bingaman, *Guardians*, 83.)

McClure had the name on his 1895 map. Ironically, the first acting superintendent of Yosemite has been honored by having his name placed on a peak that is in Inyo National Forest, although it was within the park from 1890 to 1905.

Yosemite Valley   *Yosemite Valley, Yosemite*
Upper and **Lower Yosemite Fall; Yosemite: Creek, Point** (6,936)
                             Yosemite Valley, Hetch Hetchy Reservoir

"Here we began to encounter in our path, many small streams which would shoot out from under these high snow-banks, and after running a short distance in deep chasms which they have through ages cut in the rocks, precipitate themselves from one lofty precipice to another, until they are exhausted in rain below. Some of these precipices appeared to us to be more than a mile high." (Leonard, 174.) Zenas Leonard was a member of the Joseph R. Walker party that crossed the Sierra Nevada in 1833. Francis P. Farquhar, and others, have taken this to be a description of Yosemite Valley, but I do not believe this to be correct. Their opinion is based upon that single passage; all other evidence is to the contrary.

Paden and Schlichtmann argue that Leonard was describing Cascade, Tamarack, Coyote, and Wildcat creeks, and provide a persuasive description of the route most likely taken by Walker's party. (Paden, 259–64.) Walker's party followed the Mono Trail, which for the most part kept to the top of the dividing ridge between the Merced and Tuolumne rivers.

". . . the topography of the country over which the Mono Trail ran, and which was followed by Capt. Bowling [in 1851], did not admit of seeing the valley proper. The depression or trough of the valley, and some of its dominant cliffs could alone have been discovered, and in his conversation with myself upon this subject, Capt. Walker was manly enough to say so. The experiences of Capt. Walker and his band of trappers . . . impelled them to keep the Mono Trail after it was pointed out to them by the Indians . . . ." (Letter, Lafayette H. Bunnell to the editor of the *San Jose Pioneer*, Oct. 23, 1880.) "Ten-ie-ya said that a small party of white men once crossed the mountains on the North side, but were so guided as not to see it." (Bunnell, *Discovery*, 1911: 78.)

At least two white men saw—but did not enter—Yosemite Valley as early as 1849. "While at Savage's Reamer and I saw grizzly bear tracks and went out to hunt him down getting lost in the mountains and not returning until the following evening found our way to camp over an Indian trail that lead past a valley inclosed by stupendous cliffs arising perhaps 3000 feet from their base and which gave us cause for wonder. Not far off a waterfall dropped from a cliff below three jagged peaks into the valley while farther beyond a rounded mountain stood the valley side of which looked as though it had been sliced with a knife as one would slice a loaf of bread and which Reamer and I called the Rock of Ages." (Diary of William Penn Abrams, BL.) Clearly Abrams and Reamer saw Bridalveil Fall, the three Cathedral Rocks, and Half Dome.

The author of an article in the *Stanislaus News* (Modesto) of January 22, 1875 claimed that James Savage had been in Yosemite Valley as early as June 1849, but that intelligence had been refuted long before then. "Ten-ie-ya and others of his tribe asserted most positively that we were the first white men ever in the valley. The writer asked Maj. Savage, 'have you not been in the valley before?' he answered, 'no, never; I have been mistaken, it was in a valley below this, (since known as Cascade Valley,) two and a half miles below the Yo-sem-i-te.'" (Bunnell in Hutchings *Illustrated* 3, no. 11, May 1859: 500.)

The first white men *known* to have entered Yosemite Valley were members of Major Savage's Mariposa Battalion, including Lafayette H Bunnell. The date was March 27, 1851. (Eccleston, 48, 58–60.) The valley and many of the major features in or near it were named by these men during a period of two days.

"Some romantic and foreign names were offered . . . a very large number were canonical and scripture names. As I could not take a fancy to any of the names proposed, I remarked that . . . 'I could not see any necessity for going to a foreign country for a name for American scenery—the grandest that had ever yet been looked upon. . . . that the name of the tribe who had occupied it, would be more appropriate than any I had heard suggested.' I then proposed 'that we give the valley the name of Yo-sem-i-ty, as it was suggestive, euphonious, and certainly *American*; that by so doing, the name of the tribe of Indians which we met leaving their homes in this valley, perhaps never to return, would be perpetuated.' I was here interrupted by Mr. Tunnehill, who impatiently exclaimed: 'Devil take the Indians and their names! Why should we honor these vagabond murderers by perpetuating their name?' Another said: 'I agree with Tunnehill; —— the Indians and their names. Let's call this Paradise Valley.' The question of giving it the name of Yo-sem-i-ty was then explained, and upon a *viva voce* vote being taken, it was almost unanimously adopted.

"Lieutenant Moore, of the U.S.A., in his report of an expedition to the Valley in 1852, substituted *e* as the terminal letter, in place of *y*, in use by us; no doubt thinking the use of *e* more scholarly, or perhaps supposing Yosemite to be of Spanish derivation. . . . Sometime after the name had been adopted, I learned from Major Savage that Ten-ie-ya repudiated the name for the Valley, but proudly acknowledged it as the designation of his band, claiming that when he was a young chief, this name had been selected because they occupied the mountains and valleys which were the favorite resort of the Grizzly Bears, and because his people were expert in killing them. That his tribe had adopted the name because those who had bestowed it were afraid of 'the Grizzlies' and feared his band." (Bunnell, *Discovery*, 1880: 61–64.)

"While we most willingly acquiesce in the name of Yo-Semite . . . as neither that nor Yo-Ham-i-te, but *Ah-wah-ne*, is said to be the *pure Indian* name, we confess that our preferences still are in favor of the pure Indian being given; but until that is determined upon (which we do not ever expect to see done now), *Yo-Semite*, we think, has the preference." (Hutchings, *Scenes*, 1876: 95.)

"In the first place the aborigines never knew of any such locality as Yosemite Valley. Second, there is not now and there has not been anything in the valley which they call Yosemite. Third, they never called 'Old Ephraim' himself Yosemite, nor is there any such word in the Miwok language. The valley has always been known to them, and is to this day, when speaking among themselves, as A-wa'-ni." (Powers, 361. See **Ahwahnee**.)

Bunnell named the falls and the creek, stating that the Indians called the falls "Choolook" or "Schoolook," meaning "The Fall," and the creek "Scho-tal-lo-wi," which he interpreted to mean "the creek of the fall." (Bunnell, *Discovery*, 1880: 201-2.) The problem of whether to make the fall(s) singular or plural was never resolved; it appeared both ways on various maps for more than eighty years. Eventually it was handled by providing separate names for the upper and lower falls.

Yosemite Point, just east of Upper Yosemite Fall, was first named on the USGS *Yosemite Valley* map of 1907. It was described long before that (Whitney, *Geology*, 414), and the name was in use at least as early as the 1870s. (John Conway in the *Mariposa Gazette*, April 27, 1878.) Conway began building the Yosemite Falls trail in 1873, and completed it to the north rim in 1877. He operated it as a toll trail until 1885, when he sold it to the state for $1,500. (YRL files.)

Courtesy Yosemite Research Library, NPS

General Samuel B. M. Young, superintendent of the park in 1896, and later chief of staff of the US Army.

Young Lakes   *Tuolumne Meadows*

General Samuel Baldwin Marks Young (1840–1924), acting superintendent of the park in 1896, and of Yellowstone National Park, 1907–8. Young was a veteran of the Civil War, some campaigns against the Indians, and the Spanish-American War, and was chief of staff of the US Army, 1903–4. (Farquhar; Heitman, 1,067.) The name appeared on the first *Mt. Lyell* 30' map, 1901, as "Young Lake," which applied only to the lower lake. A BGN decision in 1962 changed it to a plural and applied it to all three lakes, which is how it has appeared on all editions of the *Tuolumne Meadows* quad.

"Z" Lake   *Tuolumne Meadows*

Named in 1932 by Al Gardisky for its shape. (Spuller.) This small lake, about 0.7 mile northwest of Saddlebag Lake, is in Inyo National Forest, but was within the park from 1890 to 1905.

Old Names
Fanciful Names
Names That
Won't Be Missed

Agassiz Column   *Yosemite Valley, Yosemite*

A precariously balanced rock on the old portion of the Four-Mile Trail, below Union Point. Named for Louis Agassiz, Swiss-born naturalist and geologist who came to the United States in 1846 and became a professor of zoology at Harvard. (Matthes, *Paper 160*, 108, 111, plate 47.)

The name was used by Hutchings. (*In the Heart*, 468.) Other names for this pillar were "Agassiz Thumb" (Cumming, 173); "Ten Pin-Rock" (Muybridge 1872 stereo); and "Magic Tower" (Housework stereo, BL).

Allison, Mount   *Yosemite Valley, Yosemite*

"Two peaks have been named today. The peak south of the North Dome leaning against it has been named Mt. Allison and the larger peak to the Eastward Mt. Washburn." (Snow's Register, vol. 1, July 25th, 1871: 140.) The writer of that entry seems to have tried to name Washington Column and Basket Dome. The former was named in the early 1860s; the latter had its present name on the Wheeler Survey map of the valley, 1883.

Lake Amy   *Mono Craters*

"Probably the most perfect amongst these existing glaciers is the Dana glacier upon Mt. Dana. . . . It finally ends in a small but deep lake . . . so named by me in honor of the daughter of prof. Jas. D. Dana." (William P. Blake, "Glacial Erosion and the Origin of the Yosemite Valley," *Transactions of the American Institute of Mining Engineers*, 1889.) This now has the name "Dana Lake;" it is outside the park.

Archie Leonard Trail   *Yosemite, Merced Peak*

The trail ran east from the Wawona ranger station, paralleling the South Fork of the Merced for several miles, then bore left to the main Buck Camp Trail at the Buck Camp ranger station. Archie Leonard was one of Yosemite's first rangers. He was a scout and guide for US troops when they were protecting the park. Leonard is thought to have blazed this trail in the early 1900s. (Bingaman, *Pathways*, 27.)

Although Leonard knew the southern part of the park, he lacked familiarity with the park as a whole. He also made the mistake of guiding deer hunters while ostensibly on patrol. He was caught at it by Col. Benson, who eventually fired him for his lack of ability. (Snyder.)

Babcock Creek   *Hetch Hetchy Reservoir*

A presently unnamed stream that rises on Rancheria Mountain and flows southwest into the Tuolumne just above Hetch Hetchy Reservoir. It is named only on Benson's 1896 map. Possibly it was for John P. Babcock. See **Babcock Lake** in the main list.

Baby Basket   *Yosemite Valley*

A small arch-like formation west of the Royal Arches. Named only on the Wheeler Survey map of 1883.

The Beehive or **Beehive Cabin**   *Lake Eleanor*

The name was used by Lt. McClure in 1894 for a fenced-in meadow belonging to Miguel on the trail from Lake Vernon to Miguel Meadow. (*SCB* 1, no.5, Jan. 1895: 184.) Ranger Billy Nelson told the story of an old prospector who contracted for the building of a cabin at this place. The contractor made the door four feet high. When the prospector saw it he said, "Hell, that's not a cabin, it's a beehive." (YRL files.) The cabin is shown—unnamed—on McClure's and Leconte's maps of 1896.

The location is marked by a metal name sign, and is on the 1979 Yosemite National Park Trails Map. (Snyder.)

Beehive Peak or **Dome** (7,238)   *Lake Eleanor*

A name doubtless derived from "The Beehive." It is 1.5 miles east-southeast of Laurel Lake and two miles north of Hetch Hetchy Reservoir.

Bell, Lake   *Matterhorn Peak*

A name on LeConte's map of 1900 where the real Miller Lake is. See **Miller Lake** in the main list.

Bellows Butte   *Yosemite Valley, Yosemite*

An early name for Liberty Cap. On June 10, 1864 a party of "Ladies and Gentlemen" ate lunch on a rock midway between Vernal and Nevada falls. Referring to Liberty Cap, which was not named until the following year, the writer christened the "noble and commanding mountain . . . whose sugar-loaf cone of cream granite ascends about 2,500 feet towards the heavens," with the name "Bellows Butte." He then "broke a bottle of water upon the altar which had been temporarily erected for the occasion, and called upon the company for three cheers for the Rev. Dr. Henry W. Bellows, President of the United States Sanitary Commission, distinguished philanthropist and divine, who had rendered such eminent service to our country, and to the wounded and suffering soldiers in the army." (*Mariposa Gazette*, Sept. 17, 1864.)

Bertha Lake   *Tuolumne Meadows*

Named for Bertha Mather, daughter of Stephen T. Mather, first director of the National Park Service, when they camped there one summer. (YRL files.) Not on any maps. This is the higher of the two Cathedral Lakes.

Bishops Camp   *Yosemite*

The campsite of the Mariposa Battalion, March 25–30, 1851; named for First Sergeant Samuel Addison Bishop. (See **Bishop Creek** in the main list.) Not on any maps. C. Gregory Crampton locates the camp on Elevenmile Creek about half a mile below the Wawona Road, in sec. 32, T. 3 S., R. 21 E. (Eccleston, 56.)

Black Mountain   *Merced Peak*

The name was given in 1866 by the Whitney Survey to what is now **Madera Peak**. (Whitney, *The Yosemite Guide-Book*, 1870: 109.)

Black Rascal   *Yosemite*

This sounds like a racist name, and may well be. It refers to a place on the old Wawona Road between Chinquapin and the old Bishop Creek campground—probably at Elevenmile Creek. (YRL files.)

Black Oak Flat   *Yosemite Valley*

The flat was where the Indian village of *Ah-wah'-ne* was located. It was the largest piece of open ground in the valley (where the park headquarters now is), and the name of the village came to be applied to the entire valley by outside Indians. (C. Hart Merriam, "Indian Villages and Camp Sites in Yosemite Valley," *SCB* 10, no. 2, Jan. 1917: 205.)

Blind Pass *Tuolumne Meadows*

A designation that appeared only on Lt. McClure's 1896 map. It is meant to be a directional or guidance indication rather than an actual name. (Snyder.) It seems to indicate a pass southwest of Hanging Basket Lake; that is, just east of Vogelsang Lake. But what it apparently is saying is: Don't go this way, take the real pass. What is now Vogelsang Pass (not named on the *Tuolumne Meadows* quad), McClure designated as "Real Pass."

Blue Jay Meadows *Yosemite Valley*

Probably the meadow a quarter mile past Ribbon Meadow on the trail to Gentry's. (Snyder. See also Elliott McAllister, "Itinerary of a Route from Gentry's to top of El Capitan and Yosemite Falls," *SCB* 1, no. 4, May 1894: 134.)

Bronson's Meadow *Lake Eleanor*

Named for the first settler on this piece of ground. From its location on Hoffmann and Gardiner's map of 1863–67, it probably is in sec. 6, T. 2 S., R. 20 E.—a place that is no longer named. According to Paden, this land was later settled by Jeremiah Hodgdon in 1865. (Paden, 207–8, 214; see **Hodgdon Ranch** in the main list.) The name was on Hoffmann and Gardiner's map, 1863–67.

Brothers, The *Yosemite Valley, Yosemite*

An early name for the Cathedral Rocks. (*San Francisco Daily Evening Bulletin*, July 8, 1857.)

Bunker Hill *Mono Craters*

A name for the summit, just south of Mono Pass, marked "11805." (*Homer Mining Index*, Aug. 23, 1884.) This peak also was called "Mount Maclure" by a traveler three years earlier—because he obviously didn't know where Mount Maclure was. (Ibid., Oct. 1, 1881.)

Buttermilk Fall *Yosemite Valley, Yosemite*

"A stream heading at Ostrander's Rocks comes down near Sentinel Rock, in a kind of 'Buttermilk Fall,' or series of step-like cascades, until all the snow at its head has disappeared." (Whitney, *The Yosemite Guide-Book*, 1870: 78.)

Camp A. E. Wood *Yosemite*

Capt. Abram Epperson Wood was the first acting superintendent of

Yosemite National Park, 1891–93. (See **Wood, Mount**, in the main list.) Wood commanded the first troops assigned to protect the park. When they arrived, on May 19, 1891, they set up camp on the South Fork of the Merced just upstream from where Rush Creek comes in. The name is on McClure's maps of 1895 and 1896 and Benson's map of 1896.

Camp Placido   *Yosemite*

Apparently a resting place on the old Mariposa and Yosemite trail, about four miles above Clark's Ranch (Wawona). (Hutchings, *Scenes*, 1870: 82.) Possibly it is where the present trail crosses the head of a small creek in sec. 21, T. 4 S., R. 21 E.

Capitol Peak   *Yosemite Valley, Yosemite*

A tourist in 1859 used this name for El Capitan. "We took particular notice of Capitol Peak, 4,000 feet high, the top appearing to the eye to be leaning slightly over. High up on the mountain side can be seen the figure of a man, apparently with a blanket over his shoulders and a fur cap on his head. The moustache, whiskers, nose and eyes are very plain. The Indians call him 'Tutattinello,' and believe him to be the Great Chief who was once at the head of their tribe." (*San Francisco Daily Evening Bulletin*, May 26, 1858. See **El Capitan** in the main list for Bunnell's account of Tenaya's description of the same figure.)

Capitol Rock   *Yosemite Valley, Hetch Hetchy Reservoir*

A name used for North Dome by a tourist party in 1855. (*San Joaquin Republican*, Oct. 16, 1855.)

Cascade Avenue   *Yosemite Valley*

Below Lower Yosemite Fall the stream divides into three channels. One of these is straight for half a mile, and was once known as "Cascade Avenue" because of numerous little cascades in its course. (Hittell, 19.)

Cascade of the Rainbow   *Yosemite Valley*

An early name for Bridalveil Fall. ". . . we came opposite the falls of what has been inappropriately called the Cascade of the Rainbow." (*Mariposa Democrat*, Aug. 5, 1856.)

Castle Lake   *Matterhorn Peak*

Lt. McClure used this name in 1894 for Summit Lake at the headwaters of Green Creek. (*SCB* 1, no. 5, Jan. 1895: 171.) The name is on McClure's maps of 1895 and 1896 and on LeConte's map of 1900. See the first **Summit Lake** in the main list.

Castle Peak   *Yosemite Valley, Yosemite*
An early name for Elephant Rock. "Castle Peak, a massive column of granite, rises abruptly to a height of from 2,500 to 3,000 feet." ("The New River Trail to Yo Semite," *Mariposa Gazette*, May 2, 1873.)

Cataract of Diamonds   *Yosemite Valley, Yosemite*
Just below the Nevada Fall bridge—between the Silver Apron and Emerald Pool. (Bailey, 383; Williams, 83.)

Cave of the Spirit Voice   *Yosemite Valley*
The cave back of the base of Upper Yosemite Fall; used by Muybridge in 1868. (YRL files. See **Vestibule, The**.)

Cemetery, The   *Yosemite Valley*
A group of rocks at Union Point. (Muybridge stereo, 1872; YRL files.)

Chain Cascade   *Yosemite Valley, Merced Peak*
The springtime falls down Cascade Cliffs on the south side of Little Yosemite Valley. Named on the 1883 Wheeler Survey map of Yosemite Valley and Vicinity.

China Cañon   *Matterhorn Peak*
An alternate name for Matterhorn Canyon, used by Lt. McClure in 1894. (*SCB* 1, no. 8, May 1896: 331; on McClure's map of 1896.)

Cold Water Creek   *Yosemite*
A name used by Hutchings to identify a creek on the Mariposa and Yosemite trail, about 5.5 miles above Wawona. (Hutchings, *Scenes*, 1870: 82.) Possibly the intermittent stream shown in the lower left quadrant of sec. 15, T. 4 S., R. 21 E.

Colfax, Mount   *Yosemite Valley, Yosemite*
An early name for a point—possibly what was later named Union Point—on the south valley wall opposite Indian Canyon. In August 1865 a party of prominent tourists named it after one of their own. "That orphan printer's boy of not many years ago, whose industry, talents and perfect integrity have won for his early manhood the third place of civil trust and honor in the gift of the American people." (*Sacramento Daily Union*, Sept.

30, 1865.) The man thus honored was Schuyler Colfax of Indiana, at that time the Speaker of the House of Representatives. He later progressed to second place—vice president during Grant's first administration. But his integrity turned out to be something less than perfect. He was caught up in the Credit Mobilier scandal, and departed public life.

Courtesy Yosemite Research Library, NPS

Speaker of the House Schuyler Colfax and party in Yosemite Valley, 1865. Colfax is third from the left in the second row.

Colonnade, The   *Yosemite Valley, Hetch Hetchy Reservoir*

The cliff west of the switchbacks on the upper part of the trail to the top of Upper Yosemite Fall; that is, west of "Comimi Canyon." The name was used by John Conway in the *Mariposa Gazette*, April 27, 1878.

Columbia Creek   *Tuolumne Meadows*

The creek flowing south out of Long Meadow (on the Sunrise Trail) to the Cathedral Fork of Echo Creek. It was named only on Lt. McClure's 1895 map.

Comimi Canyon   *Yosemite Valley, Hetch Hetchy Reservoir*

The canyon that is the route of the upper part of the trail to Eagle Peak and the top of Upper Yosemite Fall. The name was used by John Conway, builder of the trail, in the *Mariposa Gazette*, April 27, 1878; also in

Cumming, 118. This natural route for a trail probably was the location of a stream flowing out of the Hoffmann Glacier during the last glacial period. (Matthes, *Paper 160*, 112.)

No one has ever provided an explanation for this name, but I suggest that it is a borrowing from the name of an important Indian village at the foot of the trail. *"Koom-i-ne*, or *Kom-i-ne.*—The largest and most important village in the valley, situated on the north side of the delta of Yosemite Creek just below Yosemite Fall . . . and extending southwesterly at the base of the talus-slope under the towering cliffs for about three-quarters of a mile, reaching almost or quite to Three Brothers." (C. Hart Merriam, "Indian Villages and Camp Sites in Yosemite Valley," *SCB* 10, no. 2, Jan. 1917: 205.)

Congress Point   *Yosemite Valley, Yosemite*
This point, now unnamed, was on the Four Mile Trail, below Union Point and above the stream coming down just east of Sentinel Rock. ("The Sentinel Rock and Glacier Point Trail," *Mariposa Gazette*, May 24, 1872.) The name was also used by John Conway, builder of the trail, in a letter to the *Gazette* of April 17, 1874.

Contemplation Rock   *Yosemite Valley*
One of two overhanging rocks at Glacier Point. (Caption for a Muybridge photo, 1872, in *CHSQ* 42, no. 1, March 1963.) The more common name for this one is **Photographer's Rock**, which see; also **Overhanging Rock**. For a geologic explanation, see Matthes, *Paper 160*, 17, 110.

Coroya Flat   *Lake Eleanor*
An early twentieth century name for a locale in the Tuolumne River Canyon about halfway between Poopenaut Valley and Hetch Hetchy Reservoir. (Foster, 25, 30–31.)

Court House Rock   *Tuolumne Meadows*
An early name for Medlicott Dome. ". . . just across either of these [Cathedral] lakes rises a mountain not less remarkable than the Cathedral. This is called Court House Rock,—a sad misnomer, for it does not resemble a court house at all—but it does look surpassingly like an old half ruined abbey . . . ." ("Beyond Yo Semite—A Trip to Cathedral Valley," *Mariposa Free Press*, Oct. 28, 1870.)

Crinoline Point *Yosemite Valley*

An unidentified point that is seen from a place on the Yosemite Fall trail where the trail makes a bend and overlooks the lower fall: "In front, the South Dome [Half Dome], Mt. Clark, Mt. Starr King, and Crinoline Point." (John Conway in the *Mariposa Gazette*, April 27, 1873.)

Crouching Lion of Yosemite *Yosemite Valley*

A one-time-only tourist appellation for El Capitan. (Williams, 67.)

Cunningham Flat *Yosemite*

Named for Stephen M. Cunningham, who was appointed Guardian of the Big Trees at the Mariposa Grove. (See Sargent, *Wawona*, 47.) Cunningham had a cabin on the flat for many years. It was at the northwest end of the present Wawona campground—the place where Camp A. E. Wood was later located. ("Yosemite's Pioneer Cabins," *SCB* 36, no. 5, May 1951: 52–53.)

Cunningham had more than one abode. "The only habitation at the big trees is a log hut occupied at present by the notable Steve Cunningham, who is said to be Sub-Guardian of the *gigantia sequoia* forest known as the Mariposa Grove." (*Mariposa Gazette*, Aug. 20, 1881.)

Decanter, The *Yosemite Valley, Yosemite*

A singular and attractive large rock on the Old Big Oak Flat Road between Tamarack Creek and Cascade Creek. (Hutchings, *Scenes*, 1870: 104.)

Deer Park *Hetch Hetchy Reservoir*

On the old Mono Trail a couple of miles east of where the trail crossed Yosemite Creek; described as a high meadow at an altitude of nearly 8,500 feet. Probably named by the Whitney Survey. ". . . descending a little [from Deer Park], we soon reach Porcupine Flat." (Whitney, *The Yosemite Guide-Book*, 1870: 92.) This probably is the meadow in sec. 32, T. 1 S., R. 22 E. The name was on Hoffmann and Gardiner's map of 1863–67, the Wheeler Survey atlas sheet 56D, 1878–79, and LeConte's map of 1893, but not thereafter.

Devils Elbow *Yosemite Valley*

The loop in the Merced River opposite El Capitan. (YRL files.) Not on maps. The name is still in use among local people, road crews, and park rangers. (Snyder.)

Devil's Gulch *Yosemite Valley, Yosemite*
On the Old Coulterville Road between Big Meadow and the Merced River gorge, where the road had been blasted out of the bluff. (Hutchings, *In the Heart*, 291.)

Devil's Maze *Tower Peak*
The name was given by Lt. McClure in 1894 to a difficult stretch of travel, apparently just outside the park boundary among the lakes northeast of Dorothy Lake Pass. (*SCB* 1, no. 5, Jan. 1895: 179, 181.)

Diamond Cascade *Yosemite Valley, Yosemite*
The Merced River below the Nevada Fall bridge. ". . . the whole river is leaping, as if in very wantonness and exultation . . . and, being seized with an uncontrollable fit of frolicking, is tossing up diamonds (of the purest water) . . . ." (Hutchings, *In the Heart*, 449.)

Diamond Flume *Yosemite Valley, Yosemite*
A narrow race above the Nevada Fall bridge. (YRL files.)

Diamond Race *Yosemite Valley, Yosemite*
"Just above the Vernal Falls comes a reach of the river known as 'The Diamond Race,'—a stream so rapid and so glittering, that it seems like a shower of sparkling crystals, each drop a separate gem." (Cumming, 178.)

Eagle Falls *Yosemite*
Another name for Chilnualna Fall; caption on a Bierstadt stereo, date unknown. (YRL files.) The caption also had the Indian name "Wepiac."

Echo, Mount *Yosemite Valley, Merced Peak*
Apparently an early name for Moraine Dome; seen from Eagle Peak by John Conway. (*Mariposa Gazette*, April 27, 1878.)

Echo Rock *Yosemite Valley, Yosemite*
"Echo Rock looms up with its picture gallery of gigantic figures." (*Mariposa Gazette*, May 2, 1873.) The name probably refers to the rock formations south of Elephant Rock.

Enchantment Point *Yosemite Valley, Yosemite*
". . . there opens up before us one of the most charmingly impressive scenes that human eyes can look upon." (Hutchings, *In the Heart*, 400.) At the west end of Yosemite Valley, looking east; now named Valley View.

Falls of Louise   *Yosemite Valley, Yosemite*
See **Bridalveil Fall** in the main list.

False Starr King (8,574)   *Yosemite Valley, Yosemite*
This dome is one half mile northwest of Mount Starr King, and is often mistaken for the real thing. The false one is what you see from the floor of Yosemite Valley; the real one is hidden behind it. It has also been called "Thompson Dome," presumably for Col. Charles G. Thompson, superintendent of the park from 1929 to 1937; also "Dusty Lewis Dome," for Washington B. Lewis, the first civilian superintendent of the park, 1916–28. (YRL files.)

Feldspar Valley   *Tuolumne Meadows*
An old name for Long Meadow on the Sunrise Trail. (See **Long Meadow** in the main list.) "We traced these boulders [found in Little Yosemite Valley] up Feldspar Valley (so-called from this remarkable granite) to their parent rock, viz: Cathedral Peak and other peaks and comb-like ridges in that vicinity." (Read before the California Academy of Sciences, September 16, 1872.) Joseph LeConte said that he gave the name, but it was already in use at least two years before that. (*Mariposa Free Press*, Oct. 28, 1870.)

Fern Grotto   *Yosemite Valley*
Just below "The Ladders" on the way to Vernal Fall. (See **Mist Trail** in the main list.) "Here a portion of the mountain has been removed, and left a large cave or grotto, in the interstices of which numerous ferns . . . mainly, one of the maiden hair species, formerly grew in abundance . . . ." (Hutchings, *In the Heart*, 453.)

Fern Ledge   *Yosemite Valley*
John Muir's name for a ledge 450 feet above the base of Upper Yosemite Fall and behind the falling water. Muir once tried to cross on the ledge between the fall and the cliff, and came near to losing his life. (Muir, *The Yosemite*, 40–42.) "This ledge is the most advanced part of the cliff, yet it is cleared by the main body of the fall, owing to the parabolic descent of the water." (Matthes, *Paper 160*, 111. See **Vestibule** in this list.)

Firefall Point   *Yosemite Valley*
The viewpoint a quarter of a mile northwest of Glacier Point from which the former evening firefalls were shoved over the edge. To reach it

Courtesy Yosemite Research Library, NPS

The new wooden stairs to the top of Vernal Fall,
and the old ladders they replaced. Photograph by Fiske.

one descended the former Ledge Trail a short distance, then followed a trail to the right. (YRL files.)

Five-Finger Falls   *Hetch Hetchy Reservoir*
A name once used for Rancheria Falls. (Williams, 131.)

Fountain Cascade   *Tuolumne Meadows*
William F. Badè suggested this name for Waterwheel Falls in 1904. (*SCB* 5, no. 4, June 1905: 292.)

Frances Lake   *Yosemite Valley, Yosemite*
The first name given to Emerald Pool, between Vernal and Nevada falls. (*Mariposa Democrat*, August 5, 1856.) The full passage is in "The First Tourists" at the end of this volume.

Frances' Peak   *Yosemite Valley, Yosemite*
James Denman used this name—no doubt for the same Frances as in the entry above—in 1857 for Half Dome. ". . . Frances' Peak looms far above the surrounding cliffs, unsurpassed in height, and unequalled in massive grandeur. The side fronting the water [of Mirror Lake] is nearly perpendicular, while the opposite one represents almost a perfect section of a half dome. " (*San Francisco Daily Evening Bulletin*, July 8, 1857.)

Gateway, The   *Yosemite Valley, Yosemite*
The name was applied to the upper end of Merced Gorge at the foot of the Old Coulterville Road—the gateway to Yosemite Valley. In a letter dated February 20, 1905, Frank Bond of the GLO wrote to R. B. Marshall of the USGS and twice referred to "the new 'Gateway.'" And in a letter written March 3, 1906, he wrote "our 'Gateway.'" (Robert B. Marshall Papers, Part I, Box III, BL.)

The name was on the first six editions of the *Yosemite Valley* map, 1907–38. It was removed from subsequent maps at the request of Francis P. Farquhar, perhaps because the name duplicated El Portal, a few miles down the road.

Gentry's   *Yosemite Valley, Yosemite*
A stopping place on the Old Big Oak Flat Road, about half a mile south of where the road crosses Cascade Creek, just outside the boundary of the original Yosemite Grant. Colonel E. S. Gentry settled there in 1870, when the route was still merely a horse trail. (See Paden, 239–40 ff.)

"The pleasant little sitting room, with its bright carpet and lace curtains and melodeon; the bedrooms, clean as clean could be and with two beds in each; the neat dining-room and good dinner; the log cabin for a linen closet; the running spring water; the smiling faces and prompt kindliness of the landlord and his wife,—what a marvel it was to find all these in this new clearing in a pine forest of the Sierra country, seven thousand feet above the sea!" (Jackson, 100.)

The place was on the Wheeler Survey map of Yosemite Valley and Vicinity, 1883, as "Gentry's Sta." It was deserted by 1886. (Hutchings, *In the Heart*, 312.)

The name persisted long after the structure was gone. "Gentry" was the location of a ranger station, and was the control point for the downbound auto traffic on the Old Big Oak Flat Road until about 1940. (Snyder.)

Giant's Pillar   *Yosemite Valley, Yosemite*
A name used by a writer who couldn't stand the name "El Capitan." "There's the Giant's Pillar . . . which some individual of a military turn has named El Capitan. . . . What a name for a perpendicular cliff three thousand feet in height! Why not follow out the simile and name some of the lesser cliffs *Lieutenants*, and so on down to *fourth Corporals*?" ("Our Yosemite Correspondent," *Mariposa Gazette*, Sept. 2, 1857.)

Giant's Thumb   *Yosemite Valley*
The prosaic early name for Lost Arrow. (Hutchings, *In the Heart*, 370, 377.)

Giant's Tower   *Yosemite Valley, Yosemite*
Another name for El Capitan, by a non-military person with giantism on his mind. (Hutchings *Illustrated* 1, no. 1, July 1856: 3.)

Glacier Lake   *Tuolumne Meadows*
An early name for the larger of the Cathedral Lakes. (YRL files.)

Glacier Rock   *Yosemite Valley*
"The Glacier Rock, with its smooth, glassy sides . . . ." (*Mariposa Free Press*, June 2, 1871.) Written by a careless tourist, who really meant Glacier Point.

Gobin's   *Lake Eleanor*
Louis D. Gobin and his son grazed cattle and sheep at Crane Flat in the

1870s. By 1874 Gobin and his wife were serving meals in their small log cabin; their stopping place for travelers later developed into a stage station. Their cabin straddled the Tuolumne-Mariposa county line. (Paden, 219–23.)

Golden Stairs *Tower Peak*
The short switchbacks on the trail coming down from Moraine Ridge into Jack Main Canyon, in part referring to all the rockwork that was necessary on this steep stretch. The trail was built under the supervision of Gabriel Sovulewski, who apparently coined the name. The name is not on the USGS map, but has been passed down orally by trail crews and backcountry rangers, and appears on the park's Trail Map, 1979. (Snyder.)

Gothic Peak *Merced Peak*
The earliest name for Mount Clark.

Green Springs Flat *Yosemite*
A locale on the Mariposa and Yosemite trail, 0.75 mile south of Westfall Meadows. (Hutchings, *Scenes*, 1870: 82.)

Guyot, Mount *Merced Peak*
An early name for **Rodgers Peak**, given by the Whitney Survey in the 1860s.

Hayes, Mount *Merced Peak*
An alternate name for Gray Peak; it was on Lt. McClure's maps of 1895 and 1896. Jim Snyder suggests that it was named by the US Cavalry for ex-president Rutherford B. Hayes, who died in 1893—during the time when the cavalry was patrolling the park.

Hell's Delight *Tower Peak*
The original name for Wilma Lake, in Jack Main Canyon. The name is carved on a tree with the date of July 4, 1877; it is the oldest dated carving in Yosemite's backcountry. During early summer, the place is a hell's delight when the mosquitoes come out. (Snyder.)

Hermitage, The *Yosemite Valley*
". . . a hollow sugar-pine that was the home of a solitary woodsman for nearly three months." (Hutchings, *Scenes*, 1870: 86.) The name was on the Wheeler Survey map of 1883 and LeConte's map of 1896. It was uphill on

the Pohono Trail from where the stage station known as "Fort Monroe" was located.

Hetch Hetchy El Capitan   *Lake Eleanor*
An early name for Hetch Hetchy Dome. (See **Hetch Hetchy** in the main list; also Matthes, *Paper 160*, plate 5.)

Hiawatha, Lake   *Yosemite Valley, Yosemite*
James Denman used this name for Mirror Lake in 1857. ". . . Lake Hiawatha, a beautiful sheet of water, covering about thirty acres. . . . The lake is filled with myriads of speckled trout, which afforded us fine sport in shooting, as they were basking in the sun." (*San Francisco Daily Evening Bulletin*, July 8, 1857.)

Hill's Point   *Yosemite*
A summit somewhere in the vicinity of Wawona, from which one has a distant view of Chilnualna Fall. Named for the artist Thomas Hill, who had a studio at Wawona from 1884 until his death in 1908. (Sargent, *Wawona*, 39, 41–42.)

Hog Ranch   *Lake Eleanor*
The original name for what is now the community of Mather. See **Mather** in the main list.

Hopkin's Meadow   *Yosemite Valley, Yosemite*
At the junction of the Clouds Rest and Sunrise trails, west of Moraine Dome. Shown only on LeConte's maps of 1893 and 1896. Origin unknown.

Horseshoe Grotto   *Yosemite Valley, Yosemite*
At the head of Illilouette Fall. (Hutchings, *In the Heart*, 440.) Not on any maps.

Hunt, Mount   *Mono Craters*, or *Tuolumne Meadows*
"Mount Hunt is a high, conical mountain, near Mounts Dana and Gibbs, and was so named by me in 1887, in honor of the late Thomas Sterry Hunt . . . for many years a member of the Institute and of world-wide fame as a writer and authority in chemical geology." (William P. Blake, "Glacial Erosion and the Origin of the Yosemite Valley," *Transactions of the American Institute of Mining Engineers*, 1899, footnote p. 11.) There are

several conical mountains in the vicinity, and it is not possible to tell which he meant.

Indian Camp
Yosemite Valley

According to Hutchings, this was the site of the principal camp of the Yosemite Indians. (Hutchings, *In the Heart*, 422.) It was about 0.4 mile southwest of Rocky Point, south and west of BM 3971, an area crossed by the modern road. The name is on the Wheeler Survey map of 1883.

Indian Lake
Yosemite Valley, Yosemite

A name used by a tourist in 1859 for Mirror Lake, as if it were the accepted name at the time. (*San Francisco Daily Evening Bulletin*, June 18, 1859.)

Jeans' Dome
Yosemite Valley, Merced Peak

"On the North by East side of the upper valley." (Snow's Register, vol. 1, 141.) This is probably what is now named Moraine Dome. The name was given by a Washburn excursion party to Snow's Hotel; it was for Jean Bruce Washburn. (See **Bruce, Mount** and **Washburn Lake** in the main list.)

Kellogg, Mount
Merced Peak

J. N. LeConte gave this name in the early 1890s to what is now Rodgers Peak. Vernon L. Kellogg was a professor of entomology at Stanford. (LeConte, *Alpina*, 10.) The name appeared only on LeConte's maps of 1896 and 1900.

La Casa Nevada
Yosemite Valley, Yosemite

Also known as Snow's Hotel. Albert and Emily Snow operated their hotel on the flat below Nevada Fall from 1870 to 1897. (Sargent, *Pioneers*, 22–23.)

Lady Franklin Rock
Yosemite Valley

Lady Franklin was the widow of Sir John Franklin, an English explorer who died in the Arctic in 1847. For more than a decade Lady Franklin organized and financed a series of expeditions in an endeavor to learn her husband's fate. Her actions created great sympathy and admiration, and after she visited the United States there was a rash of naming things for her, including the Franklin Lakes in Sequoia National Park. The rock is just a few minutes up the Mist Trail from Register Rock.

"So named because that distinguished lady visited the Yosemite in 1859, and being very feeble at the time, was carried up to this rock by the guides on a chair, and from here she viewed the Fall." (Foley, 25.)

Lake Hollow   *Hetch Hetchy Reservoir*
John Muir's name for the basin containing the Ten Lakes, which he named. (Muir, *Mountains*, 100.)

Lake of the Domes   *Tuolumne Meadows*
A tiny lake, presently unnamed, just off the Sunrise Trail at Long Meadow, ". . . that takes its name from the fact that around it stand sixteen domes similar to those of Yo Semite, four of which stand on the very shore of the lake." (*Mariposa Free Press*, Oct. 28, 1870.)

Leavitt Lake   *Merced Peak*
Now Givens Lake. The name "Leavitt" was suggested to honor Earnest P. Leavitt, assistant superintendent of the park from July 1928 to February 1929. The name did not appear on maps.

Courtesy Yosemite Research Library, NPS

La Casa Nevada (Snow's Hotel). Emily and Albert Snow and their daughter Maria.

Ledge Trail   *Yosemite, Yosemite Valley*
A one-mile-long trail from in back of Curry Village to Glacier Point. It was built by the Park Service in 1918, but had been advertised by Hutchings long before that. The trail was abandoned about 1957 because it was unsafe. Much of the trail was wiped out in 1984 by a large rockslide from the arches above Curry Village. (Snyder.)

Lightning Ridge   *Hetch Hetchy Reservoir*
In the 1870s lightning killed a large number of sheep here, belonging to a Joe Prowdy. (Farquhar files, from Ansel Hall.) Rangers Bingaman and Eastman proposed the name. (*YNN* 9, no. 7, July 1930: 67.) The ridge is northwest of Boundary Hill, and forms the west side of Bluejay Creek. The Wheeler Survey took measurements from this ridge, and called it "Kai-al-au-wa Hill" on the 1883 map. The ridge is just off the old Mono Trail, a major sheep route into the Sierra. (Snyder.)

Limerick Lake   *Tuolumne Meadows*
A name for what is now Boothe Lake. It appeared only on Lt. McClure's 1896 map.

Little Brown Jug   *Yosemite Valley, Yosemite*
See **Decanter, The**.

Little Hetch Hetchy   *Hetch Hetchy Reservoir*
An early name for a small valley on the Tuolumne River above Hetch Hetchy Valley. (*SCB* 6, no. 4, Jan. 1908: 243.) The name was on the YNP topo map, 1929. It is now under the waters of Hetch Hetchy Reservoir, where the word "Reservoir" is on the *Hetch Hetchy Reservoir* quad, south of Le Conte Point.

Little Lake   *Yosemite Valley*
The very small pond next to the trail just below Mirror Lake. (Hutchings, *In the Heart*, 385.)

Lookout Point   *Yosemite*
A viewpoint on the old Wawona Road, a quarter of a mile south of Bishop Creek at a bend in the road. This was just south of the old Eleven Mile Stage Station, in sec. 32, T. 3 S., R. 21 E. One had a view to the South Fork of the Merced and the San Joaquin Valley. (YRL files.)

Lookout Rock *Yosemite Valley*

An early name for Taft Point, used in the captions for several Muybridge stereos. (YRL files.)

Lost Lake *Yosemite Valley*

A former lake just northeast of Mount Broderick. It was shown on the *Yosemite Valley* maps, and named, from 1907 through 1938. Since then it has been nameless, and is marked as a swampy area. It was described by Ansel F. Hall in *YNN* 4, no. 14, Aug. 25, 1925: 78. For excellent information on what became—or will become—of the lake, see Matthes, *Paper 160*, 58, 104. According to Jim Snyder the transition from lake to swamp has happened more quickly on the maps than in reality, and that seasonally the lake still feeds the creek that flows between Liberty Cap and Mount Broderick.

Magee Lakes *Tuolumne Meadows*

". . . About five miles north of the last named place [Tenaya Lake], is a group of five beautiful lakes, fed by numerous springs and rivulets leaping from the rocks in miniature cascades, and shaded on all sides by tall pines and the graceful silver fir. These were named in honor of Judge Michael M. Magee." (*Homer Mining Index*, Jan. 5, 1884.) These are the Polly Dome Lakes; the old name was never on maps. The year was 1860. Magee was Justice of the Peace at Big Oak Flat during the flush years of that camp. While he and his party were camped at the lakes he found his name carved in the bark of a tree, and "recognized it as the work of his own hand, executed in 1848, while encamped on the spot as one of the 83 men who accompanied Fremont on his fourth expedition across the continent." Plainly something was afflicting the judge's memory. Frémont's fourth expedition was the one that came to a disastrous end in the Sangre de Cristo Mountains in northern New Mexico in the winter of 1848–49.

Mammoth Mountain *Merced Peak*

"A very high and massive peak was seen to the east of Mount Lyell, which it nearly equalled in altitude; it was called Mammoth Mountain, and was estimated to be 13,000 feet in height." (Whitney, *Geology*, 401.) This probably refers to Banner Peak (12,936), to the southeast, which was given its present name in 1883. "Mammoth Mt. . . . is one of the most striking peaks in the Sierra, from its great size and from the needle-like pinnacles that rise from a mountain at its southern end." (A reference to the Minarets, which were named at this time by Clarence King. From the journal of James T. Gardiner, July 12, 1866. Copy in Farquhar Papers, BL.)

Mann Trail   *Yosemite Valley, Yosemite*

Milton and Houston Mann built a trail from the South Fork of the Merced to Yosemite Valley in 1855 and 1856. The route was from what is now Wawona via Alder Creek, Empire Meadow, Westfall Meadows, Peregoy Meadow, and Old Inspiration Point. The trail is well delineated on Hoffmann and Gardiner's map, 1863–67, and on the Wheeler Survey map of the valley, 1883, where it is labeled "Old Mariposa Trail."

McClure's Pass   *Matterhorn Peak*

A pass between Spiller and Matterhorn canyons; the route taken by Lt. McClure in 1894. (*SCB* 1, no. 5, Jan. 1895: 172–75.) The pass is named on McClure's maps of 1895 and 1896, and on LeConte's map of 1900.

McLean Pass or **MacLane Pass**   *Tuolumne Meadows*

This was an early name for Tioga Pass. The name "McLane's Pass" is on Hoffmann and Gardiner's map of 1863–67, and was still in use as late as Benson's map of 1896. The name "McLean Pass" was used regularly in the *Homer Mining Index* in the early 1880s. No one has ever provided an explanation for this name, but there is a possibility. In the summer of 1852 Lt. Tredwell Moore of the US Army led an expedition against the Chowchilla and Yosemite Indians. Moore's second in command was a Lt. McLean. This command crossed the Sierra via Mono Pass, and discovered—and named—Mono Lake. On August 20 Lt. McLean and a contingent of twenty men left the camp at Mono Lake to return to Fort Miller on the Fresno River, which is where they rejoined the main party. (*San Joaquin Republican*, Sept. 15, 1852.) I suggest that Lt. McLean crossed the Sierra via Tioga Pass, and left his name thereon.

Melissa's Falls   *Yosemite Valley*

Some fool tourist lavished this fool name upon Yosemite Falls. (Starr King, 58.)

Merced Meadows   *Merced Peak*

R. M. Price and party gave this name to a meadow on the Triple Peak Fork of the Merced River in 1897. (*SCB* 2, no. 3, Jan. 1898: 199.)

Milk Ranch   *Hetch Hetchy Reservoir*

The name is on the Hoffmann and Gardiner map of 1863–67 near the head of Cottonwood Creek, in the area that is now named "Smith Meadow." The name has been used a number of times in California—and elsewhere—to indicate where someone had dairy cows and was selling milk to settlers, travelers, and miners.

Monarch of the Vale   *Yosemite Valley*

Simply a romantic way of saying "El Capitan," which name the writer already knew. (*Mariposa Democrat*, Aug. 5, 1856.)

Monastery: Peak, Valley   *Tuolumne Meadows*

For Cathedral Peak and its surrounding terrain. The names are captions on a Muybridge stereo. (YRL files.)

Mono Trail

The old Indian trail across the Sierra via Mono Pass. There were two parts to the trail: one north of Yosemite Valley, which essentially stayed on the high ground between the Tuolumne and Merced rivers, and the other south of the valley, which passed through Peregoy Meadow and went via the top of Nevada Fall to Cathedral Pass and joined the northern trail at the west end of Tuolumne Meadows. Both of these are shown, in varying degrees, on the Hoffmann and Gardiner map of 1863–67, on the Wheeler Survey atlas sheet 56D, 1878–79, and map of Yosemite Valley and Vicinity, 1883, and on LeConte's maps of 1893 and 1896.

Murchison, Mount   *Merced Peak*

A name given by the Whitney Survey to a peak just north of Mount Lyell, for Sir Roderick Impey Murchison (1792–1871), president of the British Geographical Society. A few years later the survey renamed the peak **Mount Maclure**.

Notch, The   *Yosemite Valley*

The band of rock across the Merced river over which Vernal Fall drops. (Starr King, 63.) King, a New Englander, used the word in the way it had been used in his home territory: White Mountain Notch, Franconia Notch, etc. A version of this also appears on an Anthony stereo as "The Great Notch." (YRL files.)

O! My! Point   *Yosemite Valley, Yosemite*

"At the first turn of the Old Big Oak Flat Road below the gate, where the Gentry Hotel was located." (YRL files; see **Gentry's**.) It was from this point that one had the first good view of part of Yosemite Valley, and would exclaim "O! My!"

Obelisk, The   *Merced Peak*
The Whitney Survey gave this name to Mount Clark, and the Clark
Range was sometimes called the "Obelisk Group." (Whitney, *The Yosemite
Guide-Book*, 1870: 108.)

Old Blacksmith Shop   *Yosemite Valley*
"There is a cranny little spot at the foot of the hill [where the Coulterville Road reached the Merced River], known as 'The Blacksmith's Shop,'
which consists of an irregular chamber formed entirely of huge bowlders
that have toppled off and down from the surrounding cliffs, in the 'long,
long ago.' Here the forge and anvil rang out their merry peals, while picks
and drills and crow-bars needed on the road, were being sharpened."
(Hutchings, *In the Heart*, 291.)
"Have Feusier [of the USGS] determine definitely where the 'Blacksmith Shop' is. I have seen one statement that it is at the Cascades and not
where the trail leaves the road. That would seem more reasonable to me
for the location of any kind of shop, as the other place is a mass of huge
boulders." (Letter, Hiram Chittenden to R. B. Marshall, July 22, 1904, in
Marshall Papers, Part I, Box III, BL.)
"The Black Smith Shop are [sic] just at the up turn of the Coulterville
Road about 500 [feet] S.E. from the trail down the Merced Cañon. I did not
expect to have to dive under a rock to find it." (Letter, H. C. Feusier to
Marshall, July 29, 1904, in Marshall Papers, Part I, Box IV, BL.)
So the Old Blacksmith Shop was indeed among the huge fallen
boulders—a natural shelter rather than a building. On April 3, 1982
another fall of boulders closed the old road forever. The name was on the
first six editions of the *Yosemite Valley* map, 1907–38.

Old Man of the Mountains   *Yosemite Valley, Hetch Hetchy Reservoir*
An early name for Ahwiyah Point. (*Mariposa Gazette*, June 12, 1875.)

Onion Valley   *Hetch Hetchy Reservoir*
A meadow on a fork of Cottonwood Creek, about a mile southeast of
Smith Meadow. It appears only on Lt. McClure's maps of 1895 and 1896.

Orange Lake   *Merced Peak*
John Muir gave this name to a small lake—100 yards in circum-
ference—about 1.5 miles west-northwest of Merced Lake. ("The Mountain
Lakes of California," *Scribner's Monthly*, Jan. 1879: 417.) There are no lakes
in that direction within that distance, but about half a mile farther on,
west of Echo Valley, is a granite bench where there are several small lakes.

O'Pimm   *El Portal, Yosemite*
"We learn that a new Post Office has been established on the Coulterville and Yosemite Turnpike, at a point 10 or 11 miles from the Valley formerly called Big Meadows. The name of the office is O'Pimm, and George Meyers is appointed Postmaster." (*Mariposa Gazette*, Oct. 14, 1882.) "Opim" had a postoffice from May 1882 to July 1884, located on the ranch owned by Peter Meison and George Meyers; the latter was the postmaster. "An Indian descriptive name for Big Meadows, site now known as Foresta." (*Post Offices*, 162. See Shirley Sargent, *Foresta Big Meadow*.)

Overhanging Rock   *Yosemite Valley*
At Glacier Point, just east of "Photographer's Rock." (See Matthes, *Paper 160*, 17.)

Owl Camp   *Yosemite*
A locale on the Mariposa and Yosemite trail, 0.5 mile north of Empire Meadow. (Hutchings, *Scenes*, 1870: 82.)

Paradise Valley   *Yosemite Valley*
Suggested by a member of the Mariposa Battalion as a name for Yosemite Valley. (Bunnell, *Discovery*, 1911: 68–69.)

Pelican Peak   *Yosemite Valley*
"One prominent point known as Pelican Peak, just back of Hutchings Hotel, fell with a terrible crash [during the 1872 earthquake], and scattering immense masses of boulders around but did no damage to any houses in the vicinity . . . ." (Letter from Galen Clark, May 4, 1872, in *California Farmer and Journal of Useful Sciences*.)

Photographer's Rock   *Yosemite Valley*
The famous rock whereon the daring could pose. (Matthes, *Paper 160*, 17.) See also **Contemplation Rock**.

Pilaster Rock   *Yosemite Valley*
On the hillside about one-fourth of a mile above Taft Point. The name is in the caption for a Muybridge stereo, about 1868. (YRL files.)

Pine Mountain   *Yosemite Valley, Hetch Hetchy Reservoir*
Waijau. Mount Watkins; meaning the Pine Mountain. (Whitney, *The Yosemite Guide-Book*, 1870: 17.)

sketched by Thos. Ayres, June 20, 1855—first ever taken.

GENERAL VIEW OF THE YO SEMITE VALLEY.

[From Open-eta-noo-ah, on the Old Indian Trail.]

Courtesy The Bancroft Library

From Hutchings' *In the Heart of the Sierras*.
(See the photograph on page 6.)

Courtesy The Bancroft Library

"A View From the Mariposa Trail."
Photograph by Muybridge.

Piñon Point   *Hetch Hetchy Reservoir*
François Matthes suggested this name for one of the few places in the park where the single leaf pinyon pine is found. (YRL files.) The name is not on any maps. The location is above Rancheria Falls, on the western slope of the ridge marked "6595" east of the trail into Tiltill Valley. (Snyder.)

Point Lookout   *Yosemite*
A viewpoint 1.5 miles northeast of Wawona and about 0.2 mile west of the Chilnualna Trail, in sec. 26, T. 4 S., R. 21 E. A trail was built to it by Washburn in the 1880s. (*Foley's Guide*, 1892: 45.)

Point Louisa   *Yosemite Valley*
A name in the captions of three Anthony stereos showing Photographer's Rock. (YRL files.)

Point Rea   *Yosemite Valley*
A high point on the Vernal Fall trail, beyond which Illilouette Fall comes into view. (*Foley's Guide*, 1901: 22.) The name also was used by Charles A. Bailey in the article describing how he discovered Sierra Point. (*SCB* 2, no. 4, June 1898: 218.)

Poison Meadow   *Lake Eleanor*
The northernmost of three meadows on an old trail between Miguel Meadow and Poopenaut Valley, in sec. 14, T. 1 N., R. 19 E. The name is on McClure's maps of 1895 and 1896, and on Benson's map of 1896. "A common name for meadows where the Tall Larkspur grows." (YRL files.)

Prospect Point or **Rock**   *Yosemite Valley, Yosemite*
The top of a rocky promontory just below the first turn in the Old Big Oak Flat Road below Gentry's, at O! My! Point. (Kneeland, 75.)

Pyramid Rock   *Yosemite Valley*
An early name given to Sentinel Rock. (*Mariposa Democrat*, Aug. 5, 1856.)

Randall Cañon   *Matterhorn Peak*
An alternate name for Spiller Canyon. It was used by Lt. McClure in 1894 and on his map of 1896. (*SCB* 1, no. 8, May 1896: 330.)

Rattlesnake Lake   *Tower Peak*

Lt. McClure had this name on his maps of 1895 and 1896 for what he himself named "Branigan Lake" in 1894. (Farquhar: McClure. See also *SCB* 1, no. 5, Jan. 1895: 183.)

Real Pass   *Tuolumne Meadows*

Lt. McClure's 1896 map has this designation on what is now Vogelsang Pass—an official name that is not on present maps. It's the route taken by the trail going directly south from Vogelsang Lake. McClure meant this legend and also "Blind Pass," just east of "Real Pass," as guides to the correct route rather than actual names. (Snyder.)

Register Rock   *Yosemite Valley*

A huge boulder at the intersection of the Mist Trail and the horse trail to Nevada Fall. It was named by one of the first tourist parties to visit Yosemite Valley. "Our descent [from Vernal Fall] was slow and tedious. On our route we passed a large boulder, which from its appearance, has recently been detached from the mountains and fallen nearly to the bed of the stream. It weighs many thousand tons, and on the lower side we registered our names, and for that reason it may be known as 'register rock.'" (*San Joaquin Republican*, Oct. 16, 1855; reprinted from the *Mariposa Gazette* of Oct. 11.) The name is on the Wheeler Survey map of the valley, 1883.

River View   *Yosemite Valley*

An old name for what is now "Valley View." It is on the Wheeler Survey map of 1883.

Rock of Ages   *Yosemite Valley*

Undoubtedly the first name given to Half Dome by whites: two bear-hunters, who saw it from the valley rim west of Bridalveil Fall. (Diary of William Penn Abrams, BL; see the **Yosemite Valley** entry in the main list.)

Rocket Cascades   *Tuolumne Meadows*

The Whitney Survey's name for Waterwheel Falls. "The lowest set of cascades in this group we called the 'Rocket Cascades,' because the water, striking the edges of the great plates of granite . . . was continually thrown off in great arches. . . ." (Whitney, *The Yosemite Guide-Book*, pocket edition, 1874: 155–56.)

Rocky Canyon Creek   *Tuolumne Meadows*
A name for Cathedral Creek, or at least for the upper part of it, which is all these early travelers saw. (*Homer Mining Index*, July 22, 1882.)

Round Meadow   *Tuolumne Meadows*
A meadow on the south side of the Tuolumne River midway between Soda Springs and Glen Aulin. "Here [the river] makes a bold sweep to the north, and then again to the south, including a round meadow about three-eighths of a mile in diameter." (R. M. Price, "Through the Tuolumne Cañon, " *SCB* 1, no. 6, May 1895: 202.) The name was on McClure's maps of 1895 and 1896, Benson's map of 1896, and LeConte's map of 1900—but in the wrong place. They all had it on Cathedral Creek, northwest of Fairview Dome.

Sentinel Rock   *Yosemite Valley*
The name used in 1856 by Warren Baer for what is now Grizzly Peak. (*Mariposa Democrat*, Aug. 5, 1856.)

Signal Peak   *Yosemite*
"The name given to the highest point of the Chow-chilla Mountains, lying westerly from the hotel. This suggestive nomenclature was given to it owing to the Indians having made choice of that point as a signal station . . . ." (Hutchings, *In the Heart*, 268.) Hutchings was referring to Devil Peak, which has had that name since the early 1860s. But the old name persists. The US Forest Service built a fire lookout on the peak in 1919, which is still known as the Signal Peak Fire Lookout. (Snyder.)

Signal Rock   *Yosemite Valley*
". . . adjoining [El Capitan] looms up, with broad, oval top, the Signal Rock, on which the Yosemite Indians lit their signal fires in the hour of danger." (*Mariposa Democrat*, Aug. 5, 1856.) This may be one of the two rounded summits north of, and higher than, El Capitan.

Silver Chain   *Merced Peak*
"There is a beautiful fall near the head of the valley [Little Yosemite Valley], which we took the liberty of naming the Silver Chain . . . ." (*Mariposa Free Press*, Oct. 28, 1870.) This may be what is now named Bunnell Cascade, but it is not possible to be certain.

Sink, The   *Hetch Hetchy Reservoir*
A meadow area about 1.5 miles west-southwest of Pleasant Valley,

southwest of four small lakes and a point marked "8500." The sink is formed by a debris dam that probably is of glacial origin. The area has filled in, and the creek flowing through the meadow goes underground— hence the name. The creek emerges from the rock dam at the lower end of the meadow. (Snyder.) The name is on McClure's 1896 map and LeConte's 1900 map.

Sink, The   *Matterhorn Peak*

Lt. McClure's name for a low place in the ridge that divides Slide Creek from Rancheria Creek near their respective headwaters. (*SCB* 1, no. 8, May 1896: 333.)

Sisters, The   *Yosemite Valley*

Sometimes called "Twin Sisters," an early name for the Cathedral Spires. (*San Francisco Daily Evening Bulletin*, July 8, 1857; Starr King, 50.)

Slate Creek   *Tuolumne Meadows*

The south fork of Lee Vining Creek, now named "Mine Creek." It was called "Slate Creek" in the *Homer Mining Index*, Feb. 18, 1882. The headwaters of the creek were within the park from 1890 to 1905.

Smith's Valley   *Hetch Hetchy Reservoir*

At one time an alternate name for Hetch Hetchy Valley. See **Smith Meadow** in the main list.

Smoky Jack Meadow   *Tuolumne Meadows*

This is the long meadow in Cold Canyon between Glen Aulin and Virginia Canyon. It is named for John "Smoky Jack" Connell, who at one time grazed his sheep here. (Snyder. See **Smoky Jack Campground** in the main list.) The name has never been on maps, but has been handed down from sheepherders to the cavalry to park rangers.

Soda Spgs Buttes   *Tuolumne Meadows*

A name that appears only on Lt. McClure's 1895 map—for Fairview Dome. In a sidebar McClure has both names in a list of PLACES WITH TWO NAMES.

South Creek   *Tuolumne Meadows*

The name was suggested by former BGN chairman Frank Bond to replace the name "South Fork of Cathedral Creek." "South Creek" appeared on the YNP map in 1929; it was approved by the BGN in 1932.

The longer name is the presently approved one. Neither of the names has made it onto a map. The creek rises in sec. 8, T. 1 S., R. 23 E., and flows northeast to Cathedral Creek.

Sphinx, The   *Yosemite Valley, Yosemite*
   An attractive grouping of rocks along the Old Big Oak Flat Road between Tamarack Creek and Cascade Creek. (Hutchings, *Scenes*, 1870: 104.)

Staircase, The   *Yosemite Valley, Yosemite*
   An early name for the upper part of the Mist Trail that goes up the gully between Nevada Fall and Liberty Cap; built by John Conway. "Mr. Conway also built the trail from Snows [La Casa Nevada] to the top of Nevada Falls, for Messers Washburn and M'Cready in 1871." (*Mariposa Gazette*, May 28, 1881.) This was later called the "Zig-Zag Trail."

Stand Point of Silence   *Yosemite Valley*
   Named on June 22, 1859 by the Rev. Ferdinand C. Ewer. "Left this morning before sun rise for Coulterville. I named the point on the

Courtesy The Bancroft Library

"Helmet Dome and Little Grizzly Fall." (See **Sugar Loaf.**)
Photograph by Muybridge, 1872.

Coulterville Trail where one first gains a view of the valley 'The Stand Point of Silence.'" (Ewer's diary, p. 306, in California Historical Society Library.) The spot is assumed to be on a dome 300 yards below the present-day trail from the modern Big Oak Flat Road to the Old Big Oak Flat Road at Cascade Creek—in sec. 35, T. 2 S., R. 20 E.

Ewer was traveling with a party that included James M. Hutchings, whose account was considerably more emotional. "'This verily is the stand-point of silence,' at length escaped in whispering huskiness from the lips of one of our number, Mr. Ewer. Let us name this spot 'The Stand-Point of Silence.' And so let it be written in the note-book of every tourist, as it will be in his inmost soul when he looks at the appalling grandeur of Yo-Semite valley from this spot." (Hutchings *Illustrated* 4, no. 4, Oct. 1859: 158.)

If you think that reaction a bit intense, so did others. "At a little distance from the trail, on the southern or right-hand side, a partial glimpse into the Yosemite may be obtained. It is not a satisfactory one, however, on account of the number of trees in the way, and the bend in the Valley itself, which cuts off the view of all the upper part. This point of view has been rather absurdly called the 'Stand-Point of Silence.'" (Whitney, *The Yosemite Guide-Book*, 1870: 54.)

Standpoint of Silence   *Yosemite Valley*

On the south wall of the valley, between Meadow Brook and Old Inspiration Point. It was named by the artist C. D. Robinson twenty years after the same name was given to the point in the item above. (Hutchings, *In the Heart*, 403.) The name is on the Wheeler Survey map of the valley, 1883.

Steamboat Bay   *Yosemite*

Another name for **Battleship Harbor**. A quiet stretch of the Merced River near Arch Rock where great pieces of granite appear like the prows of large ships. (YRL files.)

Stella Falls   *Tuolumne Meadows*

An old and unexplained name for California Falls. The name appears only on LeConte's map of 1900.

Studhorse Flat   *Yosemite*

The name is not on any maps. The location is where a horse trail crosses the Wawona Road about 1.5 miles southeast of Wawona, in sec. 1, T. 5 S., R. 21 E.

Sugar Loaf   *Merced Peak*

"Sugar Loaf" or "Sugarbowl Dome" were old names for Bunnell Point, on the south side of the Merced east of Little Yosemite Valley. (Hall, 82.) This dome and the unnamed dome 0.6 mile to the westward, across the river, have been called by the same name. See the next entry.

Sugar Loaf   *Merced Peak*

A presently unnamed dome 0.6 mile east by south from Moraine Dome. It was known as "Sugar Loaf" at least as early as the 1870s. (John Conway in the *Mariposa Gazette*, April 27, 1878.) It was also once called "Helmet Dome" (Muybridge photo, 1872), because two long horizontal lines running across the face of the dome make it look like a visored helmet.

". . . that remarkable dome-crowned spur of bare granite known as Sugar Loaf. Although repeatedly overridden by the glacier, this spur, which is massive throughout save for a single horizontal master joint, still stands 1,300 feet high and partly blocks the valley." (Matthes, *Paper 160*, 99; plates 31A and 45B.) The name is on the Wheeler Survey map of 1883, but was in use before that. (Whitney, *The Yosemite Book*, 94.)

Sugar Loaf   *Yosemite Valley*

An early name for Liberty Cap. (*Mariposa Democrat*, Aug. 5, 1856.)

Sugarty Bear Camp   *Tower Peak*

Jim Snyder states that this is undoubtedly the original name of Bear Valley; it may have been a hunting camp. The name appears on Lt. McClure's 1896 map, and on his 1895 map simply as "Sugarty."

Sunnyside Bench   *Yosemite Valley*

Not on maps. A bench east of the top of Lower Yosemite Fall. (YRL files.)

Sunset Point   *Yosemite*

A point southwest of the "Sunset Tree" in the Mariposa Grove, from where sunset over the Chowchilla Mountains can be seen. (YRL files.)

Surprise, Mt.   *Merced Peak*

An early name for what is now Mount Bruce. It appears only on Lt. McClure's maps of 1895 and 1896.

Table Rock   *Yosemite Valley*
The rock upon which Snow's La Casa Nevada was built. (YRL files.)

Tenmile Meadow   *Hetch Hetchy Reservoir*
On the trail from Tenaya Lake to Yosemite Valley via Snow Creek. The meadow is about two miles southwest of Hidden Lake, on a small tributary of Tenaya Creek. (Hall, 66.) The location is in the upper part of sec. 36, T. 1 S., R. 22 E. The name has never been on maps.

Third Meadow   *Lake Eleanor*
The third meadow on the old trail from Miguel Meadow to Poopenaut Valley. Named on McClure's maps of 1895 and 1896 and Benson's map of 1896.

Three Brothers, The   *Tuolumne Meadows*
A name given informally in 1895 to three domes south of California Falls, on the eastern end of Falls Ridge; not presently named. (*SCB* 1, no. 6, May 1895: 203.)

Three Graces, The   *Yosemite Valley*
An early name for the Cathedral Rocks, given when a blend of religion and romanticism was at the maximum. "Kosúkong. The rocks near Cathedral Rock, sometimes called 'The Three Graces.'" (Whitney, *The Yosemite Guide-Book*, 1870: 16.)

Transport Point   *Yosemite Valley*
"From this standpoint, not only can the entire length of the lower Yo Semite Fall be seen; but the interjacent depths and irregularities of the intervening cañon between the top of the lower, and foot of the upper fall; while in front of us the entire Upper Yo Semite Fall is in full view." (Hutchings, *In the Heart*, 476.)
This name has never been on maps. It was Hutchings' name for "Valley View Point"—which was Conway's name. (Snyder.)

Tule Meadow   *Lake Eleanor*
About two miles south-southwest of Miguel Meadow on the old trail to Poopenaut Valley—in the southwest part of sec. 13, T. 1 N., R. 19 E. (See **Poison Meadow** and **Third Meadow**.) The name was on McClure's maps of 1895 and 1896 and Benson's map of 1896.

Tunnel View *Yosemite Valley*
The viewpoint at the east end of the Wawona Tunnel. The name has never been on the maps; the location now has the official name of "Discovery View."

Tuolumne Castle *Hetch Hetchy Reservoir*
". . . a double-peaked rock of stupendous height, well named Tuolumne Castle." (*SCB* 1, no. 6, May 1895: 205.) Probably what is now named **Double Rock**, about 2.5 miles southwest of Pate Valley on the Tuolumne River.

Tuolumne El Capitan *Tuolumne Meadows*
A name used by Jennie Price in 1897 to refer to Wildcat Point on the north side of the Tuolumne River northwest of Glen Aulin. (*SCB* 2, no. 3, Jan. 1898: 176.)

Tuolumne Yosemite *Lake Eleanor, Hetch Hetchy Reservoir*
"After my first visit, in the autumn of 1871, I have always called it [Hetch Hetchy Valley] the Tuolumne Yosemite, for it is a wonderfully exact counterpart of the great Yosemite, not only in its crystal river and sublime rocks and waterfalls, but in the gardens, groves, and meadows of its flowery parklike floor." (John Muir, "The Hetch-Hetchy Valley," *SCB* 6, no. 4, Jan. 1908: 212.)

Turtle Rock *Tuolumne Meadows*
An old name for Polly Dome, in the caption for Muybridge no. 1537. (YRL files.)

Twin Cañons *Matterhorn Peak*
A name given by Lt. McClure in August 1894 to the two heads of Crazy Mule Gulch when he crossed from Slide Creek to Rock Creek. (*SCB* 1, no. 5, Jan. 1895: 178.) The present *Matterhorn Peak* quad clearly shows only Crazy Mule Gulch; there aren't two canyons. The twin canyons were found by Jim Snyder when he followed McClure's route.
The name "Twin Cañons" is on McClure's map of 1895 and LeConte's map of 1900. On McClure's 1896 map the twin canyons are shown but not named.

Twin Domes *Yosemite Valley*
North Dome and Half Dome. "At the upper end of the valley stand the 'Twin Domes'—two immense mountains, dome-shaped, and distinct

from any of the surrounding ones. The one at the right can be seen at a distance of forty miles. . . . Part of this dome has fallen away." (Hutchings *Illustrated* 1, no. 1, July 1856: 3.)

Twin Falls   *Hetch Hetchy Reservoir, Tuolumne Meadows*
The falls on Cathedral Creek just before it joins the Tuolumne River. Named on McClure's maps of 1895 and 1896 and on Benson's map of 1896.

Twins or **Two Sisters**   *Yosemite Valley*
". . . further up the valley, beyond [the Three Brothers], are the Twins or Two Sisters. They cannot be mistaken, for though when looking down through the Valley, they seem as a single rock, yet when nearly fronting them, they project two sharp projecting points . . . ." (*Mariposa Democrat*, Aug. 5, 1856.) I cannot profess to know what features this name refers to. Is that why it isn't on any maps?

Uncle Sam Point   *Yosemite Valley*
One of three points on the Four Mile Trail. See **Congress Point**; also **Union Point** in the main list. "Uncle Sam Point" was where the trail crossed the ridge running down from Sentinel Dome—the high point of the wall west of Glacier Point. ("The Sentinel Rock and Glacier Point Trail," *Mariposa Gazette*, May 24, 1872.)

Valley View   *Yosemite Valley, Yosemite*
A viewpoint on the Coulterville Trail between the Coulterville Road and the Old Big Oak Flat Road, two miles southwest of Cascade Creek. (Hittell, 51.)

Valley View Point   *Yosemite Valley*
A point on the Yosemite Fall trail above the lower fall, where the trail changes direction from northeast to north. The name was first used by John Conway, builder of the trail, in the *Mariposa Gazette*, April 27, 1878. Hutchings used the name "Transport Point" for the same place. (Snyder.)

Vestibule, The   *Yosemite Valley*
"A party of travelers went 'under' the upper Yosemite fall week before last—the first time such a feat had been accomplished. There are about sixty visitors in the valley now." (*San Francisco Daily Alta California*, July 22, 1859.)
". . . a long, broad passage behind the [Upper Yosemite] falls . . . . You

can see up behind the water several hundred feet . . . ." (John Conway in the *Mariposa Gazette*, April 27, 1878. See **Fern Ledge** in this list.)

Zig-Zag Trail   *Yosemite Valley, Yosemite*
    The stretch of trail between Liberty Cap and Nevada Fall, going up to Little Yosemite Valley. (Williams, 84.)

Courtesy The Bancroft Library

"The Vestibule" or "Fern Ledge."
Photograph by Muybridge.

Indian Names

It is not possible to launch into this list of Indian names without quoting at some length from Stephen Powers' *Tribes of California*. Powers was scorned by some because he was not a trained 'professional,' a controversy that I do not wish to reheat. But there are two things for sure: Powers had the ability to relate to Indians, and he didn't pull his punches.

"There is no doubt the Indians would be much amused if they could know what a piece of work we have made of some of their names. . . . The great grim walls of Yosemite have been made by the white man to blossom with aboriginal poetry like a page of 'Lalla Rookh'. From the 'Great Chief of the Valley' and the 'Goddess of the Valley' down to the 'Virgin Tears' and the 'Cataract of Diamonds', the sumptuous imaginations of various discoverers have trailed through that wonderful gorge blazons of mythological and barbarian heraldry of an Oriental gorgeousness. It would be a pity, truly, if the Indians had not succeeded in interpreting more poetically the meanings of the place than our countrymen have done in such bald appellations as 'Vernal Fall', 'Pigeon Creek', and the like; but whether they did or not, they did not perpetrate the melodramatic and dime-novel shams that have been fathered upon them.

"In the first place the aborigines never knew of any such locality as Yosemite Valley. Second, there is not now and there has not been anything in the valley which they call Yosemite. Third, they never called 'Old Ephraim' himself Yosemite, nor is there any such word in the Miwok language.

"The valley has always been known to them, and is to this day, when speaking among themselves, as A-wá-ni. This, it is true, is only the name of one of the ancient villages which it contained; but by prominence it gave its name to the valley, and, in accordance with the Indian usage almost everywhere, to the inhabitants of the same. The word 'Yosemite' is simply a very beautiful and sonorous corruption of the word for 'grizzly bear'. On the Stanislaus and north of it the word is *u-zú-mai-ti*; on the South Fork of the Merced, *uh-zú-mai-tuh*.

"Mr. J. M. Hutchings, in his 'Scenes of Wonder and Curiosity in California', states that the pronunciation on the South Fork is 'Yohamite'. Now, there is occasionally a kind of cockney in the tribe, who cannot get the letter 'h' right. Different Indians will pronounce the word for 'wood' *su-sú-eh, sú-suh, hu-hú-eh*; also, the word for 'eye', *hun'-ta, hun'-tum, shun'-ta*. It may have been an Indian of this sort who pronounced the word that way; I have never heard it so spoken.

"In other portions of California the Indian names have effected such slight lodgment in our atlases that it is seldom worth while to go much out of our way to set them right; but there are so many of them preserved in Yosemite that it is different. Professor Whitney and Mr. Hutchings, in their respective guide-books, state that they derived their catalogues of Indian names from white men. The Indians certainly have a right to be heard in this department at least; and when they differ from the interpreters every right-thinking man will accept the statement of an intelligent aborigine as against a score of Americans. The Indian can very seldom give a connected, philosophical account of his customs and ideas, for which one must depend on men who have observed them; but if he does not know the simple words of his own language, pray who does?

"Acting on this belief, I employed Choko (a dog), generally known as Old Jim, and accounted the wisest aboriginal head in Yosemite, to go with me around the valley and point out in detail all the places. He is one of the very few original Awani now living; for a California Indian, he is exceptionally frank and communicative, and he is generally considered by Americans as truthful as he is shiftless . . . ." (Powers, 361–62.)

Ajemu   *Yosemite Valley*
"The west side of El Capitan is called '*Ajemu*,' or manzanita, that being a place where they gather the berries of this familiar shrub." (Whitney, *The Yosemite Guide-Book*, 1870: 16.)

A-wa'-ni   *Yosemite Valley*
See **Ahwahnee** in the main list.

Cho-ko-nip'-o-deh   *Yosemite Valley*
"Cho-ko-nip'-o-deh (baby basket), Royal Arches. This curved and

overhanging canopy-rock bears no little resemblance to an Indian baby-basket. Another form is *cho-ko'-ni*; and either one means literally 'dog-place' or 'dog-house.'" (Powers, 364.)

Eleacha   *Yosemite Valley*
An alternative name for the Three Brothers. "Named after a plant much used for food." (Hutchings, *Scenes*, 1860: 94.)

Er-na-ting Law-oo-too   *Yosemite Valley*
Stated to be the name for Glacier Point, and to mean "Bear Skin." (Hutchings, *Scenes*, 1870: 169.)

Ham-mo   *Yosemite Valley*
See **Lost Arrow** in the main list.

Ham'-mo-ko   *Yosemite Valley*
"Ham'-mo-ko (usually contracted to Ham'-moak), a generic word, used several times in the valley to denote the broken *débris* lying at the foot of the walls." (Powers, 364.)

Hok-ok'-wi-dok   *Yosemite Valley*
"Hok-ok'-wi-dok [on the south bank of the Merced], which stood very nearly where Hutchings's Hotel now stands, opposite Yosemite Fall." (Powers, 365.)

Hol'-low   *Yosemite Valley*
See **Indian Cave** in the main list.

Hunto   *Yosemite Valley*
It has been asserted by some that this was the name for the Royal Arches. "From an Indian word for eye." (Sanchez, 278.) *Huntu* is "eye" in Southern Sierra Miwok. (Kroeber, 43.) "Shun'-ta, Hun'-ta (the eye), the Watching Eye." (Powers, 365.)

Kachoomah   *Yosemite Valley, Yosemite*
Wild Cat Fall. ". . . the impetuous stream . . . is thrown, or seems to spring, diagonally across towards the northern bank . . . suggesting the sudden side-spring of the animal for whom the observing red man named it." (*Bancroft's tourist Guide*, 1871: 38.) Note that this is not the present Wildcat Falls, but rather an old name for a fall about thirty feet high

halfway between Vernal Fall and Nevada Fall. The name *Kachoomah* also applied to Mount Broderick.

Kai-al-au'-wa Cliffs   *Yosemite Valley*

Between Fireplace Bluffs and Ribbon Fall, on the Wheeler Survey map of 1883. The name is also in Powers, p. 362, but no meaning is given. An alternate spelling was *Keialauwa*. (Whitney, *The Yosemite Guide-Book,* 1870: 16.)

Courtesy The Bancroft Library

"Mount Kah-choo-mah"—Wild Cat Rock—Mount Broderick.
The back of Half Dome is at the upper left. Photograph by Muybridge.

Kai-al-au'-wa Hill   *Hetch Hetchy Reservoir*

A presently unnamed summit about 1.7 miles west-northwest of Boundary Hill. The name appears only the Wheeler Survey map of the valley, 1883.

Kay-o-pha

The Sierra Nevada. "It was traditional with the other Indians, that the band to which the name Yosemite had been given . . . were descendants of the neighboring tribes on both sides of 'Kay o-pha,' or 'Skye Mountains,' the 'High Sierras.'" (Bunnell, *Discovery*, 1880: 64.)

Ke-ko-too-yem   *Yosemite Valley*
Another name for Mirror Lake, said to mean "Sleeping Water." (Hutchings, *In the Heart*, 386.)

Komah   *Yosemite Valley*
"The best view of the valley is from *Komah Point*, or *Rock*, on the Mariposa Trail about a half mile from the edge of the valley, and about 1,500 feet above it." (Hittell, 14.) Said to mean "Moon Rock." This rock is somewhere above the east end of the Wawona Tunnel. See Muybridge photo in *CHSQ* 42, no. 1, March 1963.

Kom-po-pai-zes   *Yosemite Valley*
A name for the Three Brothers. Also see **Eleacha** and **Wawhawke**.

Ko-su'-ko   *Yosemite Valley*
Cathedral Rock(s). No meaning given. (Powers, 363.) Another version was "Kosúkong. The rocks near Cathedral Rock, sometimes called 'The Three Graces.'" (Whitney, *The Yosemite Guide-Book*, 1870: 16.)

Ku-mai'-ni   *Yosemite Valley*
"Ku-mai'-ni, a village which was situated at the lower end of the great meadow, about a quarter of a mile from Yosemite Fall." (Powers, 365.)

Lah-koo'-hah   *Yosemite Valley*
See **Indian Cave** in the main list.

Le-sam'-ai-ti   *Yosemite Valley*
"Le-sam'-ai-ti, a village standing about a fifth of a mile above the last-mentioned [No-to-mid'-u-la]." (Powers, 365. This name is not mentioned by Merriam. Note the similarity to the whites' use of the name "Le-ham-ite." See **Lehamite: Creek, Falls** in the main list.)

Loi'-a   *Yosemite Valley*
Sentinel Rock. No meaning given. (Powers, 363.)

Lung-yo-to-co-ya   *Yosemite Valley*
Ribbon Fall; various spellings exist. Said by Bunnell to mean "Pigeon Basket."

Mah'-ta   *Yosemite Valley*
For Liberty Cap, said to mean "Martyr Mountain." (Clark, 108.)

Ma'-ta   *Yosemite Valley*
"Ma'-ta (the cañon), Indian Cañon. A generic word, in explaining which the Indians hold up both hands to denote perpendicular walls." (Powers, 364.)

Ma-che'-to   *Yosemite Valley*
"Ma-che'-to . . . [a village] at the foot of Indian Cañon." (Powers, 365.)

No-to-mid'-u-la   *Yosemite Valley*
"No-to-mid'-u-la, a village about four hundred yards east of Macheto." (Powers, 365. See above.)

Ollenya   *Yosemite Valley*
"*Ollenya*. Small stream between the Three Brothers and the Yosemite Fall, means Frog Brook." (Whitney, *The Yosemite Guide-Book*, 1870: 17.)

Oowooyoowah   *Yosemite Valley*
Said to be the name for Glacier Point, meaning "Great Rock of the Elk." (Hittell, 22.)

Open-eta-noo-ah   *Yosemite Valley*
For Old Inspiration Point; no meaning given. (Hutchings *Illustrated* 4, no. 6, Dec. 1859: opp. 241; Starr King, 47.)

Patillima   *Yosemite Valley*
The name for Glacier Point; no meaning given. (Whitney, *The Yosemite Guide-Book*, 1870: 17.)

Peiwayak   *Yosemite Valley*
"*Peiwayak*. The Vernal Fall; meaning, white water; spelt Piwyack by some." (Whitney, *The Yosemite Guide-Book*, 1870: 17.)

Pilliwanee   *Yosemite, El Portal*
A name for the extended cliff on the north side of the Merced River between El Portal and the Arch Rock entrance station. "Reaching the cañon, Pilliwanee, a dark and sombre cliff, menacingly overshadows you on the left." ("The New River Trail to Yosemite," *Mariposa Gazette*, May 2, 1873.)

Poo-see-na-chuc-ka   *Yosemite Valley*
The Cathedral Rocks and Spires, "meaning 'Mouse-proof rocks,' from a fancied resemblance in shape to their acorn magazines or *caches*." (Bunnell, *Discovery*, 1911: 217.)

Pútputon   *Yosemite Valley*
"*Pútputon*. The meadow and little stream, on the Coulterville Trail, first met coming into the valley; means the 'the bubbling of water.'" (Whitney, *The Yosemite Guide-Book*, 1870: 16.) Identified by Ansel F. Hall as being Black Spring. (YRL files.)

Sak'-ka-du-eh   *Yosemite Valley*
Sentinel Dome. No meaning given. (Powers, 363.)

Sak'-ka-ya   *Yosemite Valley*
"Sak'-ka-ya, [a village] on the south bank of the river, a little west of Sentinel Rock." (Powers, 365.) Note the connection between this name and the one above, which surely has something to do with their proximity.

Sa-wah'   *Yosemite Valley*
"Sa-wah' (a gap), a name occurring frequently." (Powers, 365.)

Schokoni   *Yosemite Valley*
"*Schokoni*. The Royal Arches." (Whitney, *The Yosemite Guide-Book*, 1870: 17.)

Scho-ko-ya   *Yosemite Valley*
See **Royal Arches** in the main list.

Schotallowi   *Yosemite Valley*
"*Schotallowi*. Indian Cañon; the gulch between the Yosemite Falls and the North Dome." (Whitney, *The Yosemite Guide-Book*, 1870: 17.)

See-wah-lam   *Yosemite Valley, Yosemite*
Stated as the name for Mount Starr King. (Hutchings, *Scenes*, 1870: 169.)

Tesaiyak   *Yosemite Valley*
"*Tesaiyak*. The Half Dome, generally spelt Tisayac. (Whitney, *The Yosemite Guide-Book*, 17.)

Timalula   *Yosemite*

Probably the falls of Avalanche Creek into the Merced River, half a mile below the Arch Rock entrance station. "... Timalula ... greets the ear and the eye with the melody of rushing waters, and its mad bound over a precipice, a thousand feet above." ("The New River Trail to Yosemite," *Mariposa Gazette*, May 2, 1873.) See **Tueeulala Falls** in the main list. This may be a generic name, or a generic ending meaning "falls."

Tokoya   *Yosemite Valley*

"*Tokoya*. The North Dome; meaning, the basket, so named on account of its rounded basket shape." (Whitney, *The Yosemite Guide-Book*, 1870: 17.)

Tol'-leh   *Yosemite Valley*

"Tol'-leh, the soil or surface of the valley wherever not occupied by a village; the commons. It also denotes the bank of a river." (Powers, 364.)

Too-nu-yah   *Yosemite Valley*

Said to mean "Enchantment Point." (Hutchings, *In the Heart*, 400.) This probably is where the name "Valley View" now appears, just north of the Pohono Bridge.

Topinémete   *Yosemite Valley*

"*Topinémete*. The rocks between the foot of the Mariposa trail and the Bridal Veil Fall, said to mean 'a succession of rocks.'" (Whitney, *The Yosemite Guide-Book*, 1870: 16.) The name is on the Wheeler Survey map of the valley, 1883, as "To-pi-ne-me-te Bluffs," and covers the stretch from Old Inspiration Point to Dewey Point.

To-tock-ah-noo-lah   *Yosemite Valley*

For **El Capitan**. Many spellings were used.

Tu-tock-ah-nu-lah's Citadel   *Yosemite Valley*

"A tower-shaped and leaning rock, about three thousand feet in height, standing at the southwest side of the [Bridalveil] fall, sometimes called the 'Leaning Tower,' nearly opposite 'Tu-tock-ah-nu-lah,' has on its top a number of projecting rocks that very much resemble cannon." (Hutchings, *In the Heart*, 408.)

To-tu-ya   *Tuolumne Meadows*

Maria Lebrado's Indian name, meaning "foaming water." Maria was the last survivor of the Yosemite Indians. The name was suggested by

François Matthes for Pywiack Cascade, but it was never adopted. (YRL files.)

Tululowehäck *Yosemite Valley*
"*Tululowehäck*. Illilouette." (Whitney, *The Yosemite Guide-Book*, 1870: 17.) See **Illilouette** in the main list.

Um'-mo-so *Yosemite Valley*
"Um'-mo-so (generally contracted by the Indians to Um'-moas or Um'-mo), the bold towering cliff east of Yosemite Fall. (Powers, 363.) This would seem to mean what is now called "Yosemite Point," especially since Powers goes on to say that there was formerly a hunting-station near this point where the Indians hid to kill deer. But note that the "Um'-mo" contraction is almost identical with the reported name of "Ham-mo" for Lost Arrow.

Wa-ha'-ka *Yosemite Valley*
"Wa-ha'-ka, a village which stood at the base of Three Brothers; also, that rock itself." (Powers, 365.) See **Wawhawke**.

Wai-ack *Yosemite Valley*
For Mirror Lake, meaning "rock water." (Bunnell, *Report*, 11.)

Waijau *Yosemite Valley, Hetch Hetchy Reservoir*
"*Waijau*. Mount Watkins; meaning the Pine Mountain." (Whitney, *The Yosemite Guide-book*, 1870: 17.) Also spelled *Wei-yow'*, and meaning "Juniper Mountain." (Clark, 108.)

Waiya *Yosemite Valley*
"*Waiya*. Mirror Lake. Alternate spelling of 'Ahwiyah.'" (Whitney, *The Yosemite Guide-Book*, 1870: 17.)

Wa-kal'-la *Yosemite Valley, Yosemite*
The Merced River. No meaning given. (Powers, 362.)

Wawhawke *Yosemite Valley*
A supposed name for the Three Brothers, said to mean "falling rocks," but perhaps this was confused with Rocky Point.

We-äck *Yosemite Valley*
"The obstructing rocks on the old north side trail were known as

'We äck,' 'The Rocks,' and understood to mean the 'fallen rocks,' because, according to traditions they had fallen *upon* the old trail." (Bunnell, *Discovery*, 1911: 151.)

Wis-kul'-la   *Yosemite Valley*
"Wis-kul'-la, the village which stood at the foot of the Royal Arches, and the uppermost one in the valley." (Powers, 365. Not mentioned by Merriam.)

Yan-o-pah   *Yosemite Valley*
"The Indian name [for Vernal Fall] is Yan-o-pah, meaning a little cloud, because of the spray through which the old trail passed, and because of the circular rainbow, nowhere else seen in the mountains." (Bunnell, *Report*, 12.)

Yiyanto   *Yosemite Valley*
Said to be the name for The Cascades on Cascade Creek. ("The New River Trail to Yosemite," *Mariposa Gazette*, May 2, 1873.)

Yo-wy-we   *Yosemite Valley*
Nevada Fall. Alternate spellings were used. "In this word also we detect the root of *awaia*"—meaning a lake, or body of water. (Powers, 364.)

The First Tourists

Yosemite Valley was discovered March 27, 1851 by members of the Mariposa Battalion. Yet because it received no publicity and was difficult to reach, no tourists went to the valley for another four years.

James Mason Hutchings, publisher of *Hutchings' California Magazine*, conducted the first tourist party to Yosemite, in June 1855. His major motive was to gather new and exciting information about the wonders of California to print in his magazine, and thus one of his companions was the artist Thomas Ayres, who would provide illustrations.

An account of the party's impressions was printed in the *Mariposa Gazette* for August 16, 1855, of which no known copies exist. Parts of this article were reprinted in the *San Francisco Daily California Chronicle* on August 18, under the title:

California for Waterfalls!

J. M. Hutchings writes to the Mariposa *Gazette* a description of the Yo-Semity Valley and its waterfalls. Mr. Hutchings, Mr. Ayres and Mr. Millard, both of San Francisco, and Mr. Stair, of Coulterville, formed a party to visit the place named. They appear to have started from an Indian village on the Fresno, where they procured two Indian guides. Mr. Hutchings says:

From Mr. Hunt's store, we kept an east-of-north course, up the divide between the Fresno and Chowchillah valleys; thence descending towards the South Fork of the Merced river, and winding around a very rocky point, we climbed nearly to the ridge of the Middle or main fork of the Merced, and descending towards the Yo-Semity valley, we came upon a high point, clear of trees, from whence we had our first view of this singular and romantic valley; and, as the scene opened in full view before us, we were almost speechless with wondering admiration at its wild and sublime grandeur. "What!" exclaimed one at length, "have we come to the end of all things?" "Can this be the opening of the Seventh Seal?" cries another. "This far, very far, exceeds Niagara," says a third.

We had been out from Mariposa about four days, and the fatigue of the journey had made us weary and a little peevish, but when our eyes looked upon the almost terrific grandeur of this scene, all, all was forgotten. "I never expected to behold so beautiful a sight!" "This scene alone amply repays me for the travel!" "I should have lost the most magnificent sight that I ever saw had I not witnessed this!" were exclamations of pleasureable surprise that fell from the lips of all, as we sat down to drink in the varied beauties of this intoxicating and enchanting scene.

On the north side stands one bold, perpendicular mountain of granite, shaped like an immense tower. Its lofty top is covered with great pines, that by distance become mere shrubs. Our Indian guides called this the "Capitan." It measures from the valley to its summit about two thousand eight hundred feet.

Just opposite this, on the south side of the valley, our attention was first attracted by a magnificent waterfall, *about seven hundred feet in height*. It looked like a broad, long feather of silver, that hung depending over a precipice; and as this feathery tail of leaping spray thus hung, a slight breeze moved it from side to side, and as the last rays of the setting sun were gilding it with rainbow hues, the red would mix with the purple, and the purple with the yellow, and the yellow with the green, and the green with the silvery sheen of its whitened foam, as it danced in space.

On rushed the water over its rocky bed, and as it reached the valley, it threw up a cloud of mist that made green and flourishing the grass and flowers, and shrubs, that slumbered at the mountain's base—while towering three thousand feet above the valley, stood the rugged and pine covered cliffs that, in broken and spiral peaks, girdle in the whole.

Passing further up the valley, one is struck with the awful grandeur of the immense mountains on either side—some perpendicular, some a little sloping. One looks like a light-house, another like a giant capital of immense dimensions—all are singular, and surmounted by pines.

Now we crossed the river, and still advancing up the valley, turned a point, and before us was an indescribable sight—a waterfall *two thousand two hundred feet in height*—the highest in the world. It rushes over the cliffs, and with one bold leap falls one thousand two hundred feet, then a second of five hundred feet more, then a third of over five hundred feet more—the three leaps making two thousand two hundred feet.

Standing upon the opposite side of the valley, and looking at the tall pines below, the great height of these falls can at a glance be comprehended.

About ten miles from the lower end of the valley, there is another fall of *not less than fifteen hundred feet*. This, with lesser falls and a lake, make the head of the Yo-Semity Valley, so that this valley is about ten miles in length, and from a half to one mile in width; and although there is good land enough for several farms, it cannot be considered upon the whole as a good farming valley. Speckled trout, grouse and pigeons are quite numerous.

Several other groups visited Yosemite Valley that summer and fall, and at least two of them wrote up their experiences for the newspapers. The following account appeared in the *Mariposa Gazette*, October 11, 1855, and was reprinted in the *San Joaquin Republican* (Stockton), on October 16.

The Yo Semity Valley

The main valley is almost one continuous meadow. Grass will not flourish under the oaks, and wherever the oak is found, which is generally on the sterile soil, no grass, nor in fact any other vegetation scarcely is found.

This growth is near the base of the cliff, and grows out on the barren soil made by the sand from the granite, mixed with such decayed vegetable matter as may be thrown upon it by winds, water, and other causes. Farther from the base, and in what might be called the central valley, grows grasses which might even surprise herdsmen of the most favored clime.

Large pines border the Merced River, and the small rivulets emptying into it. Other growths are common, but the several varieties of the pine predominate.

Fine timber for building or husbandry is abundant. Many varieties of berries are to be found, one of the principal of which is the strawberry. Acres and acres of the valley are covered with these. The wag of our party said that any man who would find three feet square in a space of six hundred acres, where we encamped, that did not have the strawberry on it, should have the pleasure of shooting through his old hat. The search was made for the space; but our friend says his hat will never have a hole through it from this proposition.

The valley is irregular in width; in some places it is nearly two miles wide, and in no place is the main valley less than three fourths of a mile wide. From the entrance of the valley on the West end, to the forks of the river, is ten miles; and the average breadth is about one mile and a quarter wide. The two valleys above, taken in connection with the main one, will embrace an area of ten thousand acres—eight thousand of which is good grazing land, and six out of the eight thousand, good arable land of the richest quality.

There are evidences that in high water, the water runs from the main channel through sloughs into the valley; but I don't think that much land is overflowed at such times, but merely the channels which make the "cut-off," and meet the river at a point lower down. Cupidity has induced persons to brave the dangers to be encountered in earlier times to "prospect" the valley and vicinity, but the "color" has never been found. Nature made the lovely spot, and kept from it the "dross" which alone induces man to despoil. Embowered in the mountains in its wildness and beauty, it seems desecration for civilization to intrude upon its loveliness. Even the poor Digger Indian, with all his apathy and ignorance, shows his love for the spot the "Great Spirit" has made so lovely, and hallowed as the hunting ground of his forefathers. But the restless Anglo Saxon, or rather "inquisitive" Yankee, in his onward career espies it, visits it, and *squats* upon it and *"reckons as how it'll prove a speculation."* Nature's beauties are nothing to him. That noble pine falls beneath his ax; soil which bears flowers in such profusion is upturned; and that cascade which revels in the rainbow, and leaps with joyousness from cliff to cliff, must be perverted into the power which turns his mill to grind out his "notions."

After examining all, or rather as much of the beauties as our time would allow, our party proceeded up the South Fork of the river to see the main falls. We mounted our steeds, and proceeded up some two and a half miles; where we dismounted and proceeded on foot two miles more.

As you go up, the southern valley narrows by degrees until within two miles of the falls, when it assumes the form of a cañon. Like the lower cliffs, the rocks have fallen, and the passage up the river is very difficult. We reached the falls about noon, and in nearing it, beheld the pool where the water collects after its descent. It is an ellipsis, or nearly so, and about one hundred feet in length. The water falling a distance of three hundred and fifty feet is broken into spray upon the rocks, and is collected in this pool prior to its tortuous passage through the Cañon. A constant mist spreads several hundred yards around, irrigating vegetation, which is remarkably green in the vicinity of the falls. Large boulders have fallen and been rolled up in huge masses by the water on either side of the river, and apparently without any soil, is growing upon them the real "Kentucky Blue Grass," covering the spaces and uneven surfaces between the rocks with mats, which renders it dangerous to proceed, except on "all fours;" otherwise the visitor might fall between the rocks, and be lucky to escape with a sound neck-bone. Our party went around on the side of the falls, and sat under the mist, while our draftsman passed some distance down the stream to sketch it. His effort was successful, and he produced a picture true to nature, as indeed were all the sketches he made in the valley.

The water is icy cold, and the spray as it would envelope us, caused us to draw tight our coats around us. After lunching, and allowing ourselves to take a lingering look at a sight so beautiful, we prepared for returning. Here allow me to state that our party made no effort to go beyond these falls; but I have learned that other parties have explored the river higher up, and they assert that above these falls is another, grander if possible, falling from a greater height, and that the vicinity is wilder and more picturesque than in the valley. I give the information for what it is worth, not having seen it myself. Our descent to our animals was slow and tedious. On our route we passed a large boulder, which from its appearance, has recently been detached from the mountains and fallen nearly to the bed of the stream. It weighs many thousand tons, and on the lower side we registered our names, and for that reason it may be known as "register rock." I would advise parties visiting this fall, to keep near the boulders and timber. If they attempt to go too high up from the river they will be encompassed by rocks on the way side, and if they go too near the river they will find themselves in a swamp, and in danger of meeting a "grizzly."

After reaching our horses, we mounted and went down that branch of the river until we came to the forks, when we turned up the other stream to explore it. Our guide informed us that the little stream we were then traversing was the channel, by which the Yo-Semity Lake was emptied.

The lake is situated some twenty-five miles above the junction of the rivers in the valley. It is said to be about five miles long, by about a mile in width. In the vicinity of this lake is the head quarters or rancheria of the Indians. They live on the summit of the Sierra Nevada, and make excursions into the valley to lay in their supply of acorns and grasshoppers. The tribe which gave name to the valley, was nearly destroyed during the war with them in 1851; and the few remaining have been incorporated into other tribes. Poor Indian! for a while he struggles to defend the home of his fathers; but soon is his fate swallowed up in the destiny of the white man. The poor creatures are required to leave their homes, and settle on homes *reserved* for them, and as they gaze on the covetousness of their pale-faced brother, they read the fate but too surely theirs,—Awhile they linger, and readily partaking of the vices of civilization, they are soon carried off by death, and they are forgotten and their names are blotted from remembrance.

After passing up the north fork of the river, a very fine view of the peaks is to be seen. The most prominent object at this point is Capitol Rock. It is a large bluff surmounted by a dome, rising regularly to the height of one hundred feet. To the right, is seen another dome, which is partially fallen away, and on the side next to the valley presents an uneven perpendicular appearance. In this valley are several small lakes or ponds, through which the river runs. They abound in fish, and are resorted to by every variety of water fowl.

There is some good land in this valley, and a large amount of good grazing. We penetrated some four or five miles up this valley, but were compelled to return on account of the rugged state of the cañon. Like the other valley, it gradually narrows, until the river passes through a narrow channel, hemmed in on both sides by high cliffs.

The next day being Sunday, our party rested from its labors. Monday was spent in a general hunt, in company with a party from Big Oak Flat, who came into the valley the day before. In the evening the song and jest passed right merrily, and all seemed pleased with their visit. Next day we moved to the foot of the valley, preparatory to our final exit. We determined to try a new route home, and left the valley by the trail passing on the north side of the river. About a mile and a half below the valley, the trail leaves the river and begins to ascend the mountains. The ascent is steep and dangerous, but after great fatigue and some swearing, we reached the summit.

The first day's travel was in sight of the river, but we soon learned that to procure grass we must go back to the main divide, between the Merced and Tuolumne rivers. We kept on the ridge as near as we could, and on the third day reached the settlements on Bull Creek, a tributary of the North Fork of the Merced, and the next day reached home.

In July 1856 a party led by Lafayette H. Bunnell toured the valley. Bunnell had been the surgeon with the Mariposa Battalion in 1851 when a contingent of that body discovered Yosemite Valley. It was Bunnell who named the valley and a number of other features. These names, for the most part, had not been known to the tourist parties of 1855; Bunnell's detailed history, *Discovery of the Yosemite . . .*, was not published until 1880. The account of this 1856 party, which included the first white woman to enter Yosemite Valley, probably was written by Warren Baer, one of the editors and publishers of the *Mariposa Democrat*. It filled almost the entire front page of that newspaper on August 5, 1856. It was by far the most complete description of the wonders of Yosemite that had been published to that time, and was so much in demand that it was reprinted the following year—July 23, 1857.

A Trip to the Yosemite Falls

This day two weeks, in company with Dr. L. H. Bunnell, we left the good town of Mariposa on a trip to the Yosemite Falls, nothing doubting that the sure-footed little pony so kindly furnished by Mr. Vandyke, of this town, would safely carry us over hill and dale to our lofty destination, near the base of the Sierra Nevada Mountains. Towards night, we suddenly came in view of the advanced members of our party, who had succeeded in obtaining an early start on the morning of the same day, but who had mistaken their trail, and had spent several hours wandering through the woods in search of it. As soon as we were espied, our presence was greeted with welcome shouts of joy, when we encamped for the night, and next day resumed our tramp for the Valley.

We numbered six in all, viz: Madame Gautier and Mr. Frank Williams, our hostess and host of that comfortable hotel, the Union; Mr. Craft, Mr. Franklin, and our agreeable guide, Bunnell, and our humble selves. The Chowchilla was soon crossed, and that night we encamped amid stately pines and tapering firs, some twelve miles from the Valley. We were a merry and a happy crowd, and excellent fare added to our enjoyment. We had all formed and expressed our ideas as regards the shape and extent of the Valley, and the character of the scenery on which we were to feast our sight.

But let us on to the Valley, which we reached after a hurried ride of four hours from our last camping ground. We acknowledged our inability to convey even a faint idea of the accumulated mass of grandeur and loveliness that gradually unfolds itself to the startled gaze of the eager traveler. Even now with feelings of awe and veneration we recall the gorgeous array of the vast and wonderful combined in this superb display of the beautiful and the sublime. The hand is not yet formed that, with pen, pencil, or brush, can portray even a reflection of the excessive majesty of aspect that prominently fronts the vision of the shrinking visitor. We travel to foreign climes to obtain a sight of what travelers have written of—some renowned falls, mountains or rivers—or landscapes amid the Alps of Switzerland or the valleys of Italy. We eagerly seek after books wherein some novice traveler has magnified the sight-seeings of Europe, many of which possess no wonderful attributes of greatness, save in the mind of the traveler, that will compare with the scenery, separately or in whole, of the Yosemite Valley.

We came suddenly, abruptly in view of the Valley; and then commenced our descent of the mountain, following a narrow and winding trail, until we reached the plain below. There was no danger in our path, and if there had been, we would not have regarded it, for our eyes were riveted upon the scenery that was imperceptibly spreading and brightening as we descended the trail. A little way from the top of where we began to go down the mountain, stands a pine tree, opposite to a very large bold rock. On this tree you will find a sign or blaze. The mark was placed there by Mr. Peterson, the Engineer of the Mariposa and Yosemite Water Company. It defines the height of the first falls visible from this point, and which appears, at this distance off, like a white ribbon hung over a precipice. There was a break in the timber before us, which afforded a full view of the Valley. We hope no one will attribute to us designing motives, to draw travel through this country, or treat our description of the Valley as the ravings of a wild enthusiast,—because we have no other object in view than to make known to those afar off, who may have never heard of this Valley, what a wilderness of majestic beauty they have yet to explore within the limits of our own State.

As though the enchantress of the woods had suddenly waved her magic wand o'er the mountains, was this fairy scenery opened to our view. Thrilling sensations of awe pervaded our senses, which, as we approached, gradually subsided into pleasurable emotions of wonder and delight, similar to those produced upon the soul by distant music echoing amid the hills and valleys in the quiet hours of midnight. Through the blue haze that lingered o'er the scene, we traced the bold outlines of the towering peaks of the distant range of the Sierra Nevada; while before us, or rather beneath us, spread the verdant Valley of the Yosemite, encased in lofty and picturesque walls of granite, and fertilized by the transparent waters of the Middle Fork of the Merced River. As we approached, the blue haze grew fainter and thinner, seeming to fade from the rocks we neared, only to thicken in density on the more distant summits, that ever and anon were opening to our gaze. Vainly, with attentive mind, we endeavored to catch the first sound of animated nature. We saw the cascade leaping from its precipitous terminus into the depths below. We knew that the river was flowing beneath us. Yet we heard not the voice of either. Hushed was the cooing of the grouse, and still was the moan of the turtledove. The spell of silence was flung o'er stream and hill, and we appeared like intruders into the realm of Nature's secret repose. In contemplating the grandeur of the scene, the imagination recoils back upon itself, content to follow the reach of vision, completely paralyzed by the magnitude of the expanding vista. Down, down we go, twisting, winding with the path, until we reach the meadow below. And now we first hear the gentle roar of the river, and feel the freshening breeze of the Valley. Glorious Spring was here, quickening Nature with her smiling presence, and lulling her to repose with her sportive zephyrs, sighing through the trees; while around, above, and before us—anywhere and everywhere—was written the majesty of God; and our hearts bowed in all humility to the magnitude of his greatness. Change, the handmaid of Time, was most impressively on the face of the stupendous precipices, and by the crumbling ruins scattered near their base. When first entering the Valley, the mind becomes stupefied by the immensity of the grandness to which it is opposed. Soon it begins to admire points of beauty in the rocks, or in the trees growing from the crevices of their perpendicular sides. And thus commencing with small objects, it slowly and gradually arrives at a contemplation of some particular height, and finally meditates upon their combined grandeur, blended in one universal harmony of perfect sublimity. Thus we rode along, glancing from summit to summit of towering rocks, until proceeding for about a mile and a half up stream, we came opposite the falls of what has been inappropriately called the Cascade of the Rainbow. We say this not to reflect upon the judgment of the gentleman who has ventured to bestow this fanciful name upon one of the most attractive cascades of the Valley. But inasmuch as the falls in the Valley are never of the magnitude of a cataract, and all reflect rainbows at certain hours of the day, the name might be promiscuously applied to all the cascades separately. This fall of water is nearly opposite to the famous giant of the valley, El Capitan. The stream of water which supplies it, rises in the ridge of mountains that divides the South from the Main Fork of the Merced River, and is one of the latter's tributaries. The volume of water running over the precipice will average, in summer, about three cubic feet per second, and is precipitated in an unbroken sheet of spray, and without an opposing obstacle, to a depth of 928 feet below, where the stream unites with the river, after coming through a narrow channel for a distance of three hundred yards. Viewed from any quarter or point of the horizon, this cascade is very attractive. To our mind, it resembles a cambric veil, of ample folds, of the finest texture, the purest whiteness, and fringed with silver fleece or silken floss. Sitting beside the cherry trees, at some fifty yards from the falls, we were singularly struck with the graceful motion of the water in its descent, when pressed by the breeze. Its foldings and unfoldings—its wavings and its twistings—its contractings and expandings—possess an irresistibly attractive fascination, beyond any object on which we have ever gazed, and one, too, from which the eyes are drawn with the greatest reluctance. At night, when our trip recurs to our mind, we muse on its loveliness, until we again hear the noise of its waters in their fall, and see the rainbows that follow its wanderings through the air, in its downward search for the earth and the Valley. We make bold to call it the Bridal Veil; and those who may have the felicity to witness the stream floating in the embrace of the morning breeze will acknowledge the resemblance, and perhaps pardon the liberty we have taken in attempting to apply so poetical a name to this Queen of the Valley. Nearly opposite to the Bridal Veil stands the Monarch of the Vale, the El Capitan of the Yosemite Tribe. It is the terminus of a ridge of mountains, standing out in bold relief, with perpendicular front, and rising to an elevation of 3100 feet above the level of the river that roars at his base. His stern and prominent front is the first to greet the eye of the visitor. He almost seemed to frown on us as we passed near his base; and on his bleached and rugged visage, the last beams of the setting sun linger with affectionate warmth. This monster of rocks stands on the left-hand side of the Valley as you go up the stream, and adjoining him looms up, with a broad, oval top, the Signal Rock, on which the Yosemites lit their signal fires in the hour of danger. The El Capitan projects further out towards the middle of the Valley than any of his kindred, and eclipses all of them for huge proportions and lofty bearing, and is some three hundred feet higher than the Signal Rock. Opposite the Signal Rock stand three sharp-pointed peaks, almost in the position of a triangle. They are jagged, and change their shape and location when viewed from different points. They are the Three Brothers; and further up the Valley, beyond them, and slightly thrown back or in the rear of the Brothers, are the Twins or Two Sisters. They cannot be mistaken, for though, when looking down through the Valley, they seem as a single rock, yet when nearly fronting them, they present two sharp projecting points, and are worthy of attention from the great resemblance they bear to each other.

The Yosemite Falls now make their appearance on the left-hand side of the Valley as you follow up the stream; while directly opposite these Falls stands the Pyramid Rock, which, when seen from a distance, is shaped and squared like a pyramid, but when viewed from its front, presents a flat, smooth surface. At the base of this huge monster stands a board house, of eighteen by twenty feet in length, without floor or chimney. Near this house we stopped for the night, and prepared our supper, which we ate with a hearty good relish; and after tracing the dim white line of the Yosemite Falls, which front the house on the North, and bowing in silent reverence to the Pyramid on the South, we closed our eyes for the night, and joyfully greeted the morning sun, which, when we awoke, was cheek by jowl with our friend El Capitan.

Our breakfast was soon finished, when, mounting our horses, we crossed over to the north bank of the river, and after pacing along through the luxuriant fern leaves, and elastic meadow grass, for the distance of from four to five hundred yards, we arrived at the foot of the Yosemite Falls—when, alighting from our saddles, we visited the Falls, and stood directly under the falling waters, until the dampness of the floating spray admonished us that we were scrutinizing too closely into the secrets of Nature. The whole height of these Falls is 2600 feet. Its first leap is over 1500 feet. The stream then runs foaming and roaring down a stony, steep channel, and then makes another leap of 400 feet, until it reaches a perpendicular height of 600 feet above the Valley, when, at this season of the year, it splashes, or rather drags itself down the sides of the rock, into its wide basin below. The Rapids between these Falls are nearly three quarters of a mile in length. When on the top, you can descend by a ravine, and come out under the first Falls.

It requires that one should be several hundred yards distant to justly appreciate the great elevation of this, the highest, and, during the month of May, the grandest of all the cascades. The impression made on the mind of the beholder is, that it partakes more of the wonderful than the sublime. The water of the last runs, or rather springs, over the precipice, with a languid splash, striking upon a projecting bunch of a hard strata of rock, which, when the stream above is full, it freely overleaps with great force, and in an unbroken fall.

Bidding adieu to the favorite Falls of the Yosemite Indians, we continued our tramp up the left-hand bank of the river, toward the broad and glistening front of the Sentinel Rock, at whose base the three branches of the Merced River join together; and opposite to which stands the North Dome, and behind which the South Dome rears its ponderous, towering pinnacle, unrivaled in majesty, unequaled in height, and unsurpassed in solidified grandeur—being 3300 feet from the river to the knob of the Dome. The Sentinel Rock stands at the head of the Valley, and is equally as prominent, from its position, as El Capitan. It conveys an idea of massive magnificence, and, when viewed from either side, affords an ample view of the tremendous height of its top, and the vast dimensions of its base. Keeping it on our right, we rode along the north branch of the main stream for a mile, until we reached Mirror Lake, on whose placid surface the whole of the surrounding heights were reflected, with a distinctness and a clearness unrivaled in beauty by the substantial precipices which enclose it. The water is over ten feet in depth in the center of this Lake, and has a greenish tinge—covers an area of eight acres, and is formed by the waters which flow from Lake Ten-nay-ia, some fifteen miles north of the Valley, and which have been dammed up by a fallen mass of rocks from the craggy steeps of the Sentinel Rock. We saw a great number of trout swimming near the surface of the water, and succeeded in shooting one while basking in the sunshine.

Leaving the Lake, we returned to the junction of the streams, and keeping the Sentinel Rock on our left, we dismounted from our horses, and followed the middle tributary of the river, up a narrow and rocky gorge, for a distance of nearly two miles, when we were brought in contact with the Vernal Falls. A grove of pine-trees stand clustering around the foot of the Falls, and a large pine stands like a sentinel directly in front of the descending stream. Everything is moist and green, and the surrounding mountains enclose the stream with a graceful slope, forming a small and almost perfect amphitheatre. The water falls in one unbroken sheet, over a level, perpendicular height of 350 feet; and then following a rugged, narrow and steep channel, it roaringly wends its way to the foot of the Sentinel Rock. Here the ideal and the beautiful prevail. An exquisite thrill of pleasure pervades the senses. The stream glides over the wall above with an easy gracefulness that fills the soul with admiration. All is soft, uniform and subduing. Nothing is boisterous, irregular or misplaced.

> Oh! ever green thy vale remain,
>   And sweet the music of thy flow;
> Nor ever strife thy waters stain,
>   Or dim the luster of thy bow.

These Falls are viewed from a ledge of rocks some seventy-five yards from where the water strikes the bottom in its descent. The stream runs between the observer and the foot of the Falls. From this point you turn your back directly upon the falling water, and scrambling up the mountain before your face, hugging the ridge as closely as possible, and tugging and pulling your body up the insecure steep, you reach an Indian trail. Following this path, which turns to the left through a gap in the mountain, your feet soon press a wide plateau; and from this point the beauty and the magnificence of the scenery is beyond conception. Nature is here triumphant over Art and Genius. Before you rises in stupendous grandeur the towering summit of the South Dome, the highest and the most prodigious mass of solid rock in the Valley. The North Dome is more perfect in rotundity, but fails to fill the mind with so grand an idea of immensity. Side by side, between the Dome and the Nevada Falls, stand three pointed conical rocks—that nearest the water-fall being called the Sugar Loaf. The opening between the first pillar and the Dome affords a beautiful view of a pointed mountain, which is also seen from Lake Mirror. This addition to the scene fills up the measure of awful sublimity, that startles the imagination, and renders it powerless to describe. To the right, fair in view, gently roars the Nevada Falls, descending over a perpendicular wall or embattlement of 800 feet from the stream, where the water appears as though blown over the cliff in minute particles of foam, as white and as light as the driven snow before some wintry blast. It is the Snow Drift. Here we had the beautiful and the sublime so gracefully and magnificently blended in one harmonious whole, that the "Divinity was stirred within us"— when, closing our eyes for a moment upon the vast and splendid array of Nature's mightiness, we confessed our weakness, and in mute silence acknowledged the wonders and goodness of the One Eternal and Supreme "I am!" Descending with cautious and sliding steps down from this plateau for a distance of three hundred yards, you come to a transparent sheet of water, covering two acres of land. It is a hollow basin, and lies equidistant between the Nevada Falls and where the stream pitches off the ledge, and makes the Vernal Falls.

The Vernal and the Nevada Falls are both made by the same stream, and the distance between the two is about one-half of a mile. This Lake has been called "Frances," in honor of Mrs. Jane Frances Neal—she being the first lady who had visited this Lake, and who speaks of the landscape as having fully repaid her for all the fatigue she endured in ascending to the plateau. Let no one attempt to change the name, but rather add some other record of her courage and her love of the beautiful and grand.

Leaving the Nevada Falls, you follow the stream as it runs first over a smooth, oval floor of granite, widening and spreading as it glides along, until it reaches Lake Frances. Here you sit down for a while, and watch for trout, but none are visible, and you continue to follow the stream after it leaves the Lake until it leaps over the brink; and then, resting on a balustrade of pure granite rock, you lean over and see the water as it precipitates itself down, away down below—making the Vernal the most graceful of cascades. Diamond drops flash and gleam on the surface of the descending stream, and rainbows play around its landing place. You shudder while you bend over the balustrade, but soon, attracted by the beauty beneath, your fear is changed to admiration, and you mount the rock, as did Mrs. Neal, and proudly exulting, can inwardly exclaim, that of all the piles of grace and grandeur that check the range of vision, there is none so great as this. It is a magnificent amphitheater, and the splendors of Nature's works are no where on earth manifested with such impressive richness and profusion as are here emblazoned in her giant aspect.

We left the Valley with regret, and as we ascended the mountain we took one last, fond, lingering look on the noblest and fairest scenery in the world—the equal of which we may never look upon again.

The trail leading to the Valley is free from rocks, and water, cold, pure and refreshing, can be had at convenient distances along the trail. The path is shaded by tapering firs and pines of enormous size, and is almost a direct line to the Valley. By turning off to the right-hand from the trail, say about two miles before you begin to descend into the Valley, and following a path along the mountain, the visitor can obtain a fair view of three of the Falls in the Valley, from the summits where the streams pitch over the precipices; and also enjoy a beautiful view of the Yosemite Falls. For four miles up the stream that forms Mirror Lake, the scenery becomes awfully vast and terrifically grand—the rocks running up to sharp, jagged points, and towering the air to a fearful height. There are Falls on the South stream leading into the Valley, which are about 900 feet in height, but difficult of access—a visitor having to climb over boulders all the way.

Madame Gautier, who accompanied our party, was the first white woman who visited the Valley, and to her, and our kind host of the Union, we return our sincere thanks for their kindness; and also to our friend Bunnell, for his attention.

Formation of the Valley

From the descriptions we had heard in regard to the shape and extent of the Valley, we had conceived the idea that it was a long, narrow canyon, with perpendicular rocks, the sides formed by the river's having worn or cut a channel by the constant wearing away of some softer strata of the base or bed rock, which the stream encountered in its course. In this we were most agreeably surprised. The Valley, beginning from where the Mann Brothers trail terminates at the foot of the mountain, and ending at the Sentinel Rock, at the head of the Valley, is something over eight miles in length, and will average three quarters of a mile in width. The Middle or Main Fork of the Merced River winds smoothly, with a gentle flow, between the high, perpendicular walls of granite rock, in places nearing the bases of some of the more projecting and prominent points. At the foot of the precipices are strewn fragments of rocks which have fallen from the cliffs above, displaced by the action of the frosts, or scaled off from the inaccessible sides. The stream gracefully meanders through a large area of meadowland, which, in places, is covered with a thick growth of fern and shrubbery. Here grows the oak, the fir, the hemlock, the nutmeg, the pine, the maple, the cedar, the spruce, the laurel, the arrowwood, the elder, the cherry, the plum, the poplar, the balsam, the dog-wood, and the willow. We carefully, yet vainly, sought for the wide-spreading beech tree; but we were amply repaid for this disappointment—our search revealing the bearberry, the raspberry, the strawberry, the gooseberry, and the serviceberry. Of flowers, we found many varieties, from the rose to the honeysuckle, and many plants which we never before remember having seen. The cherries were yet green, but the berries we obtained in great abundance, and found them to possess a delicious flavor. The fruit-trees and the berry-bushes were vigorously flowering on the south bank of the river, on which the snow remains longest in spring, and where the beams of the sun seldom reach. This was readily accounted for by our guide, from the fact that the Valley runs nearly due East and West in its course between the precipices, and that the fruit-trees, nourished and stimulated by the vital beams of the sun during the day, were nipped in their bloom by the blasting frosts of night. The temperature of the atmosphere would range, probably, during the day, in the shade, at seventy-six degrees of Fahrenheit; at night, the air is cool and refreshing. At the head of the Valley, three streams unite, and form the river that fertilizes its meadows. They are nearly all of a size—one being the stream that forms the Vernal and Nevada Falls—the other coming from Lake Ten-nay-ia, fifteen miles northeast of the Valley—and third from the Falls some five miles south of the junction of the streams at the base of the Sentinel Rock.

It appears evident, from an examination of the opposing fronts of the precipices, that at some period of time the mountain was joined in one continuous connection, and that all the streams that supply the Falls with water were united in one river, which was precipitated over an immense height or ridge of the mountain, at or near the top of the El Capitan rock, at the entrance of the present Valley; and that the mountain has been torn asunder by contracting influences, while the globe was in a state of refrigeration. If such is really the case, then when this dividing of the mountain took place, an immense chasm or lake must have been formed, which has been gradually filled up by the debris brought down by the streams, when swelled by the melting of the snow on the Sierra Nevada Mountains, and also by the falling boulders from the heights above. We see nothing to justify the supposition that the stream encountered a soft strata of rock in its course to the Plains, and that by continual wearing, the present bed of the river was formed. Judging from the dry channels leading from the foot of the Falls of the Bridal Veil and the Yosemite Falls, the water falling from their summits, in early Spring, must be twenty times increased in volume, and the Yosemite especially must partake more of the nature of a cataract than a cascade. By the erection of steps up the perpendicular side of the Vernal Falls, the laborious ascent of the mountain, to visit the Nevada Falls, might be avoided, and thus be rendered accessible to ladies, without fatigue or risk.

Here, then, we end our task, as conscious now as when we began this attempt, of our inability to do justice to the scene. Perhaps some poet may arise, who, in verse or prose, may, in some happy moment, stamp a page with the seal of genius, and reflect the glories of the Yosemite Valley, whose every rock is an object of study and of wonder.

Abbreviations

BGN   The United States Board on Geographic Names, established in 1890.

BL   The Bancroft Library, Berkeley

CHSQ   *California Historical Society Quarterly*

DAB   *Dictionary of American Biography*

DFG   California Department of Fish and Game

EB   *Encyclopedia Britannica*

GLO   The General Land Office was created in 1812, as a branch of the Treasury Department, to administer the public lands. It was transferred to the Department of the Interior when that agency was created in 1849. In 1946 the GLO was combined with the Grazing Service to create the Bureau of Land Management. The patent and homestead records cited are in the Bureau of Land Management's "Control Document Index" microfilm files in Sacramento.

INF   Inyo National Forest

quad   The quadrangle topographic maps published by the US Geological Survey. Each covers either 15 minutes or 7.5 minutes of latitude and longitude. The scale of the former is 1:62,500, and of the latter, 1:24,000.

SC   The Sierra Club

SCB   *Sierra Club Bulletin*

StNF   Stanislaus National Forest

USFS   United States Forest Service

USGS   United States Geological Survey

YNN   *Yosemite Nature Notes*, published by the Yosemite Natural History Association from 1922 to 1961.

YNP   Yosemite National Park

YRL   Yosemite Research Library

Bibliography

Arch. MSB. Archivo de la Mision de Santa Barbara: *Muñoz, Diario de la Expedicion hecha por Don Gabriel Moraga, Alférez de la Compañia de San Francisco, á los Nuevos Descubrimientos del Tular*, 1806. (Transcript, Bancroft Library, Berkeley.)

Badè. Badè, William Frederic. *The Life and Letters of John Muir.* 2 vols. Boston and New York: Houghton Mifflin Co., 1924.

Bailey. Bailey, Charles A. *A Trip to Yosemite and Hetch-Hetchy.* Chas. A. Bailey, 1884. This is a unique book: only one copy exists. It is hand written, illustrated with many excellent photographs, and was professionally bound. It is at the Sierra Club library in San Francisco.

Benson's 1896 map. *Yosemite National Park, 1896,* by 1st Lt. H. C. Benson, Fourth Cavalry, U.S. Army. (In *Report of the Acting Superintendent of the Yosemite National Park, 1896.* Reprinted in *Report* for 1897.)

BGN, *Sixth Report.* *Sixth Report of the United States Geographic Board, 1890 to 1932.* Washington: Government Printing Office, 1933.

Bingaman, *Guardians.* Bingaman, John W. *Guardians of the Yosemite.* Privately printed, 1961.

Bingaman, *Pathways.* Bingaman, John W. *Pathways, A Story of Trails and Men.* Lodi, California: End-kian Publishing Co., 1968.

Biographical. *A Memorial and Biographical History of the Counties of Merced, Stanislaus, Calaveras, Tuolumne and Mariposa, California.* Chicago: The Lewis Publishing Company, 1892.

Bolton. Bolton, Herbert Eugene, trans. and ed. *Font's Complete Diary: A Chronicle of the Founding of San Francisco.* Berkeley: University of California Press, 1933.

Brewer's diary. The field diary kept by William H. Brewer during his five seasons with the first California Geological Survey, in the Bancroft Library, Berkeley.

Brewer, *Up and Down.* Brewer, William Henry. *Up and Down California in 1860–1864: the Journal of William H. Brewer.* Edited by Francis P. Farquhar. 3d ed. Berkeley and Los Angeles: University of California Press, 1966.

Brewster. Brewster, Edwin Tenney. *Life and Letters of Josiah Dwight Whitney.* Boston and New York: Houghton Mifflin Co., 1909.

Bunnell, *Discovery.* Bunnell, Lafayette Houghton. *Discovery of the Yosemite, and the Indian War of 1851, which led to that event.* 2d ed., Chicago: F. H. Revell, 1880; 3d ed., 1892; 4th ed., Los Angeles: G. W. Gerlicher, 1911.

Bunnell, *Report.* Biennial Report of the Commissioners to Manage Yosemite Valley, 1889–90.

Carpenter and Gilcrist map. *Map of Homer Mining District in Mono County, California.* H. B. Carpenter and J. Gilcrist, 1880.

Chalfant, *Gold.* Chalfant, W. A. *Gold, Guns, & Ghost Towns.* Stanford: Stanford University Press, 1947.

Chalfant, *Inyo.* Chalfant, W. A. *The Story of Inyo.* Rev. ed. Bishop, California: Pinon Book Store, 1933.

Chamberlain. Chamberlain, Newell D. *The Call of Gold. True Tales on the Gold Road to Yosemite.* Mariposa: Gazette Press, 1936.

Chase. Chase, Joseph Smeaton. *Yosemite Trails.* Boston and New York: Houghton Mifflin Co., 1911.

CHSQ. California Historical Society Quarterly.

Clark. Clark, Galen. *Indians of the Yosemite Valley . . . .* Yosemite Valley: Galen Clark, 1904.

Climber's Guide. Roper, Steve. *The Climber's Guide to the High Sierra.* San Francisco: Sierra Club Books, 1976.

Coy. Coy, Owen Cochran. *California County Boundaries.* Rev. ed. Fresno: Valley Publishers, 1973.

Cumming. Cumming, C. F. Gordon. *Granite Crags of California.* Edinburgh and London: William Blackwood and Sons, 1886.

DAB. Dictionary of American Biography.

DeDecker. DeDecker, Mary. *Mines of the Eastern Sierra.* Glendale: La Siesta Press, 1966.

EB. *Encyclopedia Britannica*, Fourteenth Edition, 1940.

Eccleston. *The Mariposa Indian War. 1850–1851. Diaries of Robert Eccleston: The California Gold Rush, Yosemite, and the High Sierra.* Edited by C. Gregory Crampton. Salt Lake City: University of Utah Press, 1957.

Eleventh Report. *Eleventh Report of the State Mineralogist*. Sacramento: State Office, 1893.

Farquhar. Francis P. Farquhar. The name standing alone or followed by another name indicates that the source of the information is Farquhar's 1926 place-names book.

Farquhar, *History*. Farquhar, Francis P. *History of the Sierra Nevada*. Berkeley and Los Angeles: University of California Press, 1965.

Farquhar, *Place Names*. Farquhar, Francis P. *Place Names of the High Sierra*. San Francisco: Sierra Club, 1926.

Foley. Foley, D. J. *Yosemite Souvenir and Guide*. Yosemite: D. J. Foley, 1905.

Foster. Foster, S. L. *In the Canyons of Yosemite National Park of California*. Boston: Bruce Humphries, Inc., 1949.

Frémont, *Expedition*. Frémont, John Charles. *Report of the Exploring Expedition to the Rocky Mountains in the year 1842, and to Oregon and north California in the years 1843–44*. Washington, 1845. (U.S. 28th Cong., 2d sess. House. Ex. doc. no. 166.)

Frémont, *Memoir*. Frémont, John Charles. *Geographical Memoir Upon Upper California*. Washington, 1848. (U.S. 30th Cong., 1st sess. Senate. Misc. doc. no. 148.)

Frémont, *Memoirs*. Frémont, John Charles. *Memoirs of My Life*. Chicago and New York: Belford, Clarke & Co., 1887.

Gannett. Gannett, Henry. *The Origin of Certain Place Names in the United States*. (U.S. Geological Survey, Bulletin 197.) Washington: Government Printing Office, 1902.

Gudde, *Place Names*. Gudde, Erwin G. *California Place Names*. 3d, ed., rev. Berkeley and Los Angeles: University of California Press, 1969.

Hall. Hall, Ansel F. *Guide to Yosemite*. San Francisco: Sunset Publishing House, 1920.

Heitman. Heitman, Francis B. *Historical Register and Dictionary of the United States Army, 1789–1903.* vol. 1. Washington: Government Printing Office, 1903.

Historic Spots. Hoover, Mildred Brooke; Rensch, Hero Eugene; and Rensch, Ethel Grace. *Historic Spots in California.* 3d ed. Revised by William N. Abeloe. Stanford: Stanford University Press, 1966.

Hittell. Hittell, John S. *Yosemite: Its Wonders and Beauties.* San Francisco: H. H. Bancroft & Co., 1868.

Hoffmann and Gardiner map. *Map of a portion of the Sierra Nevada adjacent to the Yosemite Valley.* From surveys made by Chs. F. Hoffmann and J. T. Gardner, 1863–1867. Geological Survey of California.

Hoffmann's 1873 map. *Topographical map of Central California, together with a part of Nevada,* 1873. State Geological Survey of California.

Hubbard. Hubbard, Douglass. *Ghost Mines of Yosemite.* Fresno: Awani Press, 1971.

Huber. Huber, N. King. *The Geologic Story of Yosemite National Park.* (U.S. Geological Survey Bulletin 1595.) Washington: U.S. Government Printing Office, 1987.

Hutchings *Illustrated*. Hutchings, James Mason. *Hutchings' California Magazine (Illustrated).* Published from July 1856 to June 1861.

Hutchings, *In the Heart*. Hutchings, James Mason. *In the Heart of the Sierras.* Oakland: Pacific Press Publishing House, 1886.

Hutchings, *Scenes*. Hutchings, James Mason. *Scenes of Wonder and Curiosity in California.* San Francisco: Hutchings and Rosenfield, 1860, 1861; 2d ed., San Francisco: J. M. Hutchings, 1862; 3d ed., London: Chapman and Hall, 1865; 4th ed., New York and San Francisco: A. Roman and Co., 1870, 1871, 1872, 1876.

Jackson. Jackson, Helen Hunt. *Bits of Travel at Home.* Boston: Roberts Brothers, 1878.

Johnston. Johnston, Hank. *Railroads of the Yosemite Valley.* Rev. 2d ed. Los Angeles: Trans-Anglo Books, 1966.

King. King, Clarence. *Mountaineering in the Sierra Nevada.* Lincoln: University of Nebraska Press, Bison Book, 1970. (First published in 1872.)

King and Gardiner map. *Map of the Yosemite Valley,* 1865. By C. King and J. T. Gardner. Geological Survey of California.

Kneeland. Kneeland, Samuel. *The Wonders of the Yosemite Valley, and of California.* Boston: Alexander Moore. Lee and Shepard, 1872.

Kroeber. Kroeber, Alfred Louis, "California Place Names of Indian Origin," *University of California Publications in American Archaeology and Ethnology* 12, no. 2, June 15, 1916: 31–69.

Lamar. *The Reader's Encyclopedia of the American West.* Edited by Howard R. Lamar. New York: Thomas Y. Crowell Co., 1977.

LeConte, *Alpina*. LeConte, Joseph N., "The High Sierra of California," *Alpina Americana*, no. 1, 1907. (Only one issue published.)

LeConte, *"Elevations."* LeConte, Joseph N., "Table of Elevations of Peaks in the Sierra Nevada Mountains over 12,000 feet above Sea-Level," *Sierra Club Bulletin* 4, no. 4, June 1903: 285–91.

LeConte, *Ramblings*. LeConte, Joseph. *A Journal of Ramblings through the High Sierra of California.* San Francisco: Sierra Club, 1960. (Page references are to this volume. The journal also is in *SCB* 3, no. 1, Jan. 1900: 1–107.)

LeConte maps. Joseph N. LeConte. *Map of a portion of the Sierra Nevada adjacent to the Yosemite and Hetch Hetchy Valleys,* 1893; *Map of the Sierra Nevada Mountains of Central California,* 1896; *Map of the Yosemite National Park,* 1900.

Leonard. Leonard, Zenas. *Adventures of Zenas Leonard, Fur Trader.* Edited by John C. Ewers. Norman: University of Oklahoma Press, 1959. (First published in 1839 as the *Narrative of the Adventures of Zenas Leonard, written by himself.*)

Macomb, *Report*. See Wheeler Survey.

Marshall. Robert Bradford Marshall joined the US Geological Survey in 1889. He surveyed Yosemite National Park in 1893 and 1894. He was the topographer for several of the early 30-minute maps covering the Sierra Nevada. In 1904 he was a member of the commission appointed to revise Yosemite's boundaries. In 1908 he became chief geographer of the USGS, and had charge of topographic work over the entire country.

Matthes. François E. Matthes. The name followed by volume number and date is a reference to Matthes' personal diaries, in the Bancroft Library, Berkeley.

Matthes, *Paper 160*. Matthes, François E. *Geologic History of the Yosemite Valley.* (U.S. Geological Survey Professional Paper 160.) Washington: U.S. Government Printing Office, 1930.

Matthes, *Paper 329*. Matthes, François E. *Reconnaissance of the Geomorphology and Glacial Geology of the San Joaquin Basin, Sierra Nevada California.* (U.S.

Geological Survey Professional Paper 329.) Washington: U.S. Government Printing Office, 1960.

Maule. Maule, William M. *A Contribution to the Geographic and Economic History of the Carson, Walker, and Mono Basins in Nevada and California*. San Francisco: U.S. Forest Service, 1938.

McClure's maps. First Lieutenant Nathaniel Fish McClure. *Map of the Yosemite National Park*, 1895, in *Report of the Acting Superintendent of the Yosemite National Park, 1895; Map of the Yosemite National Park*, 1896, in the *Report* for 1900, 1902, 1903, and 1904.

Merriam. Merriam, C. Hart, "Indian Village and Camp Sites in Yosemite Valley," *Sierra Club Bulletin* 10, no. 2, January 1917: 202-9.)

Morison. Morison, Samuel Eliot. *The Oxford History of the American People*. New York: Oxford University Press, 1965.

Morse. Morse, Cora A. *Yosemite as I Saw It*. 3d ed. San Francisco: San Francisco News Co., 1896.

Muir, *First Summer*. Muir, John. *My First Summer in the Sierra*. Boston and New York: Houghton Mifflin Co., 1911.

Muir, *Mountains*. Muir, John. *The Mountains of California*. New York: The Century Co., 1894.

Muir, *Parks*. Muir, John. *Our National Parks*. Boston and New York: Houghton Mifflin and Co., 1901.

Muir, *Picturesque*. *Picturesque California: the Rocky Mountains and the Pacific Slope*. Edited by John Muir. New York and San Francisco: J. Dewing Publishing Co., 1889–91. (Reprint edition under the title *West of the Rocky Mountains*. Philadelphia: Running Press, c. 1976.)

Muir, *Yosemite*. Muir, John. *The Yosemite*. New York: Century Publishing Co., 1912.

Paden. Paden, Irene, and Margaret E. Schlichtmann. *The Old Big Oak Flat Road: an account of freighting from Stockton to Yosemite Valley*. Yosemite: Yosemite Natural History Association, 1959.

Post Offices. Salley, H. E. *History of California Post Offices, 1849–1976*. La Mesa, California: Postal History Associates, Inc., 1977.

Powers. Powers, Stephen. *Tribes of California*, in *Contributions to North American Ethnology*, vol. 3, U.S. Geographical and Geological Survey of the Rocky Mountain Region. Washington: Government Printing Office, 1877.

Proceedings. *Proceedings of the California Academy of Natural Sciences.*

Preuss's maps. Charles Preuss was the cartographer on Frémont's first, second, and fourth expeditions to the Far West. The Preuss and Frémont map of 1845 shows the routes of the first two expeditions. The map of 1848, although entitled *Map of Oregon and Upper California,* covers all the territory of the United States west of the 105th meridian.

Russell, *100 Years*. Russell, Carl Parcher. *One Hundred Years in Yosemite.* Stanford: Stanford University Press, 1931.

Russell, *Quaternary*. Russell, Israel Cook. *Quaternary History of Mono Valley, California.* Washington: Government Printing Office, 1889. (In *Eighth Annual Report of the director of the U. S. Geological Survey, 1886–87,* pt. 1.)

Sanchez. Sanchez, Nellie Van de Grift. *Spanish and Indian Place Names of California.* 1930. Reprint. New York: Arno Press, 1976.

Sargent, *Clark*. Sargent, Shirley. *Galen Clark: Yosemite Guardian.* Yosemite: Flying Spur Press, 1981.

Sargent, *Innkeepers*. Sargent, Shirley. *Yosemite & Its Innkeepers.* Yosemite: Flying Spur Press, 1975.

Sargent, *Lukens*. Sargent, Shirley. *Theodore Parker Lukens, father of forestry.* Los Angeles: Dawson's Book Shop, 1969.

Sargent, *Pioneers*. Sargent, Shirley. *Pioneers in Petticoats.* Los Angeles: Trans-Anglo Books, 1966.

Sargent, *Wawona*. Sargent, Shirley. *Yosemite's Historic Wawona.* Yosemite: Flying Spur Press, 1979.

SCB. *Sierra Club Bulletin,* published in San Francisco since January 1893.

Smith. Smith, Genny Schumacher. *The Mammoth Lakes Sierra.* 4th ed. Palo Alto: Genny Smith Books, 1976.

Snyder. Jim Snyder, Yosemite National Park trail foreman and historian.

Spuller. The Rev. Everett L. Spuller of Oxnard, California, and his wife, spent the summer of 1932 helping Al Gardisky manage the Tioga Pass Resort. Mrs. Spuller and Al named more than twenty lakes that summer in what is now the Hoover Wilderness, at the headwaters of Lee Vining Creek. The information and a sketch map are in a letter from Spuller to Will Neely, a naturalist at Yosemite National Park, July 2, 1956, in the park's research library.

Starr's Guide. Starr, Walter A., Jr. *Guide to the John Muir Trail and the High Sierra Region*. San Francisco: The Sierra Club, 1934.

Starr King. Starr King, Thomas. *A Vacation among the Sierras. Yosemite in 1860.* San Francisco: The Book Club of California, 1962.

Taylor. Taylor, Benjamin F. *Between the Gates.* Chicago: S. C. Griggs and Co., 1878.

Tileston. *Letters of John Boies Tileston.* Privately printed, 1922. Tileston made the first ascent of Mount Lyell, in 1871.

Trexler. Trexler, Keith A. *The Tioga Road. A History.* Yosemite: Yosemite Natural History Association, pamphlet, no date.

Versteeg. Chester Versteeg (1887–1963), lawyer, businessman, lecturer, author, and mountaineer, who devoted much of his life to furthering interest in the Sierra Nevada. He did extensive original research on the origin of Sierra Nevada place names. Many of the names he suggested are now on the maps; many more were rejected by the US Board on Geographic Names. Mount Versteeg in Sequoia National Park was named for him in 1964.

Von Leicht and Craven map. *Map of California and Nevada*, drawn by F. v. Leicht and A. Craven. 3d ed. State Geological Survey of California, 1878.

Wheeler Survey, *Report*. Wheeler, George M. *Report Upon United States Geographical Surveys West of the 100th Meridian.* Washington, 1889. See the *Annual Report* for the specified year. Atlas sheet 56D, *Parts of Central California*, Expeditions of 1878, '79, Under the Command of 1st. Lieut. M. M. Macomb, 4th Artillery, U. S. Army. *Topographical Map of the Yosemite Valley and Vicinity*, From Topographical Plat by Lt. Macomb, Nov. 30, 1883.

Wheeler Survey, *Tables*. Wheeler, George M. *Tables of Geographic Positions, Azimuths, and Distances . . . and itineraries of important Routes*, prepared principally by 1st Lieut. M. M. Macomb. Washington, 1885.

Whitney, *Geology*. Whitney, Josiah Dwight. *Geology.* Vol. 1. Philadelphia: Caxton Press of Sherman & Co., 1865.

Whitney, *The Yosemite Book*. Whitney, Josiah Dwight. *The Yosemite Book.* New York: J. Bien, 1868.

Whitney, *The Yosemite Guide-Book*. Whitney, Josiah Dwight. *The Yosemite Guide-Book.* Cambridge, Mass.: University Press, 1869, 1870, 1871, and 1874.

Williams. Williams, John H. *Yosemite and its High Sierra.* Tacoma and San Francisco: John H. Williams, 1914.

Wurm. Wurm, Ted. *Hetch Hetchy and its Dam Railroad.* Berkeley: Howell-North Books, 1973.

YNN. *Yosemite Nature Notes,* published by the Yosemite Natural History Association from 1922 to 1961.

Yosemite Road Guide. Yosemite: Yosemite Natural History Association, 1981.

You can order additional copies of this book directly from the publisher.
Price: — $12.95

Great West Books
P.O. Box 1028
Lafayette, CA 94549
(415) 283-3184

Also available from Great West Books:
Place Names of the Sierra Nevada, by Peter Browning, covering the
area from Walker Pass to the northern boundary of Alpine County.
264 pages, 15 photographs, extensive bibliography. Sewn binding, 6 x 9.
(Published by Wilderness Press, Berkeley, 1986.)
Price: — $11.95 for paperback; $19.95 for hard cover.

Shipping: — $1.50 for one book; add 50¢ for each additional book.
California residents please add the appropriate sales tax for your county.
Check or money order, payable in U.S. funds, must accompany your order.

This book was formatted on a personal computer, using Ventura Publisher®.
Page proofs were printed on an Apple LaserWriter®.
Camera-ready copy was produced on a Linotronic® 300.
The text typeface is Palatino® from Adobe Systems for use on
PostScript® printers and typesetters.

The paper is 60# Glatfelter, acid-free.

Printing and binding by McNaughton & Gunn, Inc., Saline, Michigan.